Fairweather Eden

Fairweather Eden

Life in Britain half a million years ago
as revealed by the excavations at Boxgrove

Michael Pitts and Mark Roberts

CENTURY · LONDON

This edition published by Century Books Limited 1997

1 3 5 7 9 10 8 6 4 2

Century
Random House UK Ltd, 20 Vauxhall Bridge Road, London SW1V 2SA

Arrow Books Ltd
Random House UK Ltd, 20 Vauxhall Bridge Road, London SW1V 2SA

Random House Australia (Pty) Limited
20 Alfred Street, Milsons Point, Sydney,
New South Wales 2061, Australia

Random House New Zealand Limited
18 Poland Road, Glenfield,
Auckland 10, New Zealand

Random House South Africa (Pty) Limited
Endulini, 11a Jubilee Road,
Parktown 2193, South Africa

Random House UK Limited Reg. No. 954009

A CIP catalogue record for this book
is available from the British Library

Papers used by Random House UK Limited are natural, recyclable products made from wood grown in sustainable forests. The manufacturing processes conform to the environmental regulations of the country of origin.

ISBN 0 7126 7686 4

Typeset by Deltatype Ltd, Birkenhead, Merseyside
Printed and bound in Great Britain by
Mackays of Chatham PLC, Chatham, Kent

(Drawing by John Sibbick, courtesy of *National Geographic* Magazine)

Contents

Some people think an archaeologist is a person who dons a pith helmet, travels to exotic lands, finds something valuable that solves all the big questions, and returns home to get rich on the proceeds of magazine and television interviews.

This book is dedicated to those who know otherwise.

M.W.P.

The chapter head animals are a selection from those represented amongst the bones excavated at Boxgrove. A full list begins on page 317.

Prologue

Christmas 1993

teal

Mark Roberts sat at the head of a long table, beneath the stuffed albino otter. They had booked Christmas dinner in the back room of the pub, the posh dining room, and were having the usual: drinks, jokes, candles and Christmas pudding.

There might have been a touch of sadness that the Boxgrove dig had come to an end. That week they were looking for a fossil elephant said to have been discovered a century before on the bank of the River Arun. But it was only a small private dig: the big project, the full-scale professional excavation, was over now. They were a dozen friends, some of them been together for well over ten years, almost since they left school. If there was any melancholy, it wasn't apparent.

Only Simon Parfitt, Mark's Assistant Director, was very quiet, almost in a world of his own. He'd joined in 1985, straight after his degree, and was now a leading expert in north European ice age mammals. At Boxgrove they'd dug up one of the world's best – possibly *the* best collection of animal bones dating from half a million years ago. Simon had mothered those bones right the way through.

In 1993, a year after they'd stopped digging, Mark had decided they had to do a little more at Boxgrove, to answer some tricky questions that still nagged. Just among themselves, a few small trenches, no need to involve anyone else. And in the very last trench, they had found that bone.

1

They decided to pull their crackers before the end of the meal, to get the paper hats. Simon and Mark shared one. From it a little key-ring fell onto the table amongst the scattered cutlery and shredded tissues, and dangling from the ring was a tiny plastic skeleton.

For the first time, Simon laughed.

It was just over a week since Simon had first seen the bone, and still he hadn't come out and said what he thought it was. No one beyond the friends around the table knew anything about it at all. Mark nudged him, and under the din said quietly, questioningly: 'Well go on then; is it?'

'I'm 90 per cent certain, yes.'

Mark nodded purposefully, and a grin slowly warmed his whole face. And as he held up the key-ring, amongst this group of old friends whose excavation had come to an end, there was not a sign of melancholy. No, none at all.

PART ONE

WELCOME TO
THE STONE AGE

Chapter 1

May 1995: An Excavation Begins

Deninger's bear

For over ten years a quest at once disturbing and slightly bizarre has been pursued behind the trees.

Picture an archetypal English country scene. Green leafy lanes; a scatter of villages; children waiting for the school bus; the post lady's red van perched askew, half off the road to avoid the commuting traffic; blackbirds in the hawthorn blossom. Midst all this, invisible from outside, a great swathe has been ripped out and pillaged. Beneath the pretty veneer are stores of sands and gravels – gold to our building road-laying world. And in these gravels, archaeologists have found precious relics that reach beyond our subconsciousness, just as the drag-lines delved beneath the flower beds and footpaths.

As we stand at the top of the track, the well-farmed plain dips away like a gently tipped table, blending into the distant sea. Only the spire of Chichester Cathedral far to the right, and water towers and light industrial buildings on the outskirts of Bognor Regis to the south rise above the trees. Further along the coast to the left are white cliffs where the hills behind us meet the English Channel. From there, if the air is clear, France can be seen, where the same hills rise again.

There was a time when there was no France or England, no gap in the hills, just a wide bay coming from the right to meet a long white cliff. If we could peel back the landscape before us, we would see that time: a million years of history spreading away into the blue haze.

Old gravel quarries sprawl on either side of the track. Below in the pits, beneath soft orange cliffs, shrubs cluster round weedy heaps spattered white with rain-washed flint. It's difficult to appreciate at once how the site used to be before quarries ate the land around. The most complete building is a long barn-black corrugated asbestos and iron on the roof and walls, its open side facing east. To the south is an open rectangle of flint walling, another barn, this time roofless – the tiles fell in last winter. Other buildings run off from it. A brick feeding-shed for cattle, a couple of bull pens, a stable block for four horses and more low brick and flint structures that enclose a concreted quadrangle. Dark green algae smother broken glass in a window; nettles sprout in one corner of the yard.

On the weedy concrete apron to the east of the old parlours and animal sheds, as we turn from the long black corrugated barn – is something that looks marginally newer: a pair of battered portable tin sheds. The smaller, with square wire-grilled windows, is bare inside save for an unmade camp bed and a scatter of clothing. The other's windows are covered by solid metal shutters. Its door says 'Site Office'.

And the quarries themselves, to the left of the track? There's a rattle of flints underfoot as we descend the firm, sandy ramp. Dirty clays and stones rise around in every shade of orange: rusty tones of sunset, tanned flesh, tinned fruit segments, varnished pine. New growth edges up the slopes – birch, sycamore and hazel. There is another portable hut, this time silvery, shiny, new, with shovels, mattocks and a wheelbarrow against its wall. The ground is lighter and cleaner than elsewhere. This is what we came to see.

It's like a Greek amphitheatre with fragments of bleached sculpture rolling amongst the parched weeds, surrounded by sandy red hills. Towards the west end of this part of the quarry, machines have opened up a level floor 30 by 50 metres, backed by two steps each about a metre high cut into the vertical scrubby slope of the north side. As the clays and gravels are all gone, the chalky white marl exposed beneath glares painfully in the sun. Here, 17 months and 27 days before, retired assembly line worker and archaeological volunteer Roger Pedersen found a bone that English Heritage were to tell the world's media was the greatest archaeological find of the century. And this is where today, 15 May 1995, the search begins for more of a creature known up to now only by a small part of one leg.

The old flint barn with only three walls and no roof is Ounces Barn. It's stuck out in what used to be fields on the southern edge of the chalk hills of West Sussex, circled by villages. The nearest is Halnaker; to the east is Eartham; and to the south Crockerhill – shrunken hamlets all. The largest is Boxgrove. And because the quarries are in Boxgrove parish, when news of the find was announced, on the front page of *The Times* of London of almost exactly a year before, the creature identified only by a small part of one leg was referred to as Boxgrove Man.

Chapter 2

Before Boxgrove: Myths and Men

giant shrew

As the 1960s recede they seem increasingly to be years when the basis for so much of life in the industrial west was set: economic planning, art, music, transport, education, technology (in particular computers), energy use, sex. For so many areas the 1960s seem a turning point. We wanted to forget the past because the future was good. Many thought that if only we believed in love, peace and friendship, all would be well. Yet at the same time we were being told by bestselling books that we were really aggressive, territorial animals driven by instinctive, uncontrollable urges. According to such writers as Robert Ardrey and Desmond Morris – drawing on earlier work by Raymond Dart, Konrad Lorenz and others – we were no more than jumped-up savage apes.

What happened to these two divergent schools of thought? Faith in peace and love did not last. Furthermore, some popular scientists tried to argue against the idea of the instinctive killer, too (a notable attempt being Richard Leakey and Roger Lewin's *People of the Lake*, published in 1978), while academic archaeologists abandoned it almost entirely in the 1980s. But it was an old, deeply engrained idea, and many, of all ages and levels of education, still believe, with Robert Ardrey, that the human genus 'is a predator whose natural instinct is to kill with a weapon'; and that archaeology confirms it.

This book is about archaeology, and some of the things it reveals of the northern fringe of the world occupied by hominids half a million years ago. (A 'hominid' is a member of the family Hominidae, which comprises all species from us to our remotest ancestors after the split with the apes. Pongidae, great apes, and Canidae, dogs and wolves, are examples of other families. We will use this term often, in preference to 'Early Man', for example, because it avoids any judgements about the 'humanity' of extinct species; it encompasses the australopithecines – see below – and all *Homo* species, including *Homo sapiens*.) Not so much because of the European setting, but more on account of the unique quality of the evidence, the archaeology has much to say that is new. We see in unusual detail aspects of the daily lives of these early human-like creatures and the world they lived in. We are confronted again with questions about the nature of our origins: but here the messages, if we read them rightly, are not at all what most of us would expect. We find an ancestor in the family that would not be recognized by Ardrey or Morris; but neither is it the creature that most archaeologists are now conjuring up. This is nothing to do with bones: you could say that it represents the lost intellectual link between our primate forebears and us.

Africa has played centre stage in the modern quest for what we are and whence we came. The African Rift Valley stretches from north of Sinai to the southern tip of Mozambique. About two thirds of the way down, in Tanzania, is a fissured canyon known as Olduvai Gorge. This was where the Leakey family discovered hominid fossils of major importance. They used the Swahili word 'korongo', meaning gully, for their sites and named them after members of the team. One of the most significant and contentious gullies was Frida Leakey's Korongo: FLK.

The first stone tools had been picked up at FLK in 1931, but it was not until 1959 that Mary Leakey, Louis's second wife, found there the fossilized skull that would transform the nature of their research. *Zinjanthropus*, as Louis called it, was then by far the oldest hominid remain associated with tools (at first said to be older than 600,000 years, the skull was soon dated by the then new technique of potassium-argon analysis to nearly two million years ago). However, the skull did not look in the least bit human; did this mean that tool-making predated the origin of Man? Was *Zinjanthropus* the Missing Link, an ape-like, tool-using creature that came before *Homo?* Or were these tools made by a more human-looking creature (*Homo habilis*) whose skull also appeared from the earth a few years later?

It was a scientific controversy played out in the unaccustomed glare of *National Geographic* coverage. 1959 was the centenary year of Darwin's *Origin of Species*, and Louis Leakey took the new-found skull on tour around the United States. The National Geographic Society was impressed, and responded in a style that made certain the

9

Leakeys were well funded, and any professional disagreements well publicized.

Louis had no doubts about what the tool-makers were doing at FLK. From an excavated area of more than 250 square metres came thousands of stone artefacts and animal bones. The arrangement on the ground suggested there had once been a brushwood shelter. The FLK site was a home base from which hunters had roamed the ancient landscape in search of huge grazing animals.

Louis Leakey was making assumptions that were implicit in just about every archaeological discussion in the 1950s and 1960s of finds such as those from Olduvai Gorge: our early ancestors were hunters; the males brought kills back to camps; at these camps the meat was shared out with females and children. Indeed, it is probably true that most of us still imagine our distant ancestors behaving in some way like that. It was these assumptions that Robert Ardrey exposed and inflated in a gripping tale of scientific conspiracy published in 1961 called *African Genesis*.

He espoused what had been the lost cause of an Australian anatomist, called Raymond Dart, who had ended up in South Africa. Late in 1924, Dart was given some rocks from a lime quarry at Taung, near Kimberley. Among these he recognized the cast of a brain that looked half ape and half human, and some skull fragments that fitted onto it. His name for this fossil creature, *Australopithecus africanus*, was accepted, and the australopithecines are now seen as lying at the core of the hominid tree, originating over four million years ago ('Lucy', found in Ethiopia 50 years almost to the day after Dart got his first Taung specimen, is probably the best known) (*see* fig 1).

Even now, few if any stone tools have been found unequivocally associated with fossils of these creatures. Dart, however, became convinced that the australopithecines he was finding in South Africa had used *bone* tools. His evidence consisted of the broken animal bones, jaws and antlers found with the hominid fossils, ready made weapons, he thought, for a life of bloodthirsty killing, in which australopithecines ate both other animals and their own kind. It was on this that Ardrey built his idea of the killer ape, the instinctive murderer whose progress marked the early stages of hominid evolution and whose urges still lurk in the modern human psyche. In his own words: 'We are Cain's children, all of us.'

Twenty years ago, after Ardrey's 'confirmed killer' idea had been so publicly promoted, some of archaeology's leading intellects

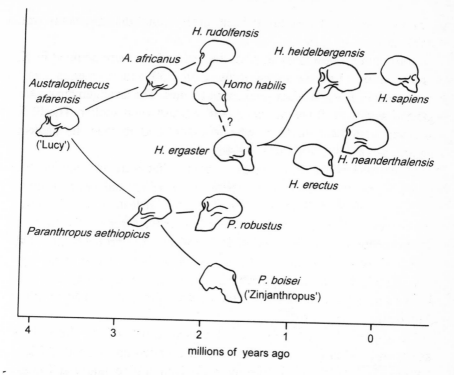

fig 1: Perhaps the one thing on which anthropologists who study hominid evolution agree is that any attempt to picture a complete evolutionary tree is destined rapidly to become history. Current opinion tends to favour a multiplicity of species, anticipating the discovery of new fossils that will add to the complex paths of evolutionary changes and extinctions. In the view that we follow here, *Australopithecus afarensis* evolved into two groups, from one of which emerged the first *Homo* species, which evolved through other forms, including regional variants that became extinct (*neanderthalensis* in Europe, *erectus* in Asia). *Homo sapiens* may be the only species in hominid history to have existed in isolation. (adapted from I Tattersall)

considered the issues again. How *did* the earliest hominids behave? How strong is the evidence for hunting and meat eating? Indeed, is it even possible to tell?

When the evidence from Taung was critically examined, it did not support Dart's or Ardrey's case. Bob Brain, director of the Transvaal Museum in Pretoria, showed that Dart's supposed australopithecine carnage was no more than an imaginative interpretation of a natural accumulation of debris. None of the bones showed any artificial working or damage – just crushing under the weight of the cave fill and gnawing and crunching from carnivores. No object could be held up as an artefact that had been used to attack another creature. One of the few genuine sudden deaths was that of a hominid taken by a large cat: a skull cap had distinct punctures that fitted the teeth of a leopard jaw found in the same deposit. Meanwhile, Richard Leakey, pointing to the large grinding teeth in the back of the *Zinjanthropus* jaw, wrote in the pages of *National Geographic* that some early hominids (*Zinjanthropus* is now seen as an australopithecine offshoot: *see* fig 1) were vegetarian and not carnivorous at all.

But it was in east Africa where most of the action was to be found. Glynn Isaac, sometimes working with Richard Leakey, excavated important sites there in the 1970s. He is particularly well known for projects at Koobi Fora and Olorgesailie, where he found well preserved and extremely ancient deposits (ranging between about three and one million years ago) that consisted of large amounts of stone tools and animals bones, with very occasional hominid remains. He called these deposits 'dense artefact-plus-bone patches'. When first found in the 1960s, such deposits were automatically taken to be occupation sites where, amongst other things, hunters retired to consume their kills. But, said Isaac, how right were they to make such assumptions? 'The notion that in times before civilization', he wrote, 'men were mighty meat-eating hunters, is deeply embedded in the folklore, sacred myths and philosophy of West European cultures.' So were archaeologists just peddling a fable? What, asked Isaac, did these 'dense patches' really mean?

One of the first things to be noticed by Isaac and his colleagues was that many of the animal bones had what appeared to be cut marks: fine grooves and scratches that suggested the action of sharp stone tools. Animals ranging in size from gazelles to elephants had been dismembered and filleted. One researcher working with the bones from the Olduvai *Zinjanthropus* site found two or three hundred fragments with such marks. And, interestingly, cut marks were sometimes found at sites where there was otherwise no indication of a hominid presence.

There was plenty of argument about the significance of these scratches. Some came to feel that early claims had exaggerated the number of genuine knife marks. Some might be from the effects of gnawing rodents or damage caused by trampling by other animals. Nonetheless, some cut marks refused to go away: there could be no doubt that somebody had been removing animal flesh with stone tools. But this threw no light on how the creatures had died, whether naturally or killed by hominid hunters.

As a result, every aspect of these excavated sites was taken apart. If some of the animal bones had been butchered, what about all the others that had not? Was it just coincidence that stone tools had been found in the same deposits? And anyway, why did so many bones and stones accumulate in one place, regardless of how the animals might have died, and whether they had been eaten by hyenas or leopards, or carved up by tool-wielding hominids?

The debate was not just an academic exercise. Archaeologists learnt to make stone tools, dissected elephants, threw things into rivers, crawled into hyena dens and hung around African water holes after dark. For Isaac, the outcome was that 'dense patches' probably did, after all, have something to do with early hominids gathering at 'home bases' or 'central foraging places'. But he found no evidence for big game hunting. Rather, he felt, hominids were efficient scavengers of dead animals.

'This research movement began with the aspect of a drawing-room card game', wrote Isaac in 1983, only a couple of years before his untimely death; 'but the recent entry into the stakes of a well-known player has brought the game to a much wider audience.' That renowned punter was American anthropologist and archaeologist Lewis Binford, who subtitled his first book on the subject 'Ancient Men and Modern Myths'. He wasn't just destroying legends: he promoted his own tales, but with scrupulous attention to material evidence.

Binford was as sceptical of visions of savage hunters as Isaac. Finding animal bones with stone tools was no reason to assume that the makers of the tools had killed the beasts. As he said, three-and-half-million-year-old footprints of hominids beside those of animals, found remarkably preserved in fossil ash at Laetoli in Tanzania, did not mean the former herded elephants.

Isaac, a South African who had studied archaeology at Cambridge, England, had a background of excavating in Africa; Binford of living with Arctic Inuit, talking to hunters and trappers in remote parts of Alaska. When he looked at excavation reports, Binford remembered scenes he'd witnessed in the Arctic: men hunting caribou and wolves tearing at flesh. He thought of people sitting round fires in modern southern Africa, gossiping and sharing food. But he couldn't see the hunters in the boxes of old bones and stones. Like Isaac, he thought it more likely that early hominids had scavenged carnivore kills or natural deaths. But, unlike Isaac, he couldn't see a home base either.

He chose Mary Leakey's excavations at Olduvai to test his ideas (he wrote to the Louis Leakey Memorial Institute – by then Louis was dead – for help, 'but never received answers' to his letters). After looking at the way in which different body parts of animals were variously represented in the collections, he felt he had 'demonstrated what will most certainly become a point of controversy – a new and perhaps "unflattering" view regarding the nature of tool use' among the early hominids.

'Earliest man', he wrote, 'far from appearing as a mighty hunter of beasts, seems to have been the most marginal of scavengers.' They began by using unshaped stones to break bones for the marrow (picking over what was left at kills after lions, hyenas and other carnivores had gone), then over many generations came to appreciate the potential of broken stones for cutting meat. But they showed no abilities to plan and cooperate in a hunt, and had no 'camps': tools occurred in heaps simply because animals tended to die in restricted places, such as near water holes.

Binford later analysed another excavation, at Klasies River Mouth in South Africa. Here, he argued, was evidence that only 40,000 years ago, the first anatomically modern humans were still living largely by scavenging. And when he came to consider European excavations, Binford found the same thing: no convincing evidence for hunting much before the era of *Homo sapiens*. Hunting, in fact, had little to do with ancestral hominids at all.

So Binford and Isaac, and their supporters and detractors – mostly American – battled it out. The high profile of the debate meant that by the early 1980s hardly anyone in academia contemplated an early hominid past of brutal killing. Discussion centred on the type of scavenging. Did they actively seek out and defend carcasses against carnivores, or did they salvage what they could after other creatures had had their fill? Research had shown that, at least in contemporary Africa, a life of scavenging would be viable. Robert Blumenschine, an American working at Olduvai, had argued for two opportunities for early hominids: big cat kills in woodlands near rivers, and carcasses of very large animals that died of disease or by drowning.

The relative importance of animal products in the diet remains an open question – direct evidence for plant foods just does not survive. Parties are still divided on matters of detail. A paper published while we were writing this book, for example, reconsiders (again) the evidence for the differing roles of hominids and carnivores in accumulating bones at the FLK *Zinjanthropus* site. But the creatures that Raymond Dart described as 'human . . . in their love of flesh, in hunting wild game . . . slaking their ravenous thirst with the hot blood of victims and greedily devouring livid writhing flesh'; such chimeras, it seems, are dead.

It was a major shift in attitude, prompted by thinking carefully

14

about how to make sense of archaeological assemblages, studying finds from excavations and experimenting. Mary Leakey was unmoved. 'I never thought interpretation was my job,' she said in a recent interview. 'What I came to do was to dig things up and take them out as well as I could'. But the debates echoed round the world of palaeolithic archaeology, which would never be the same again.

Of course in 1980 nobody had even heard of Boxgrove. Still less would anyone have guessed that one day, consideration of animal bones and stone tools from over a decade of excavations at this site, would be prompting another major change in thinking. There were always a few eccentrics almost obsessed (as some other archaeologists saw it) with making stone tools. But it would have surprised most academics 20 years ago to learn just how much new understanding of this most ancient of technologies is affecting the way we think about early hominids. And to understand *that*, we will have to get right into the heads of the creatures who made those tools. Impossible? As we will see, there's more to a flint axe than meets the eye.

PART TWO
FOUR CENTURIES OF FOSSILS

Chapter 3

Boxgrove: a Fossil World

wild cat

Mark Roberts' first small survey at Boxgrove was in 1982, when he was still a London Institute of Archaeology undergraduate struggling to find money for beer and pencils. Two years later his work attracted English Heritage funding. Since then he had been digging every summer with teams of students, six or seven months of opening new test pits, expanding areas already started in previous seasons, following the archaeology while trying to keep ahead of the quarrying. All this time the geology and the extraction programme had acted together in his favour. The layers the archaeologists were most interested in were sandwiched between two much thicker commercially valuable deposits of gravels, above, and sand below. Amey Roadstone Corporation (now ARC) would remove the coarse gravels down to just above the archaeology-rich silts, making these readily accessible to Mark and his team. It might be months or years before ARC later moved in with their machinery to extract the sand; in some areas, it was not clean enough or deep enough to be worth taking out at all.

The result for the archaeologists was an extremely rare, if not unique situation. At a typical dig – for example, at a Roman villa a few centuries old – you start at modern ground level and hope to find, preserved beyond the reach of ploughs, or of sewers or the foundations of buildings, evidence that people in the past had themselves dug that deep, and left clues to what they were doing in their pits and trenches and the rubbish that filled them up. Almost everything that occurred in Europe in the past 10,000 years – since the last ice sheets moved north into the Arctic or high into the Alps and the Pyrenees – did so on the same ground that we know today. About 8,000 years ago hunter gatherers chased deer in the forests that grew in the soils where Boxgrove is now, and fished in the streams that still flow out to the same sea channel. Neolithic farmers cultivated these soils, and generations came and went as the forest slowly fell away to first the stone axe and then the bronze. Then 3,000 years ago people built chalk-banked enclosures on the hills above Boxgrove to defend their stored grain and stock from attack; the grass covered banks are still there, the subterranean store pits filled with refuse. Around 2,000 years ago, to connect their city at Chichester with London, Roman engineers laid a road at the foot of the hill, and cars today drive this route. Boxgrove is a village with church, shops, school and sports field. This community began before the Norman Conquest. By the time of its entry in Domesday Book in 1086 the meaning of 'Boxgrove' may already have been forgotten, so that only a probably coincidental hint at a grove of box trees remains. What in the twelfth and thirteenth centuries was a huge sprawl of sophisticated ecclesiastical architecture that grew from a church first built around 1115 as an outpost of a Benedictine Abbey in Normandy, is now largely ruinous, except for part of the priory that today is still a place of worship for parishioners. These people from past times have shaped the landscape we see today, and left their clutter in the buildings, the roads and ditches and even the language that make this present world.

But all of this is very, very remote from the times that Mark was trying to reach in the gravel quarries. Deep in the ground below Ounces Barn, the special geological history at Boxgrove meant that there was another completely separate land surface, a parallel world to the 10,000 year palimpsest of the present, buried and preserved hundreds of thousands of years ago. This surface was a fossilized storehouse of information, beyond the reach of Victorian drains or cable television trenches. If an ancient hominid knelt down and chipped out a flint axe, the debris they left might well still be there in a scuffed heap. And as you knelt on this same surface once all the layers above had been removed, carefully trowelling out the fine silt, you were in a very real physical sense on the Earth of 500,000 years BC.

Chapter 4

The Dawn of Archaeology

robin

In these days, when finds of ancient human fossils regularly make headlines, we are comfortable with the idea of measuring our human family tree in millions of years. But little more than a century ago this notion was shatteringly new.

That tools and weapons (or indeed circumcision instruments) could be made from stone was familiar to a people who set beliefs by the Old Testament. 'Make thee knives of flint,' says Joshua. Even the idea that there was a time when metals were completely unknown had a long pedigree. The Roman philosopher Lucretius could write in the first century BC that before the discovery of bronze, and then of iron, men went to war with hands, nails and teeth, and branches broken from trees – and rocks.

Furthermore, generations of Europeans working the soil had turned up stones of such shapes that needed explaining. Objects we now recognize as products of ancient craftsmanship were given such names as elf-bolts or fairy arrows. Neolithic axes are sometimes found carefully placed at Roman temples or in the walls of medieval chimneys: things to be feared, venerated or simply collected, but not really understood.

Scholars ventured scientific glosses on folk typologies. Sixteenth-century Italian Ulisse Aldrovandi's definitive description of a thunder-stone explained how 'an admixture of a certain exhalation of thunder and lightning with metallic matter, chiefly in dark clouds ... is coagulated by the circumfused moisture and conglutinated into a mass (like flour with water) and subsequently indurated by heat, like a

21

brick'. But the days of indurated bricks falling from the sky were passing.

Once stone tools had actually been seen by Europeans in use in the Americas they became a physical, not just a philosophical reality, and the first records of this change date from the seventeenth century. In 1655, Isaac de la Peyrère proposed that 'thunderbolts' were in fact primitive tools. Robert Plot, in his *History of Staffordshire* (1686) recommended his readers look at North American Indian artefacts to see how prehistoric stone tools were hafted. Antoine de Jussieu read a paper to the Paris Academy of Sciences in 1723 on 'the origin and use of thunderstones': he had seen such weapons in use in contemporary Canada and the Caribbean.

There are many similar instances from all over Europe: their frequency suggests that the point was slow to take hold. But when Dr Johnson, so scornful of antiquarians, compared stone arrowheads he'd been shown on his 1773 tour of the Scottish islands with implements made in the Pacific, we may guess that wide acceptance had been achieved. Peoples skilled in a stone technology lost to Europe for millennia had unwittingly set off a chain of arguments, research and discoveries whose implications still divide the world.

As stones survive the weathering of time so much better than bones, it is no surprise to discover that the first known printed description of a truly ancient European human relic was of a flint axe. It is equally to be expected that the writer, though correctly recognizing the flint as a product of craftsmanship, had no idea what his friend had really found. Antiquary John Bagford told in 1715 how a chemist and antique dealer, Conyers, had some years before (apparently at the end of the seventeenth century) found a 'British Weapon' and the remains of an elephant near Gray's Inn Lane in London. Armed with this flint, the 'Head of a Spear, fastned [imagined Bagford] into a Shaft of a good length', the Ancient Briton had defended himself, clearly with dramatic success, against an elephant brought in by the Emperor Claudius.

It is in fact not unlikely that the elephant was an extinct species of vastly greater age than anyone at the time could have imagined; and furthermore that the maker of the axe was itself *a different species from modern humans*. A century later, when John Frere found what we now call handaxes in a gravel quarry at Hoxne, in Suffolk ('Hoxne' rhymes with 'oxen'), he was beginning to understand how old these things might be. In a layer of sand above the axes were huge bones. The flint weapons, as he thought them, were buried beneath 'different

fig 2: Stone 'handaxes' (sometimes called 'bifaces') were being made by early *Homo* species throughout Africa, western Asia and Europe over a period many times longer than the existence of modern *Homo sapiens*. The oldest in Europe date from around 500,000 years ago. This flint specimen (length 16.5 cm) was the first to be described in modern times. It was found at the end of the seventeenth century by a Mr Conyers in central London, and published in 1715 (with what John Evans, who commissioned this woodcut in 1859, described as 'a rude engraving'). At the time of discovery it was thought the 'weapon' might have been used by a native Briton to fight Roman invaders. The axe is now in the collections of the British Museum.

strata ... formed by inundations happening at distant periods', and came from so deep in the quarry, that he was tempted 'to refer them to a very remote period indeed; even beyond that of the present world'.

Only the year before – 1796 – a paper titled *Mémoire sur les espèces d'éléphants vivants et fossiles* had been published by prominent French zoologist Georges Cuvier. He explained how he compared fossil bones to bones from living animals, and was thus able to reconstruct creatures once living but no longer to be seen. Quite possibly he was unaware of John Frere's modest little letter: he did, however, know of the work of pastor Johann Esper, and was not impressed. Esper had published descriptions of his explorations around Bayreuth, southern Germany, in 1774. He claimed to have found a human jaw and shoulder blade deep in the deposits of the Gailenreuth Cave, below fossil animal bones. This was evidence he'd been actively seeking: an aboriginal human buried under – and thus older than – the remains of animals drowned in the Deluge, just as Moses told it in the Bible.

Cuvier had two principal objections to claims for fossil humans. The bones were wrongly identified (for example, a Swiss physician's case for *Homo diluvii testis*, or Man Who Was Eyewitness to The Flood, fell apart when Cuvier showed that the bones in question belonged to a crocodile); or the bones, recognized to be genuinely human, had somehow got mixed up with fossils of far greater antiquity. This second argument could also be levelled against stone tools. Esper, dead and defended only by his inadequate records, could be contradicted on both fronts.

By the 1820s claims for human remains or ancient stone tools found with bones of extinct animals were being made all over Europe by more or less eccentric collectors and amateur scientists. Even the Russian ambassador to Vienna, Count Rasoumovsky (better known as a violinist and patron of Beethoven) was reported to have found human skulls with extinct animals near Baden. But the two great geologists of this era, Georges Cuvier in France and a certain William Buckland in England, continued to deny the possibility of fossil humans. 'Everything attests', wrote Cuvier, 'that when the revolutions buried fossil remains, the human species was simply not present.'

Chapter 5

October 1993: Trench Five

common spadefoot

When in 1993, already behind schedule on the major excavation report, Mark started to think about digging again – just a small hole or two – he didn't see why anyone needed to know. For one thing, there was obviously no point in asking for sponsorship: the quarrying had virtually stopped, and English Heritage had made it clear there was to be no more fieldwork. But there was something he still did not fully understand about the geology. Not knowing bugged him, kept edging into his mind as he walked around the quarries and sat at his desk reading reports on animal bones, gravels and flint tools.

He decided to bang in some test pits and get a section through the deposits. If they dug a long line – five or six pits in a row, each pit four metres long – they should see what happens. And he knew just the man to do the job.

Roger Pedersen first worked at Boxgrove in 1989, in his summer holiday. Born in Copenhagen in 1929, he still retained a clipped accent. He had no particular skills, no special insights, just put himself into the right place at the right time. His is the story of countless dedicated amateurs who have been an integral part of decades of field archaeology in Britain; the barrow-man (they *are* mostly men), the driver, the sandwich-maker, the senior volunteer of student teams directed by young professionals, the experienced, hardened digger.

'OK,' said Mark, 'Simon and I will survey you in and you can get started.'

Out in the quarry it was cold, dark, windy and wet (one day, by counting the buckets, Simon Parfitt – Mark's Assistant Director – and

Roger calculated that they had bailed out 900 gallons of rainwater). But in his quiet unemotional way Roger was happy. He had another trench to dig. Wrapped in his coat, his green army sweater, his woollen hat, and his thick blue woollen socks, he lowered himself down onto his hands and knees, and started to trowel out Trench 5.

Chapter 6

Buckland and the Hyena Cave

spotted hyena

The Reverend William E. Buckland, Reader in Mineralogy at Corpus Christi College, Oxford, and afterwards Professor of Geology and Dean of Westminster, was excited by caves. In a landscape he believed devastated by a universal Flood, caves preserved vignettes of former life, 'antediluvial' scenes (to use Buckland's word) like period pieces in a museum. His immense reputation as a geologist (as distinct from that as an inspired lecturer, eccentric or defender of Old Testament theology) owed a great deal to his study of a single cave. But even before this was discovered, he had proclaimed what he would find there – or rather, what he would *not* – in his inaugural lecture at Oxford in May 1819.

He had been appointed to a readership in mineralogy – in the absence of a teaching post in geology – six years before. His reputation as a teacher spread fast. He had all the makings of a modern television scientist: he possessed immense, if idiosyncratic command of his material; he was an eccentric dresser (known for emphasizing the importance of work in the field, he would leap into crumbling quarries in top hat and flowing academic gown); and he was given to dramatic gestures, whether lost on horseback and dismounting to seize a handful of earth to cry 'Ah yes, as I guessed: Ealing', or rising with a large bagful of bones to address the Geological Society at an annual dinner. He had a vivid sense of humour, so that his audiences were not infrequently left wondering at what point the script was to be taken

27

literally, and when not – as was said after one address, he 'enlarged on the marvel with such a strange mixture of the humorous and the serious that we could none of us discern how far he believed himself what he said'.

The newly promoted Professor Buckland delivered his address on the subject of 'The Connexion of Geology with Religion Explained'. His thesis stripped down to two key points. Geology was not antithetical to religion, but on the contrary could be shown to support the accounts of the creation and a universal deluge. Furthermore, all research confirmed that the origin of mankind could on no account be supposed to have occurred 'before that time which is assigned to it in the Mosaic writings' – that is, in the First Book of Moses, or Genesis. This was no vague reference to an unmeasurable past. Several calendrically minded clerics had tackled the Bible as if it were a human genealogical timetable, computing the first arrival to 4004 BC.

His chance to argue these points further from geology came a couple of years later, when Buckland heard of a newly discovered cave at Kirkdale, between Kirbymoorside and Helmsley, overlooking the Vale of Pickering in Yorkshire. Hurrying to the scene, 'at the end of one of the most rainy seasons ever remembered', he found that quarry workmen had uncovered the mouth of a narrow fissure, previously choked with rubble and hidden by shrubbery. Bones – thought to be the remains of cattle that had died in a recent epidemic – had been pulled from the cave and used to improve the muddy tracks outside. But Buckland could see at once that these bones were no domestic cows. He plunged out of the wet into the tunnel.

Crawling in the darkness, he explored a string of connected caverns 75 metres long. The passage was sometimes less than a metre across, at other times it swelled to a ceiling more than four metres above. The floor was cool, smooth clay. But what most caught his attention were the bones. From end to end, wherever he dug, the ground was thick with fragmentary bones and teeth. The scene was like a huge subterranean dog kennel.

On examining his finds, Buckland made a number of startling discoveries. Altogether he was able to identify 24 different species. Many of these were extinct; and there was not a scrap of human bone. One animal in particular dominated the collection, and its presence could explain both the crushed nature of the bones and the frequency of what looked like indications of gnawing. The new Oxford Professor of Geology had acquired what was perhaps the largest group of hyena remains outside Africa, and they had all come from a cave in Yorkshire.

This was, of course, hardly the first time anyone had found old bones. But whether they were identified as parts of dragons or giants, such finds had always been difficult to relate to a real world, past or present. However, Buckland recognized that he had what we would today call a death assemblage: the bones came from creatures who were, more or less, alive in the area of the cave at the same time. A catastrophic flood – *the* Catastrophic Flood – had, he surmised, killed off the last of the animals, and removed all evidence for their presence. Only in the depths of the tunnel, where the waters had not reached, were remains still to be found. So what were they doing in there?

'We can only suppose', he wrote, exercising his case in a letter to Welsh amateur geologist Miss Jane Talbot, 'the Bones to be the wreck of Animals that were dragged in for food by the Hyaenas; not that I suppose an Hyaena could kill an elephant etc., but that as we know they do not dislike putrid flesh we may conceive they took home to their Den fragments of those larger animals that died in the course of Nature, and which from their Abundance in the Deluge gravel we know to have been the Ante Diluvian inhabitants of this country.

'I hope', he added doubtfully, 'you will get some converts to this theory of mine or supply a better.'

To further test his idea, Buckland took a special interest in living hyena. His first stop was a travelling circus visiting Oxford. He managed to persuade the owner, Mr Wombwell, to allow him to feed South African hyena in his care. Down the gullets of the beasts went bones of oxen and sheep, and then spars of wood. Everything was scrutinized, from the chewed splinters spat onto the floor to the digested scraps that fell from the other end. Next he obtained his own live hyena, intending to kill and dissect it, but sentimentality intervened: Billy lived another 25 years until he died of a goitre only a decade before his master.

Billy earned his keep by littering his den with parallels for everything that Buckland had found in his excavation. He 'performed admirably on shins of beef, leaving precisely those parts which are left at Kirkdale'. Bones chewed for their marrow were identical to fragments from the cave. His rolling and pacing rubbed the floor and walls so that they took on the appearance of the limestone in Yorkshire. And he demonstrated with copious evidence that pale coloured calcareous balls from the floor of the cave were fossil hyena droppings.

Buckland also corresponded with contacts overseas. Even the chewed hyena bones could be accounted for: the voracious creatures had actually been observed munching on their own tails and toes. 'Buckland has got a letter from India about modern hyaenas', reported one geologist to another, 'whose manners, habitations, diet etc., are everything he could wish, and as much as could be expected had they attended regularly three courses of his lectures.'

In fact, the only outstanding problem at the cave was 'the extreme abundance of the teeth of water rats': 'for modern Hyaenas, at least two that I have tried, will not eat land rats'.

(His Oxford residence in Tom Quad, Christ Church, echoed to the noise of animal observation. On one occasion, an evening dinner party was brought up sharp by crunches emanating from beneath the sofa. 'Don't concern yourself with that', said the Dean to his clearly concerned guests. 'It will only be the hyena eating one of the guinea pigs.' He also had a pet bear.)

In 1822, Buckland described his assemblage of bones from the Kirkdale Cave to a meeting of the Royal Society. His hyena den theory was widely, if not universally, accepted, and he received the prestigious geological award, the Copley Medal, for his efforts. The paper formed a substantial part of a famous monograph published the following year, entitled *Reliquiae Diluvianae; or, Observations on the Organic Remains Contained in Caves, Fissures, and Diluvial Gravel, and on Other Geological Phenomena, Attesting the Action of an Universal Deluge.*

One of the criticisms he had to face stemmed from the difficulty some people had in visualizing elephants, lions, tigers, hippopotamuses – not to mention the hyena – roaming about Yorkshire, antediluvian or not. This was a conundrum that had previously been solved, to the satisfaction of some, at least, by resorting to the great Flood. The planetary waters had swept all before them, depositing in Europe the corpses of creatures that could have been picked up just about anywhere. But Buckland was saying that his cave had *not* been flooded: the animals had died where they had been found.

Were these animals, now found living together only in southern Africa, evidence for a different climate in the past? Or could they, asked Buckland, have been adapted to a modern Yorkshire winter? It was too early to tell: more information was needed, and, doubtless, in time, would come. But this was not important to the argument for evidence of the Flood.

It could also have been said, as did Paul Tournal, championing the cause in France for fossil man, that the argument for evidence of the Flood was not important to his interpretation of the contents of Kirkdale. 'The work of Mr Buckland (*Reliquiae Diluvianae*) . . . will always be an admirable model of description . . . to which one cannot take any exception, save perhaps with the title.'

But for Buckland the title was crucial: and soon he would find himself in conflict with the excavator of more bones from another cave, over just this aspect of his work.

Chapter 7

November 1993: Roger's Discovery

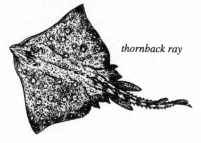

thornback ray

The geology in Trench 5 was different from the start. The layers were more complex. As Roger Pedersen trowelled down they got whiter and chalkier, hard, at times almost cemented by carbonate from the spring water that flowed from the north. He was right in the middle of the puzzling geological feature that had prompted this last furtive cut in the Boxgrove quarries.

Mark and Simon had laid out four trenches in a row, whose combined long faces would contribute to a big section through the silts. As they worked east, the weather deteriorated. When it came to peg out string for a fifth trench, things were so bad – the short days, the cold and rain, hardly the best environment for an arthritic man approaching retirement – they considered stopping. But Roger wanted to continue. So they laid out a new trench. It seemed then this really would be the last one, so instead of tagging it on in the row next to Trench 4, they left a gap and placed it where Trench 6 would have been: that way they would be sure of getting a good look at the spring deposits.

A couple of weeks into this hole 12 metres down in the bottom of the quarry – it was slow work, planning in every artefact, measuring its orientation, carefully filling out the labels, and in weather that would keep the average hardened digger tucked up in bed, or at least in the pub – Roger found a bone. It was Friday 13 November straight after lunch. He sat back on his heels, put down his trowel and considered the situation. It was a huge big bone, he could see that already. Like most of the bone at this level, it was not well preserved. The bones at Boxgrove are not strictly speaking fossils. A true fossil is a permanent mineral replacement of organic tissues. At Boxgrove less perishable components of bones are simply preserved by the chalkiness of the water percolating through the silts and gravels. Sometimes to the naked eye a bone looks and feels not unlike a modern specimen. More often it is fragile and crumbly. In some layers bones do not survive at all. Roger couldn't just grab one end of his bone and pull it out (not that that was an option), or even scrape carefully around it to expose it so he could lift it. He knew he had to get it to Ounces Barn in a block of protective silt. But if he tried to dig this thing up by himself, he would be very, very late getting home.

Back in the shelter of the barns, he found a good cardboard box, a stout brown box about fifty centimetres long with a separate lid, of the type used for storing finds from the dig. Also in the barns was Darren Norris, a local tree-surgeon who'd helped them out in previous winters. He asked Darren to lend a hand. It was hard work, even for two of them. As they scraped out the block of silt holding the bone, Darren began to speculate on its significance.

'Suppose it *is* human?'

It was certainly big enough, and bones this shape and size were not common. Roger shrugged, and made no comment. Later, he admitted that a mental block had prevented him – a trained nurse – from seeing the obvious, that Darren was right. But he wasn't into conjecture. It was just a bone, and if they didn't get it out soon it would be totally dark for his ride home on his blue 50cc Yamaha.

Normally Mark would be down at the site at the end of every day to check on Roger's progress. This weekend, however, he'd flown to France, for an international conference at Tautavel (an event that was itself to play a significant role in the Boxgrove story, as we shall see). He'd left Roger a slip of paper with two phone numbers on it. One of these was the 'Hominid Hotline'. It'd been a long-standing joke on the dig. One day they would find a hominid bone. Drama usually happened when you weren't around, and Mark was always sure to leave a number where he could be contacted for the good news. Then everything finished and no one had ever had to use it. But even for this last small return to the quarry in the depth of winter, Mark had followed his own protocol, stuck to the rules as he always did: on this occasion, the Hominid Hotline went to France. The other number was for Roger to call if he found something of less immediate significance. It was Simon Parfitt's.

The next morning, Roger telephoned Simon in London. Simon was in the bath.

'I've got an interesting bone,' said Roger. 'Any chance it might be human?'

'I can't tell from here, Roger. It's probably a deer bone.' Or maybe a bear, thought Simon, climbing back into his bath.

Chapter 8

McEnery and Kent's Hole

fallow deer

In September 1824, a Mr Thomas Northmore, visiting Torquay from Exeter, saw a popular book casually left on his brother-in-law's table. It was a copy of Belzoni's work on the Egyptian pyramids. Only a few years before, nearly 2,000 people had paid half a crown each to see Belzoni's collection on the first day of its exhibition in London. The brother-in-law also had a book by a Reverend Buckland, about finding bones in caves. Inspiring, too, in a different way.

Two weeks later, Northmore was digging inside a cave known as Kent's Hole (it was said the cave was so long that a dog got lost once, and came out in Kent). His theory was simple. He supposed the Hole was once a Mithratic Cavern for the Druidic Priesthood, where could be found pellucid water for baptismal regeneration, just as at the Pyramids of Egypt and the Tower of Babel. The following year, he organized a tour around the cave. One of his visitors was local chaplain Reverend John McEnery. McEnery was born in Limerick in 1796 (though his gravestone says 1797). When his father took his family to the United States, John went to Torquay in Devon. In 1822, he was appointed chaplain to the Cary family at Tor Abbey, an imposing house with a grand view of the sea. Kent's Hole was a couple of kilometres to the east. Some time later (exactly how much later is not clear, as he never dated his notes) McEnery wrote about the experience.

'As soon as the party was assembled in the vestibule, Mr Northmore ascended a rock, from which he delivered instructions to the group

35

around him.' He also lectured on the subject of Druids and Mithratic Temples (when someone found a piece of wood, and McEnery dubbed it the 'Druid's sandal', Northmore seems to have taken it seriously). The team set to grubbing about in the flickering darkness. But there was an iron hard floor of stalagmite, and McEnery could see that more was needed than bare hands.

'Perceiving that it was in vain to look for the fossils, without first piercing through the crust which stood between them and the mould under foot, I betook myself alone, to a spot which had the air of having been disturbed. It was one of those perforations in the floor which further observation enabled us to trace to burrowing animals.'

There was a heap of dirt thrown out beside the hole, and he could see what he soon realized were animal teeth glinting in the candle light.

'On tumbling it over, the lustre of enamel . . . betrayed its contents. They were the first fossil teeth I had ever seen, and as I laid my hand on them, relics of extinct races and witnesses of an order of things which passed away with them, I shrank back involuntarily – Though not insensible to the excitement attending new discoveries, I am not ashamed to own that in the presence of these remains I felt more of awe than joy – but whatever may have been impressions or the speculations that naturally rushed into my mind, this is not the place to indulge them – My present business is with facts.' He went on: 'I pursued my search in silence and kept my good fortune a secret, fearing that amidst the press and avidity of the party to possess some fossil memorial of the day, my discoveries would be damaged.' Or stolen. For he wanted to send them straight to Oxford.

In fact, these weren't the first bones from the cave to reach Buckland. Northmore wrote to the Professor immediately after his original discoveries, and Sir Walter Trevelyan, only a month later, delivered some bones that he had himself dug up. Encouraged by these communications, Buckland was in the cave in January 1825 when he found some bones and a flint tool, and again in the summer, this time with McEnery.

Before the end of 1825, McEnery had commenced a large scale excavation in the cave, with the assistance of the Cazalets, a local couple. Some rare sabre-tooth canines turned up the following January. In June (after the Cazalets had moved out of the area) he put it about that he was preparing to publish his results. What with one thing and another, however, his intentions in this respect were never fulfilled.

For a start, it was tough, and dangerous. When he wrote that 'the work demanded ... a constitution inured to fatigue, and proof against the chills incident to sustained exertions in unwholesome vaults', he was not thinking of his duties as a chaplain. He seems to have survived three potentially fatal accidents. On one occasion, he unsettled a large boulder which nearly crushed him. On another, to the horror of his colleagues behind him, he disappeared through the floor of the cave.

There was a system of subterranean passages, and he could reach more than 15 metres up the main arm – 'much incommoded, of course, by the crumbling of earth from the roof, and occasionally jammed up, too, by the projection of rocks from its sides, or straitened by the contraction of the passage'. When he fell through, he tried to find a way out at this new level. It didn't work.

'I had only gone about 100 paces, when owing, it is to be feared, to foul air, my light was extinguished, and I was deprived of my senses – my friends supposed me lost, and despaired of drawing me out. I was, however, extricated by my faithful fellow labourer Walsh, to whom I am indebted for my life. I suffered for some weeks from the consequence of imprudence, and it was some time before I was able to revisit the cavern.'

His rescuers suffered, too. 'The most robust of the workmen were generally more sensibly affected with nausea and vomiting.'

McEnery was driven on. Once, when he tried to reach the end of a lower passage, where it suddenly expanded into a large grotto, he met with more trouble. 'The hollow floor gave away like a pitfall with my weight and sank into a cleft of the rock. I shall not dissemble my terror at my sudden descent, my efforts to escape would but cause the ground to sink still deeper and deeper into deeper abysses ... The crash routed some animals from their subterranean abodes – I heard them forcing their escape towards the outside ...'

'The spectacle presented by these tunnels', however, 'was almost worth the risk.' As he crawled and shuffled in the dank labyrinth, one hand held out with the candle, the other feeling for the edge, he brushed fossil bones projecting from the floor and sides – he could identify some twenty species of quadrupeds. 'The roof, too, exhibited the appearance of being studded with teeth and jaws which occasionally protruded forwards. The effect was still more striking, when the soil became dry, and mouldering from exposure, parted from the fossils, leaving them quite bare hanging to the ceiling. The remains thus exposed to the action of the air, were decayed and discoloured: the enamel of the teeth showed it most, by their greenish streaks . . .'

McEnery also found a wide range of human artefacts. Some of these were quite familiar – fragments of Roman pots, corroded metal, evidence for burning and even for human burials. But the stone tools and debris from their manufacture were not so familiar. And, most significantly, unlike the other evidences for a human presence in the cave, these stone tools were to be found mostly beneath the dense, amorphous stalagmite – with the extinct animals.

McEnery was not a man to turn to dogma in the face of a conundrum. One senses that actually he would have relished a good, logical consideration of the evidence and the issues it raised. Instead, he was forced largely to work out his ideas, privately, in manuscript, so that future readers would interpret hypothesis as contradiction.

Like so many in Britain at the time, for geological advice he looked to Buckland. *His* comment on the stone tools was that McEnery had obviously got it all wrong – that the artefacts had been introduced from above, perhaps by people digging ovens. But McEnery knew this was nonsense. And he had reasons to believe that the Professor knew, too.

'On several occasions', he wrote, he was assisted 'by Dr Buckland, to whom I was desirous to point out, on the spot, the position of flint knives, and the alternation of the stalagmite with mould in certain chambers.'

He continued, with yet greater care, to seek confirmatory evidence for himself.

'Having cleared away on all sides the loose mould and all suspicious appearances, I dug under the regular crust – and flints presented themselves in my hand. This electrified me. I called the attention of my fellow labourer, and in his presence extracted, from the red marl, arrow and lance heads.'

Scrabbling in the debris with mounting excitement, as others in the cave responded to his shouts, he found a tooth.

'About three inches below the crust, the tooth of an ox met my eye (I called the people to witness the fact), which I extracted before Master Aliffe – and not knowing the chance of finding flints, I then proceeded to dig under it, and at about a foot, I dug out a flint arrow head. This confirmation, I confess, startled me. I dug again, and behold: a second, of the same size and colour (black). I struck my hammer into the earth a third time, and a third arrow head (but white) answered to the blow. This was evidence beyond all question. I then desisted – not wishing to exhaust the bed – but in case of cavil, leaving others an opportunity of verifying my statements.'

But of course, the others he had in mind were not really interested in any verification, as McEnery knew. 'It is painful to dissent from so high an authority, and more particularly so from my concurrence generally in his views of the phenomena of these caves.' But dissent from Buckland he must.

While McEnery was fatally slow in getting into print, Buckland was less so. In April 1826, the *Edinburgh Philosophical Journal* published a story headed 'Professor Buckland's notice of the Hyaenas' Den near Torquay'. Kent's Hole was like Kirkdale, with all the evidence for hyenas – but 20 times the size. There was no mention of flint tools.

A year later, Buckland visited Torquay and did a deal with McEnery. They would share the costs of producing 18 plates, and they could each use them for their respective publications. The plates were drawn in 1828. Around the same time, McEnery issued a begging prospectus, explaining that he now wished to have 30 plates to show his bones and flints. Unsure how to address his controversial finds, he had delayed the problem by enlarging the burden.

At least partly on account of the strains from working underground, McEnery's health began to suffer. Twice he went to Europe chasing a cure. In Paris in 1831, he presented Cuvier with bones from Kent's Hole. He rode back into Torquay in December, just as, an hour or two's brisk canter to the west, a young amateur naturalist by the name of Charles Darwin was leaving Plymouth in H.M.S. Beagle. His second period of sick leave took him from his friends for four years, until he returned to England in the spring of 1839.

In a sudden burst of good health he found a new determination to settle the cave controversy. Buckland was too busy, so he would do it himself.

'There remains to me therefore no other alternative than to yield to the duty, which my discoveries impose on me, towards science, by publishing an account of what I know of the cavern. I avail myself of the return of health accorded to me by a merciful Providence, to record those researches, from which illness not improbably occasioned by them has long compelled me to desist.'

But by the autumn of 1840, he was a complete invalid. He died, quietly in his chair at Tor Abbey, on Thursday evening, 18 February 1841.

Others rapidly took on the duty towards science. In March 1840, while McEnery was yet struggling with his health, Mr Robert A. C. Godwin-Austen read a paper to the Geological Society in London. There followed a discussion between him and Buckland as to whether it was lions or hyenas that had brought bones into the caves. Six months after McEnery's death, Godwin-Austen was addressing another meeting, this time in Plymouth. In the discussion, Buckland was again able to get on record his view that 'in Kent's Hole, the Celtic knives and human bones were found in holes dug by art ... which had disturbed the floor of the cave and the bones below it'. The following year, Godwin-Austen stated firmly that 'the bones and works of man must have been introduced into the cave before the flooring of stalagmite had been formed'. But he muddied the issue by suggesting that the flint tools might still be younger than the fossil animals. For the time being, at least, the argument had been won by the Oxford Professor.

Chapter 9

December 1993: Revelation and Doubt

wigeon

It had become a tradition at Boxgrove to have a little Christmas project. Anyone available would go down to Chichester and they'd get together for a bit of fieldwork and a bit of socializing, and at the end they'd have a party in a local pub, this year the Anglesey Arms in Halnaker.

Simon remembered Roger phoning him in London a few weeks before to say he'd found a big bone. He'd thought then he'd wait until he was down in Sussex for the Peppering dig (their goal was to find fossil elephant bones, dug up – and re-buried by a hawthorn tree – over a century ago). Every piece of bone they'd found that could possibly be hominid he'd pored over. Each could take half a day's work, and none had passed the tests. By that time he'd given up hope of finding a hominid fossil – well, they all had, Boxgrove was over now the quarrying had stopped. Roger's bone was safe in the barn, it was out of the ground, out of the weather, off the site. It was OK. Better to get on with his studies of all the bones in London.

But when Mark showed him Roger's bone, buried in its block of dirt in its brown cardboard box, it seemed to Mark that Simon went off into a silent world of his own. Simon had a toolkit: a tried selection of modelling tools, fine plasterer's gadgets, bits of wire, a lighter and a packet of fags. You really couldn't see much at all, just a few patches exposed in the top of the block – there was no way that anybody could have said it was hominid (or anything else for that matter). He could see a fracture in the middle of the bone, and that its two ends were missing. What was exceptional was the completeness: most bones were just scraps, but this was big, as Roger had said.

He worked in the office for two or three hours, gently scraping away the fine silt, exposing a tiny bit more bone with each spoonful of dust removed, gingerly lifting the fragments and laying them out beside each other in a tray just as they'd been in the block. By then it was fairly late. The others were watching a film on television, about a group of newly rich friends who'd clubbed together and bought a house to restore and sell at great profit. The film ended when the house collapsed.

It was so fragmentary, so many flakes and splinters, probably crushed by the pressure of the sediments it lay in, that it was totally unrecognisable. All he could say was that it was a large bone. So with little dabs of UHU, he gently rebuilt Roger's find, until there were essentially just two parts, the two halves of a long bone, a long longbone, broken across the middle. Then Simon drew the two lengths gently together.

Bang. That's it: it's human.

But the size – massive. There are no hominid limb bones of this age from anywhere in Europe, so no one could say exactly what to expect. But this was big.

Simon carefully packed all the pieces into secure boxes, picked up his ashtray and cigarette, and joined the rest of them to see the end of the film.

The next day Mark was getting curious. First Simon said nothing then he sent him off to Chichester to find a human leg bone.

Back in the barns, Simon compared the two bones, one a hardened, kippered looking thing a few centuries old, the other soft, broken and . . . a bit older. So far so good. The two bones were very similar, apart from that little problem with size.

It was that night they gathered around a long table at the Anglesey Arms to celebrate another year of companionship if not, now, another year of digging, and a skeleton fell out of a cracker.

Come Friday morning Simon wasn't anything percent *certain*. The most likely alternative to human was bear, but he didn't have any bear bones at the site with which he could compare the specimen. The problem was that the tibia was so heavy, so thick and robust: it wasn't at all what he would have expected for a hominid. Physical anthropology is littered with over-enthusiastic announcements, and

Simon needed to be quite sure of his identification before the news got out.

Chapter 10

Brixham and Abbeville

extinct vole

On 15 January 1858, in a limestone quarry above the fishing village of Brixham, across the water from Torquay, a drill was lost down a crevice. When the proprietor, John Lane Philp, saw where the tool had gone, he had an idea that he could make more from this cave than its valuation in tons of rock. Philp was naturally a scoundrel, charging the public to see the cave, selling off fossils and already creating fakes. Pengelly had seen them in his display case: 'skulls, etc. of animals probably not dead a week, certainly not dead a long time; but which he at first affirmed were found by him in his cave; subsequently . . . he confessed that they were forgeries . . . smeared . . . with cave earth to give them the requisite colour'.

A Cornishman, William Pengelly was in Torquay at that time to improve his lot by teaching. On 29 March he convened a meeting of the newly formed Torquay Natural History Society, of which he was Secretary. The principal business was to discuss the fissure, now being called the Bone Cavern at Brixham. It had been immediately apparent that no one had entered this cave for a very long time; there was a deer antler on the floor, partially embedded in stalagmite; the cave promised a large haul of completely undisturbed fossils, and – who knew? – perhaps evidence that would settle the flint tool controversy raised by John McEnery 20 years before.

The Society formed a committee, consisting of Pengelly, and local men with faith in the improving qualities of an interest in geology and antiquities. Pengelly was delegated to negotiate a lease with Philp. They wanted exclusive access to the cave for six months, and the right to keep anything they found, to add to the new collection.

A few weeks later, Falconer and Everest, geologists from London, were in the area on a cave tour of the south west. Brixham Cave had been in the news, and Hugh Falconer met with Pengelly, visited the cave and was duly impressed with its significance. Falconer and his assistant then returned to London.

Mindful of the success of an earlier McEnery fossil auction, Philp was not to be bought off for cheap. He wanted £100 for the cave lease. On 15 May the Torquay committee dropped the idea as beyond their means. The next day, Pengelly got a letter from Falconer, proposing that the Geological Society approach the Royal Society for funds, and appoint a committee of senior and respected geologists, including, of course, Dr Falconer and Mr Pengelly. 'I trust', wrote Falconer, 'it will not be disagreeable to you to cooperate.'

The posters were rushed off. 'The "Ossiferous Cavern" Recently discovered on Windmill Rea Common, will be exhibited for a short time only, by Mr PHILP, who has just disposed of it to a well-known scientific gentleman. Those who delight in contemplating the mysterious and wonderful operations of nature, will not find their time, or money mis-spent, in exploring this remarkable Cavern, and as the fossils are about to be removed, persons desirous of seeing them had better apply early. HYENAS, TIGERS, BEARS, LARGE FOSSIL HORNS ...'

Wednesday, 1 May 1859, Joseph Prestwich, ever cautious but determined amateur geologist and London wine trader, 47 years old, was waiting at the railway station at Abbeville, France. He had arranged for friends and colleagues from the Geological Society to meet him, it was dark, and not one had appeared.

The previous November, Prestwich had received a letter from Falconer, posted in Abbeville. Dr Falconer was combining a geological tour with a bid for health, swapping the clean Mediterranean climate for the winter smog of London (he found the fossils in Italy, but not the cure: within six years he died horribly of rheumatic fever). 'Abbeville is an out-of-the-way place, very little visited', he had written. He had been shown around a vast private collection of fossils, flint tools, curios, pots and paintings, antique furniture, you name it. The owner had taken him to some local gravel quarries where, he claimed, he had found flint tools and bones of extinct animals together at great depth. There was none to be seen on this trip, but M. Boucher de Perthes' collection was enough to convince. 'Flint hatchets which *he had dug up with his own hands* mixed *indiscriminately* with the molars of *E. primigenius*': mammoths and handaxes

BRIXHAM.

GREAT NATURAL CURIOSITY.

INTERESTING EXHIBITION ! !

THE

"Ossiferous Cavern"

Recently discovered on Windmill Rea Common, will be exhibited for a short time only, by Mr. PHILP, who has just disposed of it to a well-known scientific gentleman.

Those who delight in contemplating the mysterious and wonderful operations of nature, will not find their time, or money mis-spent, in exploring this remarkable Cavern, and as the fossils are about to be removed, persons desirous of seeing them had better apply early.

Many gentlemen of acknowledged scientific reputation, have affirmed that the stalactitic formations are of the most unique and interesting character, presenting the most fantastic and beautiful forms of crystallization, representing every variety of animal and vegetable structure.

Here too, may be seen the relics of animals that once roamed over the Earth before the post-tertiary period, or human epoch.

THE BONES AND TEETH, &c., OF

HYENAS, TIGERS, BEARS,

LARGE FOSSIL HORNS

of a Stag, all grouped and arranged by an eminent Geologist.

N.B. Strangers may obtain particulars of the locality, &c., of the Cavern, on application to Mr. BROWN, of the Bolton Hotel; or at the residence of the Proprietor, Spring Gardens.

THE CHARGE FOR ADMISSION TO THE "CAVERN," SIXPENCE.

Children will be admitted for FOURPENCE.

Ated. Brixham. June 10th. 1858.

EDWARD FOX, PRINTER, &c., BRIXHAM.

fig 3: A limestone cave near Brixham in Devon was one of a handful of sites that proved crucial in establishing the idea of a long ancestry for modern humans as an alternative to Old Testament myth. It was discovered by John Philp's workmen in 1858. Had Philp not realized there was money to be made from the fossils it contained, the cave may never have been excavated (although his high fee nearly achieved the same result). In the event, bones of extinct animals were found convincingly associated with ancient flint tools. (Poster reproduced courtesy Torquay Natural History Society) together, and in a deep, open quarry, not in the depths of a cave where no one seemed prepared to believe you. This was what they had been looking for. 'Let me strongly recommend you to come to Abbeville ... I am sure you would be richly rewarded. You are the only English geologist I know of who would go into the subject *con amore*'.

John Evans, 35, had escaped the Folkestone ferry at Boulogne in the early evening, after 'as rough a passage as the strongest stomach could desire'. He had had to wait for an hour and a half, alone, for the next train to Abbeville, then settled back for the 80 kilometre ride, winding down the coast through every little village, could he but see them, past the beach resorts, over the swamp south of Étaples, eventually swinging inland a little along the flat of the Somme to Abbeville. 'Think of their finding flint axes and arrowheads at Abbeville in conjunction with bones of Elephants and Rhinoceroses', he had written excitedly to his fiancée. 'I can hardly believe it.'

Evans and Prestwich met a little before midnight, and they went straight to bed.

The cave excavation the year before had been everything they had hoped for. Falconer wanted animals, lots of them, well sealed in the deposits and well recorded, and the bones had just piled up. Pengelly had seen to the recording, which had been conducted with unprecedented care (despite Edward Vivian who, not content with publishing a garbled version of McEnery's notes – just out – had tried to sink whopping great shafts through the complex deposits). Pengelly and his Devon colleagues were interested in stone tools. On 29 July, a fortnight into the dig, the first flint had come up, from beneath three inches of stalagmite. Brixham Cave had the lot, and it was the best recorded archaeological excavation, bar none.

The Geological Society Brixham Cave Committee had presented their results at the September British Association meeting in Leeds. Pengelly had spoken on the methods and rationale of the work: delicate, horizontal excavation was necessary if deposits of different age were not to be mixed, but it was slow, and they were running out of money. Professor Ramsay, reading from a paper compiled by Falconer, Pengelly and himself, had pulled no punches: they had found flint knives with rhinos and hyenas.

Pengelly had been ecstatic. He wrote home to his wife: 'all the great geologists' were there; he had been 'very much complimented ... by sundry persons'.

Falconer, however, had been less sanguine. Impressing again on the

Devon workers the importance of careful recording, he had left England in search of corroboratory evidence. He had found it in Abbeville.

Jacques Boucher de Crêvecoeur de Perthes was an eccentric, Molière-like character, aware of his aristocratic ancestry (acquiring 'de Perthes' to perpetuate the otherwise threatened name of an ancestor who had married Jeanne d'Arc's first cousin), striving for public recognition in a post-Napoleonic Paris, without understanding what it was that would have brought him real status there. He collected anything and everything, he wrote endless plays and ballads (which by all accounts deserved not to be performed), he travelled in Russia and Ireland and wrote about that. He amassed fossils and flints. In the 1830s, he published five volumes claiming that antediluvian man would soon be found. In 1847 he had the first volume of *Celtic Antiquities* printed, in which he described how he had found him.

While McEnery begged for help with 30 immaculately drawn plates, de Perthes threw his wealth at 118 sheets of graffiti, sandwiched within nearly 2,000 pages of text in three volumes. The illustrations to *Celtic Antiquities* are enough to explain the scorn of the Paris intelligentsia. There, supposedly, were to be found weapons, symbols of an antediluvian hieroglyphic language, models of dolmens and Druidic standing stones, animals and birds – all these represented by broken flints from the quarries.

He had, though, found one champion for his cause – albeit short-lived. A highly sceptical geologist, Marcel-Jérome Rigollot, was entrusted by a local Academy with the task of assessing his antediluvian claims. In 1853 he dug at St Acheul and St Roch, down the road from Abbeville at Amiens. To his surprise, he found stone tools with rhinoceros bones. On 15 November the following year, he publicly recanted his contempt to the Society of Antiquaries in Picardy. Two weeks later, he wrote to de Perthes with enthusiastic apologies for ever having doubted the significance of his discoveries. In December he was dead.

When they rose at seven the next morning, all three of them had reason to be excited. The 70-year-old de Perthes, sensing the history of the occasion, had obtained a new visitor book for the two English gentlemen. After breakfast his museum curator took Evans and Prestwich to see some quarries, but they found nothing of interest. More impressive was the large town house where de Perthes lived, containing the local Société d'Émulation, the museum, and, officially the *raison d'être* of it all, the Excise Office. Evans, the great Victorian flinter, saw enough to satisfy even him: 'the number of the flint implements that has been found is almost beyond belief'.

They travelled direct to Amiens to meet local dignitaries, in time to see a flint handaxe still firmly jammed into the quarry face three and a half metres from the surface. 'It was quite impossible', Evans later reported, 'that the implement could have been inserted into [the gravel] by the workmen for the sake of reward.' A quick photo, then on the train back to Abbeville. More quarries and sandpits the next morning, then back to London in the afternoon. At midnight on Friday they settled down to sleep in the railway hotel at Euston, mission accomplished.

Prestwich was now convinced. Early in May, he wrote to de Perthes confirming his opinion, and on 26 May he presented a detailed paper to the Royal Society. Evans was not impressed with his performance. 'His voice was hardly audible in that room ... I had written an antiquarian letter to him to incorporate in his paper, and this he dexterously managed to leave behind him'. So the younger man stood up at the end, and did the job himself. There were 'a good many geological nobs' present, including Charles Lyell and Thomas Huxley.

Evans had his proper chance on 2 June, when he summarized the geology and described the flint implements to the Society of Antiquaries. A few days before, Pengelly had detailed the Brixham Cave findings to the Royal Institution. On 29 May, a second and larger delegation had set out to Abbeville, in which Prestwich was joined by Flower, Mylne and Godwin-Austen. It was snowballing.

On 22 June, at an extraordinary meeting of the Geological Society, the gang continued the attack. Flower presented handaxes he had found at St Acheul, and Prestwich detailed the Brixham Cave excavations. Falconer, back from Sicily, described the results of his dig in a cave at Maccagnone. Public critics were publicly put down. Ramsay defended the authenticity of flint handaxes in the *Athenaeum*; Flower his St Acheul find in *The Times*.

Meanwhile in Abbeville, Boucher de Perthes was preparing his latest address in which he would again claim that the existence of diluvial man was finally proved.

In the summer, the Brixham dig finished and the story told, Britain's most influential geologist, Sir Charles Lyell, followed the well beaten path to Abbeville. And at the British Association meeting at Aberdeen, on 18 September 1859, he laid out his endorsement. This was the turning point, the official acceptance from a highly regarded and long sceptical pillar of the intellectual establishment.

At the same session in Aberdeen, Lyell announced the forthcoming publication of a new book that would focus public debate on the history and antiquity of the human species like nothing had before, though it contained few references to *Homo* and none at all to handaxes. It was *The Origin of Species*, by Charles Darwin, published on 24 November.

Chapter 11

Homo heidelbergensis

elephant

When you consider that human fossil sites in Britain can be counted on the bones of one finger, you will appreciate there are not many careers in early British hominids. Actually that is a little unfair. By including all remains from up to the end of the last glaciation – a mere 10,000 years ago – there are quite a few finds. Indeed, the Paviland skeleton (from a cave in South Wales), now dated to nearly 30,000 years ago, was the first human fossil to be excavated in Europe. Of course at the time (1823) the discoverer was not about to proclaim the great antiquity of this find. He was a geologist and a Dean, the Reverend William Buckland.

Other fossils followed the Welsh cave discovery. There was, for example, the complete skeleton from a chalk pit at Galley Hill in Kent, found in 1888 (proved modern in 1948 by fluorine analysis). Or the woman from Hunstanton, revealed in the face of a gravel pit on the Norfolk coast in 1897 (and shown to be Anglo-Saxon, by radiocarbon dating, in 1994). Or again, Henry Prigg found part of a fossil skull (from 'an undersized poorly developed individual of middle age, probably of the female sex') at Westley in Suffolk in 1882. He sent it in the post, with some flint implements, to his friend Worthington G. Smith. Unfortunately when returned to Suffolk the skull was found to be smashed to pieces: the two friends decided that the authorities, in search of explosives at a time when London's railway stations were being subjected to terrorist attacks, dropped the contents of the parcel and threw them back without a care. 'Bad fortune', wrote Smith, 'seems to attend nearly all discoveries of very ancient human relics of bone.' That one might have been genuine – unlike Piltdown Man, exposed as a fraud in 1953.

Outside Britain things have been different. The neanderthal lineage, for example, is represented by hundreds of fossils from all over Europe and the Near East, including a dozen or so quasi complete skeletons. At but one site in a complex of caves and fissures currently under excavation at Atapuerca in Spain, archaeologists might find three hundred hominid bones in a single field season only a month long. Meanwhile, up to 1993, British archaeologists have found only a few early neanderthal teeth in Wales and parts of a skull in Kent.

The Piltdown head was a modern human skull with the jaw of an orangutan. In 1912, when this confection was proclaimed a revolutionary addition to the story of hominid evolution, it could be accommodated (given the will) within the known picture. Today we have a much better idea of the pattern of early human variation in Europe. Controversies, and there are some, concern issues unthought of fifty years ago (fig 4).

Hominids first reached Europe out of Africa anything between two million and half a million years ago (dating is a major controversy). The genus is firmly *Homo*, and the species is probably some form of late *erectus* or a parallel evolutionary development known as *Homo heidelbergensis*. By a process of fairly rapid change, probably in part as an adaptation to the cold environments dominant in northern Europe, and apparently also in response to a physically strenuous lifestyle, over many generations the body evolved into what we now refer to as the neanderthal physique. The first signs of *Homo sapiens neanderthalensis* (or *Homo neanderthalensis*) appear over 200,000 years ago. It is much later, less than 50,000 years ago, that we first see modern looking humans. Still known in many school books as the Cro-Magnons (after a French cave where some bones were found in 1868), these fossils are generally agreed to represent a second hominid migration out of Africa. The break in Europe at this point (in both hominid fossils and artefacts) is perhaps uniquely clear. What is less obvious is what happened to the existing neanderthal population. Did they interbreed with the new *Homo sapiens*? Did the two hominids

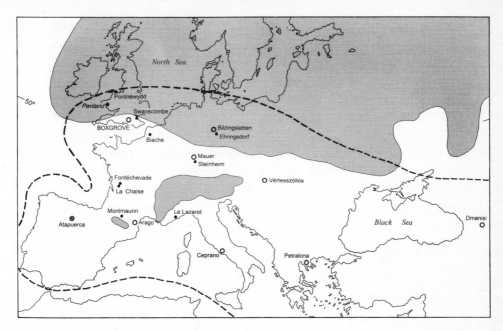

fig 4: Well dated pre-neanderthal fossils are rare in Europe. Sites of finds are here divided into those older than 400,000 years (circles) and more recent, up to about 125,000 years ago (spots). Neanderthal remains, found throughout the area enclosed by the dashed line, are much commoner, and date from around 115,000 to 35,000 years ago. Also marked is Paviland, a cave in Wales where the first fossil skeleton was excavated in 1823 (it was a modern human, or 'Cro-Magnon').

The shaded areas represent the approximate extent of permanent sheet ice during the severest cold periods of the ice age. At the time of Boxgrove, a land bridge joined England and France at their closest points. This was broken through during the subsequent Anglian glaciation (*c.* 450,000 years ago) by water flowing south west from an ice-dammed lake in what is now the southern North Sea. (map based on Stringer and Gamble)

fight over limited resources? Or did the neanderthals just gradually die out in the face of an ecological take-over by a somehow better adapted species?

Our main concern here, however, is with the earlier hominids, the ancestral neanderthals – sometimes referred to as 'archaic *Homo sapiens*', an unfortunate term implying a halfway limbo between earlier hominids and modern humans. It is the view of prominent anthropologists Ian Tattersall, Chris Stringer and Bernard Wood, among others, that these 'archaic *sapiens*' in fact represent a separate species; a species which possibly evolved in Africa, and is ancestral both to the neanderthals (a change undergone in Europe) and to modern humans (an African transformation). This species, for historical reasons, is named after a chinless jaw found in 1907 at Mauer, near Heidelberg in Germany: *Homo heidelbergensis.*

Early hominid fossils are rare in Europe, and because most of the important recent finds have yet to be fully published and described, it is not possible to give precise evolutionary status to every known bone. What we can say is that available evidence allows for all remains to be thought of as examples of *Homo heidelbergensis,* with specimens later in date showing signs of features that become characteristic of the neanderthals. The earliest *heidelbergensis* in Europe would then not really be 'European' so much as the northerly fringe of the world population of this creature. Ancestral to both modern humans and neanderthals, these remains are taking us pretty close, especially from a European perspective, to the primal human root. Or, if Simon Parfitt was right about the bone found by Roger Pedersen, the primal human leg.

Early Monday morning, 20 December 1993, Simon was in the basement of the Natural History Museum, shuffling through the collection in the Osteology Room, with Victorian glass fronted cabinets and skeletons mounted on wire frames for company. He looked at bones of bear, deer, lion, anything in the right size range. But there were no bones exactly like this in the whole Museum.

Spanish archaeologist Antonio Rosas had been the first outside the Boxgrove coterie to hear of the tibia, when Simon had rung the Museum from Boxgrove, and now he was the first to see it. He picked up some fossil cave bear for comparison; bear bones are notoriously variable in size and shape. He agreed: hominid.

At one o'clock, Simon found human anthropologist Chris Stringer. Chris prevaricated – this wasn't the sort of tibia he had expected to see, although he had heard it was very robust. He was astonished. He considered all the possibilities again. He looked at a neanderthal tibia, and at broken human tibiae. After half an hour, Chris too agreed that it was hominid. A feeling of gentle elation spread around the Palaeontology department. Simon went out to find something to eat. He could now tell Mark but his phone was engaged; he left a message with a friend.

So late Monday just before Christmas 1993, English Heritage received a call from Mark. Suddenly they too realised that Boxgrove was not yet over.

Chapter 12

May 1994: The News Breaks

3-spined stickleback

When the news got out, Chris Stringer was in Gibralter, Simon was in Poland and Mark was about to set off on a fishing trip. They hadn't planned it that way.

Since his student research in the 1970s, Chris Stringer's special interest had been the evolution of hominids in Europe and the Near East, in particular the place of neanderthals. He had probably studied and measured as many ancient human remains as anyone alive. But he had never, yet, fulfilled an ambition to find his own ancient fossil hominid.

On 17 May 1994, Chris was digging in a cave on Gibraltar for the Natural History Museum. At lunchtime somebody approached him with some news. They had heard on BBC World Service radio that a fossil human leg bone had been found in Sussex, England. There were ten days to go before the media release of the Boxgrove find, but what else could it be? He couldn't call out – mobile phones didn't work that side of the Rock. And it was hardly worth dragging all the way down, out along the tunnel and back to the hotel, only to return that same afternoon. He'd find out when they finished work.

It was a stunning conference, held in Poland to honour Professor Kazimierz Kowalski, on ice age and modern mammals in Europe. Simon had been invited to attend. He displayed Boxgrove, with a few photos and some typed text. As he listened to the lectures, and talked with other delegates, he realised in a way he had not quite realised before, how very special their site was. No one had bones like his.

In the middle of the second lecture, he felt a tap on his shoulder. He turned to see one of the conference organizers – call London.

Had someone died? Had the story been leaked to the press? Had the bone been stolen, or destroyed? But Simon couldn't get a line. Confused and isolated, Simon had no idea what was happening in England.

Mark had been drinking at a reception the evening before – so when the phone rang at 7.10 am he didn't wake with fired enthusiasm. It was his Mum.

'Well done Mark, you're on the TV.'

Telephone again. Now what?

'I can't tell you that', said Mark, 'it's embargoed till May 26. *Nature* has first rights.'

'You can forget that, mate. It's all over the front page of *The Times*.'

'Hello, is that Mark Roberts? English Heritage Press Office. I've got Professor Wainwright for you.'

'Geoff. What's happening? ... But I'm going fishing!'

'Well, I'm telling you to change your plans and come to London.'

'Are you telling me I'm not going fishing?'

'Yes.'

'But I haven't got a tie!'

On 16 May – when it was difficult to imagine their three key specialists being less available for reasoned comment – English Heritage had issued a news release, announcing that 'the oldest human remains ever found in Europe' were to be revealed on 26 May. They had invited journalists and TV crews to the Boxgrove quarries. This advance notification was risky, but they were off-guard when *The Times* published the discovery the next morning – followed immediately by just about every radio, TV and press channel in the country. 'It grieves me greatly', said a spokesman for English Heritage. 'For some reason *The Times* has broken the embargo. This presents us with a problem because we promised not to release anything until the paper had been published in *Nature*'.

For *The Times* News Desk the advance invitation – 'the oldest human remains ever found in Europe will be revealed at a news conference' – was not itself material of a type that could be controlled. 'Had there been an actual release giving embargoed information', says archaeology correspondent Norman Hammond looking back, 'they and I would of course have been bound by it'.

The Times itself took its cue from the press release. ENGLISH HERITAGE FINDS THE OLDEST HUMAN IN EUROPE – AND HE IS ENGLISH.

'Here was not the short and stumbling figure of Neanderthal Man, who stood no more than five feet seven with a short, stocky body', opined *The Times*. 'A moment like this is not one for chauvinism. But every Englishman may walk a little taller in the recognition that he is descended from such a striking creature'.

It was the biggest archaeological story given to modern British media, but perhaps it is no surprise that within a few days, people were beginning to wonder what the fuss was about. 'Who cares?' asked *The Economist*. 'Dear Sir', wrote one of many correspondents to *The Times*, 'How far is Boxgrove from Piltdown?'

When *Nature* magazine finally lead with the scientific report from its front cover on 26 May, the immediate news story was over. If only the journalists had known what was *really* exciting about Boxgrove. And that, the product of more than ten years of dedicated teamwork, is what the rest of this book is about.

Chapter 13

The Cave Men

extinct lion

Kent's Cavern – as Kent's Hole is now known – is no longer a dangerous place. The floor is smoothly concreted, with rubber strips to stop you slipping in the wet. Electric lights make the most of the spooky tunnels, the fantastic shapes and colours of the stalactites and stalagmite, the dark corners. It's all so clean, it looks dusted and polished. And you emerge from the end straight into the souvenir shop. What of McEnery's conclusions? He wrote, considering early man: 'As he was not likely to associate with [beasts of prey], it is vain to look for his remains among theirs – but it is not impossible that his remains may yet be found collected together where whole communities perished by the same catastrophe that overwhelmed the races of elephant, rhinoceros, hyena, tiger and bear'. He had found the animals, he had found the tools, but he saw no reason why he should have found the people themselves.

Like McEnery, Phillipe-Charles Schmerling, a French doctor, had found animals now extinct in a cave. Unlike McEnery, he had actually recovered human bones. And even less like McEnery, he'd managed to publish some of his work. Not that this was the route to acceptance: unsold copies of his *Researches into Fossil Bones* were bought by a grocer for wrapping cheeses and boudin.

In his *Antiquity of Man* (which, with Huxley's *Man's Place in Nature*, appeared in 1863), Sir Charles Lyell included a warm testament to Schmerling's determination. This was by way of an apology to the explorer, whom he had visited some 30 years earlier –

'a passing traveller', as he put it – without then appreciating the significance of his finds.

To be let down, as Schmerling was, day after day, by a rope tied to a tree, so as to slide to the foot of the first opening of the Engis cave, where the best-preserved human skulls were found; and, after thus gaining access to the first subterranean gallery, to creep on all fours through a contracted passage leading to larger chambers, there to superintend by torchlight, week after week and year after year, the workmen who were breaking through the stalagmitic crust as hard as marble, in order to remove piece by piece the underlying bone-breccia nearly as hard; to stand for hours with one's feet in the mud, and with water dripping from the roof on one's head, in order to mark the position and guard against the loss of each single bone of a skeleton; and at length, after finding leisure, strength, and courage for all these operations, to look forward, as the fruits of one's labour, to the publication of unwelcome intelligence, opposed to the prepossessions of the scientific and as well as of the unscientific public; – when these circumstances are taken into account, we need scarcely wonder, not only that a passing traveller failed to stop and scrutinise the evidence, but that a quarter of a century should have elapsed before even the neighbouring professors of the University of Liège came forth to vindicate the truthfulness of their indefatigable and clear-sighted countryman.

Schmerling and McEnery looked for ancient bones and stone tools in caves, just as William Buckland found a hyena den in a cave in Yorkshire, or Johann Esper, in the previous century, found remains in the Gailenreuth Cave. In the 1860s in the Pyrenees and, especially, in the golden limestone cliffs beside the River Dordogne, also in France, antiquarians explored caves to find astonishingly rich collections of artefacts and bones and, on the walls, paintings and engravings. Early antiquarians turned to caves as we might search attics for relics of our more immediate ancestors. It took years of exploration, of the development of concepts and attitudes as much as of field and laboratory techniques, before meaningful data could be found and understood in the open landscape.

PART THREE
BOXGROVE DISCOVERED

Chapter 14

Ancient Beaches

blue fin tuna

6 April 1825. 'WEDNESDAY – Attended an exhibition of ventrilo-quism at the Star Inn. A fine elephant's tooth found at Kemp Town near Brighton.'

Diarist Gideon Algernon Mantell was a contemporary of John McEnery. A medical practitioner of astonishing energy, he achieved fame (and, for him, the important accolade of the Copley Medal from the London Geological Society) for his discovery of the iguanodon and other extinct giant lizards in central Sussex.

Living close by, he was often out on the Kemp Town shore. Once he was called to attend to a young man recently drowned. On another occasion, he went to see a whale hauled in by the fishermen. On New Year's Eve 1829, with his 'kind friend, Mr Lyell' – a man destined for greater geological fame than Mantell – he 'walked under the cliffs as far as Rottingdean ... and returned to Brighton in the Fly'

Gideon Mantell was the first person to describe the geology of these cliffs, which had an unfortunate habit of falling in loose lumps to the beach and thence out to sea. That long bank of chalk hills that runs behind Boxgrove continues eastwards to Brighton, where, but for the English Channel, it would connect with chalk in France. Now white cliffs rise and fall until they reach their majestic peaks at the Seven Sisters and Beachy Head.

The Kemp Town cliffs, and Black Rock in particular, rose shakily some 24 metres into the sky, but, said Mantell, had only four or five metres at the bottom that were actually chalk rock. Resting on this was a bed of about a metre of fine sand; then a layer of flint shingle that might be as much as two and a half metres deep; and covering everything, 16 or 17 metres of the 'Elephant Bed'. This was a mixture of collapsed chalk, clay and broken flints, and was known to yield fossils. (He had also heard of bones in West Sussex, found high above the River Arun: '... the bones, and several grinders of elephants, have been found in a bed of gravel, on the estate of John Drewett, Esq., of Peppering'. The finder planted a hawthorn tree to mark the spot.)

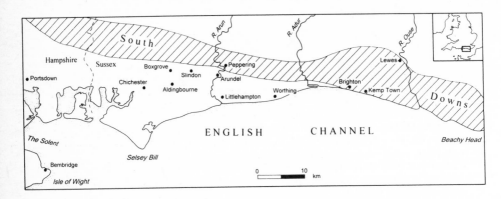

fig 5: The coast of modern Sussex

On the map, the Sussex coast is a long gentle curve, bordered at either end by the points of Beachy Head and Selsey Bill. But while the chalk cliffs to the east tower 160 metres above the water, at Selsey the crumbling little step is barely enough to keep out the waves. At least as far as records go back, land and property have been tumbling into the sea.

Frederic Dixon, another local amateur naturalist, reported that large blocks of granite lay on Selsey's beach, that could not have been locally derived. 'The general opinion is,' he noted, 'that they have been transported by ... frozen masses' of ice, presumably floating up the Channel. Like Mantell he found elephant bones. And by exploring quarry pits along the coast, he discovered a 'stratum of brownish sand and pebbles' which 'may be the remains of an old beach' running all the way from Selsey to Brighton.

So, at Black Rock and at Selsey Bill, where there was active erosion, beach pebbles and sand were falling into the sea. But the old beach was at a higher level than the present one, so it must have formed when the sea was also higher. To add to this were bones of elephants and other animals found in the cliffs, and the suggestion that glaciers had been floating by. However, neither Mantell nor Dixon could have had any sound reason for understanding the meaning of such things, or when the events behind them had occurred.

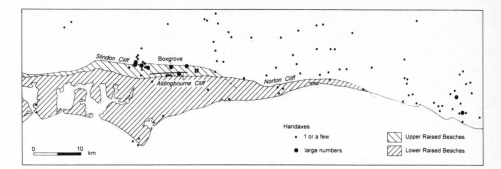

fig 6: The coastal plain of Hampshire and West Sussex was formed by a succession of high sea levels at warm periods in the ice age. Each sea left its own cliff in older deposits. Two of these, the Slindon cliff and the Norton cliff, though very much eroded, still form slight undulations in the modern topography. Between them lies the less visible Aldingbourne cliff line, and to the south others probably lie undiscovered (one has recently been identified in bore holes). Sands and gravels left by these seas have long been quarried. Open pits provide opportunities for local geologists and archaeologists, who found the first flint handaxes in the 1870s. The known distribution of axes today undoubtedly reflects the concentration of gravel pits on the upper beaches. It is important to note that flint tools that may be contemporary with Boxgrove are found all over the region. The Boxgrove hominids are likely to have moved through a variety of landscapes in search of food and other necessities.

In 1855, Robert Godwin-Austen reckoned to discern two different beach levels inland near Chichester, separated by an old weathered cliff line. Other geologists ignored, or failed to notice, this observation, and it wasn't until this century, first in 1913 at Portsdown in Hampshire and then in the 1930s in Sussex, that its truth was confirmed. Geologist the Reverend Joseph Fowler and schoolteacher/ amateur archaeologist Bernard Calkin found *three* beaches: while the shingle at Brighton was a mere seven or so metres above present sea level, the gravels in pits at Aldingbourne and at Slindon (both near Boxgrove) pointed to seas that once stood at 25 and 40 metres higher respectively. And not only were the beaches now seen to reach well into Hampshire: already in 1870 Thomas Codrington had found a raised shingle deposit on the north coast of the Isle of Wight, at Bembridge.

Meanwhile, people had been finding ancient flint handaxes. Codrington reported the first, from the brickearth which covered the ancient beach at Bembridge. Then in 1876 Ernest Willett found an axe in the chalky material above the Brighton beach. They continued to pop up, from the plain south of Chichester (1897), from terraces of the River Arun (1905), from the beach itself at Brighton (1914), and from the higher beach platforms at Slindon Park (1925) and Aldingbourne

(1929). By 1933, a century after Mantell's *Geology of the South-east of England,* the plain was well covered.

What did it all mean?

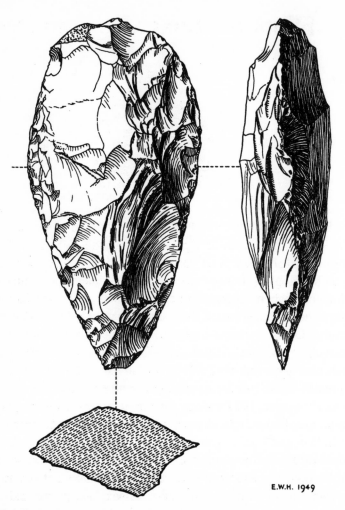

E.W.H. 1949

fig 7: This fine flint handaxe from Slindon, found by Edward Pyddoke in 1947, was the first to be found in Penfold's Pit (length 18.5 cm). (drawn by Eric Holden)

Chapter 15

Flints on Boxgrove Common

rabbit

By 1986, as we shall see, Mark had achieved an understanding of the complex geology in the Boxgrove quarries that still forms the basis of our knowledge today. Such an understanding is absolutely essential if the archaeology is to be properly interpreted, and it was one of Mark's prime goals when he first went there in 1982. When artefacts were first discovered at Boxgrove in the early 1970s, however, the geology was a muddle. This was one reason why the full significance of the discoveries was not at first appreciated. On the other hand, that as much was achieved as it was is testament to the quality of the work conducted by the first investigators in these huge pits.

On 15 August 1977 tour organizers geologist Roy Shephard-Thorn and archaeologist John Wymer led their group to Brighton, attracted by the famous cliff exposure of the raised beach first described by Gideon Mantell, for a night in the country. The next day of the tour was devoted to raised beaches. As well as visiting Black Rock itself, they went to two quarries in West Sussex, one near Slindon and the other on Boxgrove Common. There was little to report at Black Rock, but further west, on the higher or 'Goodwood' beach as it was then known, there was much news.

For some time Shephard-Thorn, an officer of the Institute of Geological Sciences in London (and later of the British Geological Survey), mappers of geology and land resources, had been visiting with friends and colleagues, trying to understand the quarries' geological story.

There were several outstanding questions about these high marine sands and gravels thought to date from perhaps 250,000 years ago. They added up to the admission that geologists still didn't really understand what the beaches were doing there.

Geoff Kellaway, a close colleague, thought he had the answer in glaciers. The Goodwood beach, he said, was not a sea beach at all, but a platform left by a hitherto unrecognized glacier that had carved up the English Channel from west to east. In the Slindon pit was a layer of grey clay with freshly broken flint nodules that looked to Kellaway like a glacial boulder clay, a deposit left by retreating ice sheets. Could this also be evidence for a Channel glaciation? Other geologists talked of a sea cliff, but no one had actually seen it: perhaps it did not exist. In 1859, a year already crammed with activity for this energetic geologist, Joseph Prestwich had found time to publish an angular block of hard chalk from a local quarry, which he thought part of a marine reef. But if it were so angular, how could it have come from a reef? Was not an ice raft more likely? And, while we're at it, said Kellaway, were not the alien stones at Stonehenge much more likely to have been brought from Wales by another unrecognized glacier than dragged all that way by primitive peoples?

One important contributor to the unravelling of the complex stratigraphy in the quarries at that time was not actually a geologist, but an archaeologist. Andrew Woodcock had come to Chichester in 1970 as Curator of the District Museum. Almost at once, he began work on his PhD. His topic was the palaeolithic of Sussex. Woodcock was supervised in his research by Derek Roe, Director of the Donald Baden-Powell Quaternary Research Centre at Oxford, who had made his name in the 1960s when, as a doctoral student at Cambridge (helped by travel money from *The Times* as their first archaeological correspondent) he motored over 80,000 kilometres around the British Isles in search of palaeolithic artefacts in museums and private collections. Such was his success that when he conducted a detailed study by measuring more than 5,000 handaxes (and analysing the results without the aid of pocket calculators or computers), he used but a small sample of the myriads he had diligently catalogued.

Roe's monumental achievement in recording all those artefacts posed a problem for other British archaeologists interested in the palaeolithic: now that he had finished, what was there left to do?

The way forward, it seemed, was to paint Roe's grand tour with local colour. Things looked pretty bad for Sussex. While neighbouring counties Hampshire and Kent scored 7,000 and over 29,000 artefacts in Roe's gazetteer respectively, Woodcock read of a mere 622 palaeolithic flints from his new county. A lot of those had come from the gravel pits around Chichester, so before long, Woodcock was out in the field looking for more. He was not to be disappointed.

The best known palaeolithic site in Sussex was then at Slindon, where several flint tools, some in mint condition, had been found earlier this century in the old gravel pit in the Park – the first when the pit was re-opened in 1912 for the rebuilding of Slindon House. In fact, as we shall see, Slindon has given its name to two of the critical deposits (from an archaeological point of view) at this highest raised beach.

Much of Woodcock's effort was devoted to an excavation at Slindon. He expected this to be his most important site, but a surprise discovery at another pit changed that. His first call was routine: as little had been reported, his expectations were not high. At that time the entire pit was in the parish of Eartham. More than 50 visits later, and after he had scrabbled over some 15 hectares of sand and muddy gravels, it had expanded westwards into the adjacent parish of Boxgrove.

Woodcock was struck by the enormous quantities of flint flakes in the coarse gravels. Then he started to find handaxes in very fresh condition, and finally a few razor sharp pieces that could be fitted back together. All this was in a large, active quarry, and Woodcock could not fail to appreciate that his flints were turning up in several different geological deposits, frequently distinguished by radically different colours and textures. He recorded huge sections through the sands and gravels, and called in geologists for help – among them Roy Shephard-Thorn and Geoff Kellaway.

There was no doubting the importance of Woodcock's discoveries. Such undisturbed flintwork was very rare anywhere in Britain; there were a few animal bones contemporary with the handaxes (identified by a young geologist from London, Mike Bishop, as various voles and a possible bison); the rich geology held out promises of charting the changing climate of the time; and the range of specialist skills displayed by the geologists and their colleagues excited Woodcock. His small excavation had been tantalizingly successful. 'The concentration of artefacts . . . on the banks of a small stream channel seems . . . indicative of a temporary camp . . . Alternatively, it is possible that the artefacts were hastily manufactured in the vicinity of a "kill" prior to its butchering . . .'

In fact it was so important, Andy Woodcock was not quite sure what to do about it. Geologists and archaeologist alike were faced with a simple dilemma. In discovering the riches of the Eartham pits, which went so deep into the higher beach deposits, they had realized how simplistic earlier interpretations in the Sussex quarries had been. Whatever others thought of the glacier theory (and the two geologists found that some colleagues minced few words in voicing their opinions – the theory is now long abandoned), the notion that the history of the deposits was longer and more complex than previously thought was difficult to deny.

Later, as Woodcock moved to East Sussex, and the geologists to studies elsewhere in Britain, a student would be down in the quarry looking for flint axes. And over ten years after that he'd still be there, looking.

Chapter 16

Mark Roberts

roe deer

Mark Brian Roberts was born in Chichester in 1961. His family lived in East Preston, an in-between rural suburbia that grew around a medieval church, a cluster of old houses and a railway station on the coast between Littlehampton and Worthing. He was the first of four children. The older of his two brothers was to become a partner in their father's plumbing business.

Mark attended the local County Primary School until the family moved to Worthing, and he to Elm Grove School. He was bright, and good at sports: at Elm Grove he was in the football team.

He passed his Eleven Plus and entered Worthing High School. The move was a traumatic experience. It was run like a small Public School, with a high academic reputation. The pupils were split into four Houses named after early medieval invaders. Roberts was a Saxon of average academic achievement who enjoyed Latin but missed the football.

Schoolwork went down the pan in his third year. He had a job as a greengrocer's boy, which thrust him into adult company. O Levels didn't seem relevant any more. He collected fossils in the chalk pits and read about volcanoes, but this didn't help in school. When it came to sit exams, the authorities were so sure he would fail English Literature and History that his father had to pay for him to sit them – but he passed. So he stayed on for A Levels, but still didn't enjoy it: just got lazier and lazier. Yet he was able to take an unusual selection of subjects that broke the academic strangle of the Level system of schooling, and it was this that ultimately woke him up again.

He says he took Religious Studies because it was popular with pretty girls ('I was the class atheist'). His second subject was Ancient History, and the third Geology. For Geology they went on field trips, looking at rocks, recording, travelling away with friends and teachers. Mark loved these trips. He started playing rugby, this time with enthusiasm. He gave up his term job at the greengrocer's, and instead started digging people's gardens.

Then one afternoon, he was shovelling a patch of earth at the front of a house in west Worthing, when the owner asked him, in a kind fatherly sort of way, what he was going to do when he left school. Join the army, was the reply. 'So why do A Levels, my boy?'

Mark's response was that he wasn't an idiot, he could get an army bursary for university and become an officer. The garden belonged to Con Ainsworth, a television engineer by trade but archaeologist and teacher by passion, with evening classes all along the Hampshire and Sussex coast. It was immediately apparent that Mark was more impressed with the medieval pottery that poured from his garage in old boxes and bags than with his garden. Mark told him he was expecting to work with his Dad on a building site in the summer, as he had before. Con had a different idea. Had he thought of trying archaeology?

So it was that in the summer of 1978 Mark was a volunteer – not a job, but it was only for a couple of weeks – on an archaeological excavation high on the chalk downs overlooking Newhaven in East Sussex. It was a revelation. All the trophies of a dig were there. The trays of finds by the manicured trench sides, polythene bags in the huts, tape measures, red and white ranging rods, shovels, barrows and pointing trowels. It was a novel use for trowels. A brickie needed a good slab of metal to hold the cement, and sharp tip and edge for tidy pointing: but these archaeologists graded each other by their trowels' shrinkage. The old hands had things that looked from a distance like handles with no blade at all.

The site was a classic example of a fascinating series of small farming settlements that had survived as lumps and bumps in the turf *since the bronze age*. No one had sown the downs around these farms for 3000 years. That is until the 1939–45 war, when the tide of land pressure rose so high that the thin soils of these ungrateful low hills began once again to be opened up. Today farm subsidies move in where the War did not reach. In 1977 Peter Drewett, Director of the

Sussex Archaeological Field Unit, started a three-year dig to record the vestiges of such a farm before they went for good; the site was known as Black Patch. One of his volunteers was a school boy in field dress with a shaven head. As the days passed, Mark could see the plans of little round huts appear on muddy sheets of graph paper as on photographic prints in a developing tank. He could join in discussions about how these people made do so long ago, on the significance of pot sherds scattered on the hut floors and on whether the villagers were buried in barrows on the higher ground around. Peter Drewett was an inspiring teacher. The life was fun, the work gripping. And so that was that. When Drewett warned against the limitations of such a career, Mark said, 'Someone has to do it'.

He took a year off after he had passed his exams, working for his Dad, pulling petrol at a garage and fitting in a little more fieldwork with the Sussex Archaeological Field Unit. Already, in 1979, he had his first experience as a Supervisor, working for Owen Bedwin, a Unit Field Officer, on a dig on the chalk downs not far from his home. SAFU was based at the Institute of Archaeology in London (then independent, later to merge with University College), where Drewett was a part-time lecturer as well as being the Unit's Director. So the choice of London for his degree was easy: besides, noted Mark, at University College, which was also in Bloomsbury just across the road from the Institute, there was a strong rugby club.

He began his degree in 1980. The very first break he was back down in Sussex, part of a team of Institute students under Peter Drewett digging bronze age barrows north of the Downs. Further south, the Field Unit were opening little trenches all over Halnaker Hill, a few miles east of Chichester, to investigate a barely surviving prehistoric enclosure on the top and field banks down the sides. Over at the chicken factory, down the road near the village of Halnaker, an iron age earthwork needed looking at before it was damaged by a new factory extension.

The Halnaker project continued for two more years, running concurrently with Mark's degree. Godfrey Udell of Amey Roadstone Corporation (ARC) reported finding a ditch and some Roman pot sherds from their gravel pit at the foot of the hill. At the quarries since the 1930s, foreman for ever it seemed, Godfrey was still looking for things, finding pottery, fossils, bits and pieces that accumulated on window sills in the offices. His ditch had to be followed up. In fact, it became the focus of Institute activity in 1982 and 1983: and for the first year Mark was the excavation Supervisor. They found a substantial Romano-British farmstead. ARC could not have been more helpful. The archaeologists did not even have to put up their own site huts: there were some old buildings at the quarry which they could use for offices and storage – Ounces Barn. The site of that excavation has been quarried away, now. Amey's Eartham Pit, they called it then. Better known these days simply as Boxgrove.

On the long summer evenings in 1982, camping in the quarry, sometimes the students would look for 'palaeos': not archaeology, really, just souvenir hunting. They were rewarded with battered handaxes from the coarse gravels. But for Mark it became more than a game.

They had to choose a topic for a written dissertation in their third year. Trowelling out Roman post-holes by day while heavy machinery massed in the pit below, and down there searching in the still safety of the evening light, Mark decided to write about the handaxes. He understood how important the site might be from a thesis by the curator of Chichester Museum, published only the year before. In London he had watched lecturer Mark Newcomer, an American outdoorsman turned palaeolithic archaeologist, actually make hand-axes – at that time Newcomer, always amongst the highest regarded knappers, was the only one teaching in a British university. And Mark was fascinated by the geology.

Out there in the pits he was certain there was something really radical, if only he could understand it.

Chapter 17

In the Beginning

wild boar

Why did Mark Roberts want to dig a hole in the bottom of the quarry at Boxgrove?

Archaeology is tough in England. You get cold, wet, bored, you struggle with absurd levels of funding, and all for what? A small heap of junk that people will look at and say: 'You did all that for *that*?' Even other archaeologists will tell you they would've done it better, they would've dug *there*, not *there*. And if you publish it no one ever seems to read it and, if you're really, really lucky, it gets a review in an academic journal subscribed to by a few hundred institutions.

By the time Owen Bedwin recruited him as Supervisor for the Roman farmstead beside Ounce's Barn, Mark had worked on excavations of virtually every 'period': bronze age, Saxon, iron age, medieval . . . but he'd never worked in the palaeolithic. But mucking about in the quarries after work, playing a bit of football, they started finding handaxes and big flint flakes. At the far end of the eastern quarry, near the area where Woodcock had dug a small hole, it seemed you just tripped over the things – it was a few years since any archaeologist had been down there looking for them. One day they had an official visit from the Department of the Environment's Chief Archaeologist, Geoffrey Wainwright (this was shortly before English Heritage was formed). Mark had to show him around the site (they'd spent hours straightening all the pit sides, sweeping up, polishing buckets) and, just for fun really, they'd washed a few of their palaeolithic flints and arranged them on a table. There was no thought

75

of showing Wainwright where they'd come from, but it was pleasant to see that he was interested. Not everyone was.

Some students at the Institute were crazy about flint knapping, making their own tools, but not Mark. What he liked to do was dig: to be out in the open, at large in the thick of it, helping to set up, plan the campaign, lay out the trenches (the military careers of the two great inspirers of modern excavation techniques, General Augustus Pitt Rivers and Colonel Mortimer Wheeler, left their legacy in field jargon). But slowly it dawned on him that what they were finding in the bottom of the quarry was not just a collection of flints: it was a huge, complex (even dangerous with the towering quarry walls and heavy machinery) archaeological site, into which the Roman excavation would just disappear like a pebble in a pond. Mark was starting to get interested in the palaeolithic.

One day he bumped into Roy Shephard-Thorn, the geologist from the Institute of Geological Sciences who was working on the survey of Sussex. Roy had popped into the pits to have a scratch around, as he often did, and had told Mark what he and his colleagues were doing, explained the stratigraphy of the pits, and showed him (as best as he knew) where flint artefacts had been found. For Mark this was a critical meeting: Roy could put the quarries into the broader context of the whole coastal plain. He'd refer Mark to publications where he could read about the geology, and explain why he thought the original ancient cliff had been so high – there was just so much chalk rubble in the pits. They were wary of this huge cliff theory, then, but everyone who spoke to Roy Shephard-Thorn found him very helpful.

Although few students did it that way, it was quite natural that Mark's undergraduate dissertation be based on an excavation. For a week or so shortly before Christmas 1982, there were six London students down in the Eartham pit, including Mark (the others were Martin Bates, Richard Champion, Simon Hornby, Phil Perkins and Tony Tynan). They were there for a small survey. With Peter Drewett's help, Mark had applied to the Sussex Archaeological Society for some money. Their privately endowed Margary Fund had given him £100. In addition a friend lent him £300. This was the first capital to be spent on archaeology in the quarries. The weather was dreadful, wet all the time; it was dark by 3 o'clock.

Flint tools in mint condition had been reported from the bottom of the pit. For this to happen, thought Mark, there had to be a preserved land surface – a rare phenomenon that held exciting prospects for large scale exploration. This is an important concept and the key to the quality of preservation at Boxgrove. The modern ground surface is, more or less, the same surface that would have been cultivated or built on by, say, a Roman villa owner 2,000 years ago or a bronze age farmer 4,000 years ago. But because both natural processes and human interference are continuous, what was once a 3,000-year-old field will today be a modern soil, with none of the ancient field in evidence. Sometimes, however, time is frozen. If the bronze age farmer builds a burial mound, throwing dirt and rocks into a heap, the surface underneath is trapped. Nothing can now reach it, and until it is disturbed by the removal of the mound, it stays there as a fossilized record of a lost landscape. Hundreds of thousands of years ago, no one constructed earth mounds. But in an age of ice, the Earth itself could move and bury an entire world.

The students' goal in December 1982 was to see if there was such a surface at Boxgrove. They dug seven small holes, in a line running south from as near to the imagined ancient chalk cliff as they could get. They didn't find the cliff. And neither did they find the land surface. Then, in the last hole, two of them were cleaning the pit side when a shovel hit flint with a loud 'whack'. A second try, and 'whack' again – the flint had not moved. They crouched down to look, and saw a handaxe, stuck in the silts where it had been dropped thousands of years ago, yet still fresh as new. They didn't then know why it was there, or what had preserved this ancient surface; but Mark had his dissertation. And they were hooked.

In the summer of 1983, Mark Roberts, BA (hons) worked as a Senior Supervisor on a deep excavation at Peel Castle on the Isle of Man, helping to organize the careful removal of deposits that ranged in time all the way from Viking to medieval and later. In September he was back in the pit. Maybe that handaxe was a fluke.

He had a further £500 from the Margary Fund, so they were able to mount a proper excavation: the same group of friends, this time with a dozen student volunteers on subsistence money. Now Mark was Director. And he got his own Supervisor (not that either of them actually got paid). Duncan Lees had just finished his first year as an undergraduate, and like many students at the Institute, knew about Mark and his quarry dig. There was something attractively subversive about it all: this guy had got a good degree, he was a brilliant digger, yet he liked loud punk music and seemed to attract little support from 'grown-up' archaeologists. He wasn't interested in money: he just wanted to dig. Duncan Lees became the first Supervisor at Boxgrove, an experienced excavator who wanted to join Mark because of what he'd seen and heard. They shared the barns with Owen Bedwin, directing his second season at the Roman site.

First they dug a seven by seven metre trench near where they had found the handaxe the previous Christmas. Then they dug several more little test pits, photographing everything, measuring in their finds. It all fell into place, like a well oiled military machine. They were driven people, on site at 6.30 in the morning, working hard.

Mark knew what they'd find as far as the geology went. The first little pits they'd dug were to explore just that – they called them Geological Test Pits or GTPs – and were for the sections, the pit sides that showed the different layers of silt and sand and gravels piled one on the other. But the archaeology was different. To understand that, to see how big an area it covered, they needed to examine everything that came out of the ground. The main trench looked small, but as it went down, it seemed to grow. They had never done any three-dimensional recording before, and they didn't really know what to expect. It was only in the last couple of weeks that they found a lot: suddenly there were tons of flint flakes all over the place, and every single one had to be individually surveyed and levelled in. They recovered precisely 990 flint artefacts, including two handaxes, all in mint condition. Chris Bergman, an American Research Fellow at the Institute studying flint knapping, was able to fit together several flakes, as if they had only just been struck apart. If the rest of the quarry was like this, the preserved land surface must cover at least 1,000 square metres.

Then Mark's money ran out.

Chapter 18

Reinforcements and Recognition

European mink

'It's time you got a proper job', said his father. 'Get yourself a proper job', said uncle. So he went back to London, to be near the Institute of Archaeology – if not for work, at least for comfort. He fell out with his girlfriend, and stayed in a Housing Association flat in Borough with his old Supervisor, Duncan Lees. It was a long walk from the house to the Institute, where he would just sit in the library and read. He'd break the drag back, when the library closed, with a beer at the Cittie of York: one pint could be made to last a long time. When it came, the job turned out to be a security guard in the City, haunting an office building site in 12-hour shifts. Any job was better than the dole: but this one? Half hour walk, over the Thames and back again, and the pay was atrocious. Things really were desperate. And then one day, sharing a drink with an old student friend who had been at the original Christmas 1982 dig, it hit him. Mark drained his pint and stood it back on the table; he *knew* he had to get back to digging at Boxgrove.

And from that moment security guarding was a challenge – the walk out and back an intellectual assignment. Visits to the Institute library had purpose, even a trip to the launderette was a chance to leaf through some old notes again. For Mark was planning an excavation. He read and re-read his undergraduate dissertation; he calculated a budget (he didn't have any money, but it was as well to know what he couldn't get); he worked out who would be able to come with him, what tools they would need, where they would dig and how much they could do in how many days. He wrote to the ARC pit manager, John Horrocks. He scrutinized quarry charts, borrowed Woodcock's thesis from the library. He'd show them: they *had* to support a dig.

The better to read the story of Boxgrove, the time has come to get close to the quarries, to enter the world of trenches, test pits and sections: to learn the grammar of excavating.

Look at the first map (fig 8). It shows Boxgrove Common in 1975: the point when Andrew Woodcock was researching palaeolithic Sussex and Geoff Kellaway and Roy Shephard-Thorn were studying the geology. Ounces Barn, still surrounded by fields, is near the middle of the map, accessible by straight farm track from the road to the north. The route into the quarry is from the Plant Site to the south east.

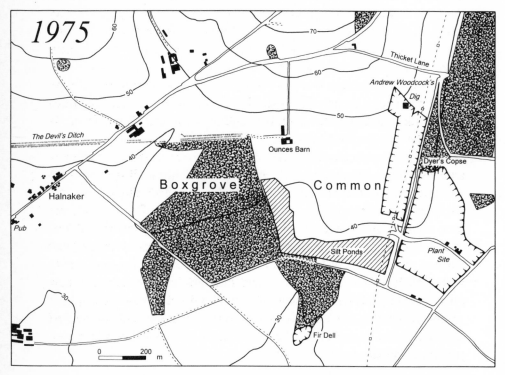

fig 8: Andrew Woodcock, then Curator at Chichester Museum, was the first archaeologist to dig in the gravel pits on Boxgrove Common.

In a straight line, it is about 1.2 kilometres (three quarters of a mile) from the barn to the pub in Halnaker village. Down the centre, the contours show the bottom of Halnaker Hill coming in from the north at about 75 metres above sea level, and the slope gradually flattening, as the contours space out, with a small valley starting to the south of Ounces Barn. Fir Dell itself is an old overgrown gravel pit; one of many tiny, non-commercial pits that were dug for local building and road mending or, if on chalk, for liming the fields.

The most ancient feature of the surface landscape is Devil's Ditch, the iron age dyke which now runs through the chicken processing factory, where Mark will be a student volunteer on the Field Unit's first excavation on the Common (though once a true 'common', all the land in the area has long since been divided up into fields and is privately owned). Pylons carry high power electricity cables across Thicket Lane; other tracks across the common remain unmetalled.

Quarrying has started to eat into the landscape from the east. The Eartham pits were begun in a small way in the 1920s by James Penfold, a local man whose four sons expanded the business thirty years later, after the War; the Amey Group took them over in 1965 (Consolidated Goldfields swallowed Amey in 1972, and merged them with Roadstone to form Amey Roadstone Corporation; since 1989, ARC – as they are now known – have been part of the Hanson Group). The Plant Site, a secure area with offices, showers and other facilities for the men, grading and loading machinery for gravel and so on, is established in one of the old Penfolds pits.

Quarries are generally backfilled with local refuse or unwanted material from newer workings; so you cannot always tell from looking at a map whether or not the original ground has been dug out. In fact the field to the south of the Plant Site was another old Penfolds pit, this time refilled and put back to farming. The recently exhausted pits south of Ounces Barn are now silt ponds, where watery muds from washed gravel can settle and dry. Soon they too will be spread over with topsoil, which is scraped off and stored in heaps whenever a new pit is opened, and farmed again. The huge pit beside Dyer's Copse is where Woodcock has a small excavation in progress. This is the first archaeological dig in all of the Eartham pits; he will find eight well preserved handaxes.

The summer of 1984 was unusually warm and dry. Listening to cricket on his portable radio, concentrating on the grains of sand and gravel Mark gently scraped out with his trowel – by now well worn down – he began to realize the enormity of what he had done. He arrived on 5 May. The regulations meant he couldn't sign on for welfare money, as he had resigned from his job. His old man helped out with the odd fiver. Some of the men went shooting in the quarries Friday nights, and he'd wake up with a couple of rabbits on the ground outside his tent. But food wasn't his only problem.

In 1979 ARC had opened a new pit on Boxgrove Common, north of the Devil's Ditch. By 1984 there was around 40,000 square metres of hole (fig 9). The pit that Woodcock had explored in the 1970s was now a gigantic silt lagoon, but fresh quarrying had opened ground to the north and west. The geology seemed more complex than ever, the opportunities for finding archaeology greater – until the current pits were finished and gone, as they would be before long – and Mark trowelled gently by himself in his little trench while circling iron behemoths threw dust into the sky.

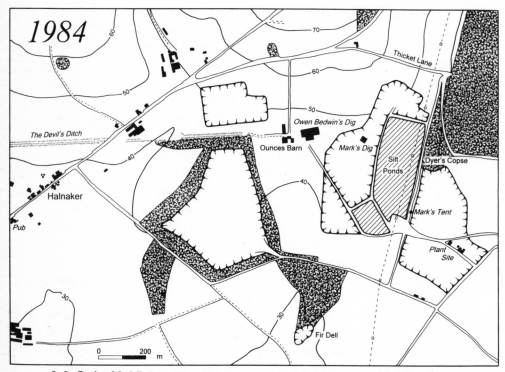

fig 9: Student Mark Roberts directed his first small digs at Boxgrove in 1982 and 1983. In the early summer of 1984 he went back to the quarries with no funding, but determined to continue the work.

Once again, the Sussex Archaeological Society kept him going with a grant (this time £750). Then, ten days before the main excavation was due to start, he heard he had English Heritage support. They dug for exactly eight weeks from 8 July. Mark had about 20 students and former student friends for help, among them Greg Bell, Duncan Lees, Tony Tynan and Frank Wenban-Smith (who was to be the senior staff member in the final two dramatic years). They expanded the previous winter's main trench, opened some more test pits and extended the Beach Section – but the ancient cliff continued to prove elusive. They also opened some test pits in the newer quarry north west of Ounces Barn (which we will call the West Quarry to distinguish it from the original East Quarry). They found more debris from flint tool manufacture, and confirmed the exceptional preservation conditions. In one of the small test pits in the East Quarry they found the first animal bone of the project – like some of the few bones found in the 1970s, a small relic from a bison.

Mark's official position was Temporary Assistant Field Officer. Peter Drewett was worried that they wouldn't find enough to merit continuing beyond August. Then one day, as they sweated in the dust and the heat, they had a visit from English Heritage's Chief Archaeologist. On his decision rested the long term future of the excavation. Peter had briefed Mark in an attempt to ensure he said the right things. But Geoffrey Wainwright had already met Mark in the quarries, two years before, on his routine visit to Owen Bedwin's excavation of the Roman farmstead. And though now working from an office in London, in earlier years Wainwright had directed some of the largest prehistoric excavations ever seen in Britain.

'Ah yes,' remembers Wainwright, still Chief Archaeologist over 15 years later. 'Mark was a determined, pugnacious, obsessed young man. He was absolutely fascinated by the palaeolithic. He said "Do you have a few minutes?" and took me down to his test pits in the quarry bottom. It was immediately apparent he had a fossil landscape, with bifaces and animal bone in excellent condition. Most impressive.'

Mark didn't know it, but Wainwright himself had happy student memories of looking for handaxes (or bifaces) in the Sussex quarries. He is well known in the profession for his work on 'henge monuments', huge earthworks approximately contemporary with Stonehenge, and could recognize in Mark a skilled field campaigner.

In 1984 Geoff Wainwright was President of the Prehistoric Society. In the very month that a penniless Mark Roberts had pitched his lone tent in the Boxgrove quarries, this Society had completed a report aimed squarely at the newly formed English Heritage. One of its recommendations was that 'the discovery of an undisturbed open-air palaeolithic occupation site would warrant total excavation by highly-skilled specialists,' although they were concerned that 'recognition of such sites may ... be beyond the capabilities of most field archaeologists'.

Mindful of the Society's report, Wainwright was on the look-out for just such a site with someone like Roberts attached.

Late in August 1984, Mark learnt that English Heritage were commissioning from him, through the Institute's Field Archaeology Unit (it had by then dropped the 'Sussex'), a 12-month assessment of the quarries, to be known as the Boxgrove Lower Palaeolithic Project. On 1 September 1984, gathering his equipment together, he left Boxgrove for a fishing holiday in Ireland. He needed to think things through.

Chapter 19

'Major Dig on Unique Site'

elephant

September is not the best time of year to begin an outdoor project in Britain. One of the first things they did with their new money was to buy a shelter to cover the trench in the East Quarry, in anticipation of what was becoming an increasingly important and delicate excavation needing protection over the winter. It was a horticultural greenhouse, a 30-metre tunnel of translucent polythene held up by curved metal pipes and closed at either end by more sheeting supported on wooden slats. By the close of that 1984 summer, the British were talking of a drought – it hadn't rained for weeks. The day the cover arrived in the quarry, the heavens opened. There were ten pipes each side to be sunk into the brickearth, and every day of two weeks it took to put it up it rained. The huge polythene sheet had to be persuaded into place in a howling gale.

Once up the shelter offered psychological as well as meteorological defence: safe from wind and rain, stray dogs, wandering deer and anything else loose in the quarries, you could lavish the ultimate care on the excavation. The fine sand could be scraped away with modelling tools, every tiniest piece of flint left in place and marked with a little flag for measuring in later, and the slightest change in colour or texture of the deposits could be noted and recorded at leisure. The digging of exploratory pits could be continued outside, including in the West Quarry, where animal bone started to appear in quantity. This in fact was the pattern for the next 12 months: good bone West Quarry; good flints East Quarry (fig 10).

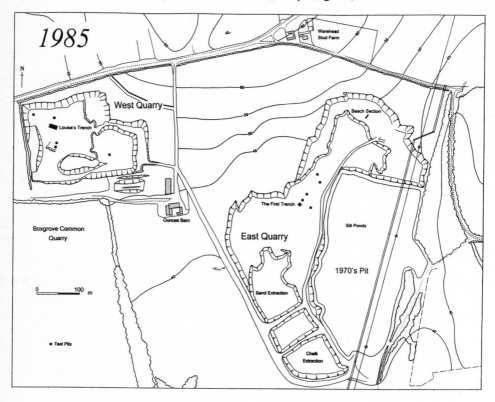

fig 10: The first 12-month project at Boxgrove, funded by English Heritage, ended in the autumn of 1985. Mark extended operations into the West Quarry, which had been opened by ARC late in 1979.

The shelter was no help, however, against the cold, and that winter it got so cold, your pick bounced up off the frozen gravel. Peter Drewett was worried for the safety of the diggers camped out in barns, and ordered them to stop. They packed up for a couple of weeks over Christmas. They were back in early January, when they found the shelter good protection from heavy snow. One week the thermometer never rose above freezing at all. With all water supplies gone, they had to collect snow and ice to melt for drinking and cooking. They'd come back in for a mid-morning break and find the tea and tea bags frozen into the pot. 'Can't afford it,' said Mark when someone suggested heating, so they borrowed an old gas heater from the pub in Halnaker. That wasn't the full answer, however, for first they had to vaporize the gas. The least dangerous method they tried was to hang the spare bottle on a rope above the burning heater. There they'd sit, searching for feeling in their fingertips until, one evening, the rope broke and a full gas bottle dropped from above and smashed the heater. After that they bought their own. But the worst problem was rats. They were everywhere, in your sleeping bag, in your clothes, in the kitchen, perhaps, they joked, even in the stew – Mark shot anything that moved.

Bidding for English Heritage money the previous summer, Mark'd had to put together a written proposal – some short notes, a map, fill in a few forms – and he remembered meeting Geoff Wainwright at a conference and taking the opportunity to show him a plan of the quarries detailing all the test pits he hoped to dig. When they had the team and they were excavating pits all over the place, things moved more slowly than anticipated. There was archaeology everywhere, and plotting all those flints took time, a lot of time. The bones made it even worse. There were animal bones wherever they dug in the West Quarry, and they really hadn't been expecting them. The bones were not well preserved, so they had to be lifted in blocks of silt, wrapped in aluminium foil and plaster. When it came for Wainwright to make a formal inspection visit, Mark was so worried about the discrepancy between proposal and reality that he had all the pits on the original plan opened up in the quarries: not dug out – just opened. So when Wainwright stood at the top of the West Quarry in the drizzle and looked across the heaps of gravel and scrubby weeds, he could see an array of neat pits laid out on a grid (Mark had correctly reckoned on him not feeling the urge to climb down into this quarry). They called those pits their cardboard tanks, after a campaign in the African desert when airborne aggressors were confused by mock fighting tanks on the ground.

The ploy seemed to work: or perhaps Geoff Wainwright knew what was going on all along, and that their delay was in fact a reflection of the quality of the site. In any event, late March, 1985, the *Chichester Observer* carried what is probably the first Boxgrove media story. Under 'Major dig on unique site', they explained that English Heritage had granted more than £41,000 for the excavation, which would continue to 1987 (what they didn't say was that Mark's contract was renewable annually). The site was one of the best of its kind in western Europe. The local *Observer* series gave them good coverage throughout the project, occasionally beating the national media to a story. Now, as the lengthening days at least held the promise of warmer weather, the paper was reminding Mark that his site had already become public property. It seemed only a matter of time before someone would say, openly, it was too important for Roberts.

It wasn't just the newspapers. Other archaeologists were starting to visit, the first – and in some ways the most significant – arriving as early as November the previous year. As the gentle, skeletal man with a black beard climbed the field from the south, Geoff Wainwright turned to him and said: 'Be warned, Clive, the excavator's a bit of a rough diamond.'

The excavator hauled himself out of a red van as the pair approached.

'I wondered when you buggers would show up.'

It was plain to Geoff Wainwright that Clive Gamble was his man for advice on Boxgrove. Like Mark, Clive already had experience of excavating when he reached university. In particular, he had been the recipient of the first 'rescue' grant for a palaeolithic dig in Britain. Within a month of joining the staff at Southampton University, early in 1975 he had found himself at Red Barns, Hampshire, with Arthur ApSimon, a senior lecturer, exploring what might be the same raised beach that he could now see at Boxgrove; they were given £100 from the Department of the Environment's Rescue Budget. Clive Gamble was to remain a key adviser to the end, establishing a link with Southampton that the University was to become increasingly keen to foster.

The two visitors were back in the quarries in the spring, with a high level tour put on by the Prehistoric Society celebrating 50 years (Wainwright was still President; Gamble, Secretary). Among the guests were prominent archaeologists Australian Peter White and Americans Kent Flannery and Lew Binford. Beneath the plastic cover, they picked their way in shoeless feet between the flints and the flags on the palaeolithic 'floor', the perfectly preserved land surface that Mark had always said was there. Later in the Anglesey Arms, Binford was thumping the table with excitement. This great bear of a man, an inspiring talker as well as writer, had met a kindred spirit.

Mark never had doubts about his field skills. He could manage teams and budgets, plan campaigns, dig like the best. But the background stuff, holding his own in the pub with the likes of Binford and Gamble, understanding the specialists: that was different. If he'd not learnt it all as an undergraduate, now was the time. He joined the Quaternary Research Association, an ice age think tank. He threw everything into understanding climate and geology. And that summer, as the whispering campaign to remove him from the site began, he put the learning to work in the first of many meetings for which the project was to become justifiably famous. The way to hold on to Boxgrove was to invite the world in.

Supported by the Institute of Archaeology's then director, John Evans, he convened a meeting in London. There were a dozen or so of them: English Heritage staff, geologists, palaeolithic archaeologists, Institute lecturers – all people that Mark wanted to convince that *he* was the person to dig Boxgrove. They looked at slides of the site, handled flint axes, talked about the bones and the geology – what date were the deposits? did anyone believe this old glacier idea of Kellaway's? – and argued about how it should be studied. Then afterwards in the pub, listening to Geoff Wainwright talk excitedly about the project, Mark knew his team had them. Boxgrove was theirs.

The next thing was to invite people down to Sussex. The excuse was a conference to think about the ancient land surface, to suss it out: What was it? Why was it there? There was no questioning its existence. Richard Macphail, a specialist in sediments, had at first said bare mudflats. But the excavation was now producing bones of small mammals and amphibians which were incompatible with salt water. So Mark had brought down from London Macphail, Chris Bergman (flint knapper), Simon Collcutt (geologist), Andy Currant (zoologist studying the animal bones) and Rob Scaife (botanist working with preserved pollen grains). They stayed a few days, wandering about the quarries, looking at the vertical sections. In the end the problem was solved by analogy with the present. By the time of the tour, they had been sieving the fine silty clay for a few months, and a wet heap of it had spread out on the pit bottom. Growing at the edge were thick grasses. Even on the bare gravels trees had taken root. The ancient surface had to have been left by a slowly falling sea, but then been quickly colonized by vegetation. The animals implied this, too: large herbivores like rhinos and bison, which they had already been finding, needed vast tracts of grazing. The excavation trenches were windows on a long grassy plain between the cliff and the marine estuary.

All those bones needed looking at. Over the winter, Mark had taken some to London to show Don Brothwell (a lecturer at the Institute known for his work on both animal and human bones and his interest in disease). Brothwell was excited by what he saw: could he come down to the site in the summer? Which he did, with his wife and young children, camping in the quarries in their caravan. He also brought an assistant, a newly graduated student called Simon Parfitt.

Mark had earlier taken to muttering 'the voleman cometh'. When Simon appeared in white polo-necked sweater and black Wellington boots, looking like a U-boat captain from an old black-and-white War movie, they called him Otto Voleman. The name stuck. As did Simon, from volunteer, to Supervisor with responsibility for fauna in 1986 and eventually to Assistant Director. His rise reflected the enormous significance to the project both of the animal bones and of Simon himself.

In 1985 he created an immediate impact, by playing about with chemicals. As a student he had learnt the importance of thinking very carefully about retrieval techniques for bones on archaeological excavations. How to ensure the best recovery of this precious evidence at Boxgrove? He tried breaking down the sediments in solutions of bicarbonate of soda and hydrogen peroxide, but found the most effective way was the simplest: dry the silt, by spreading it out in the sun on plastic sheets, then gently wash it with clean water through a series of increasingly fine stacked sieves. The early implementation of such tricks was significant, one reason in itself for the high esteem in which Boxgrove is now held for its animal remains alone. Over the entire project, many tons of sediment were sieved, and thousands of bones identifiable to animal species were examined by Simon with a binocular microscope. What stories those bones had to tell . . .

The season closed at the end of September, and Mark immediately returned to London to write the first major report. It was an extraordinary opening year by any standards. Geology, archaeology, animal bones, staff, a management partnership – achievements everywhere. Mark Roberts was then 24; Simon Parfitt 22.

Chapter 20

The Giant Tooth

great auk

Midsummer 1986. They'd been drilling holes through the bottom of the quarry pit – augering. Along the north west edge of the pit they'd been hitting something. The auger wouldn't go through it, it must have been the chalk. Mark suggested digging a hole to get a section through the deposits: to reveal what was going on down there.

The archaeologists weren't the only ones digging in the quarry. The real excavators weren't just poking about in the pit, they were *making* it. They took the red gravels, first, with a drag-line. When the gravels were gone, there was a bunch of clays and silts in the way – brickearth that could be pale yellow or reddish brown, thin layers of grey sand and light brown silts, lenses of small rounded flint pebbles – and underneath, more valuable material – this time up to six metres of fine, clean, brownish-yellow sand. The junk between was hauled off with a box scraper, a huge machine dragging its belly over the floor, rolling up the quarry bottom and dropping it off at the east side of the pit. Here the clays were moulded into 'bunds', settling ponds for the silt-rich water that flowed from the gravel washing.

They called it 'the archaeology'. Walking across the quarry floor after the silts had been shaved off, scanning like a hawk, Mark spotted a worked flint. 'Hey, we've hit the archaeology.'

Faces turned towards him expectantly.

The 'archaeology' was mostly between the bottom of the brickearth and the top of the sands. Gravels were removed when a client wanted to buy. There wasn't usually much of a hurry to get out the sands underneath, giving the archaeologists time to study the surface, open a few thoughtfully placed trenches, clean up the section faces. There was a distinctive marker horizon between the brickearth and the silts, a thin, dark brown, almost black line. Sometimes it was still hidden underfoot, where the box-scraper had left a little clay; sometimes it had been ripped out. Sometimes it had never been there, taken away by more recent geology. This was the Fe Horizon, the iron-rich layer. The best archaeology was just below: traces of human and animal activity undisturbed for hundreds of thousands of years.

Walking back from lunch towards the trench they were digging, Greg Bell took a circuitous detour, crunching his heavy black boots down a slightly deeper machined area. Then he spotted something perched on the tip of a wheel rut ridge. It was a huge molar: a prodigious back tooth. Most of the time they found bones of small mammals or bits and pieces that were difficult to identify. This wasn't a small mammal, such as a vole or mouse, it wasn't even a horse, or a deer: it was bigger than that. And it still had some Fe stuck to it, so it came from the 200,000–300,000-year-old land surface.

'Simon! Where are you?!'

Chapter 21

Simon Parfitt

giant deer

Later the same day Simon left for London, by train. The railway track ran straight and flat across the old sea plain, through fields of ripening wheat, fenced and ditched but, since Dutch elm had ravaged the hedgerows some ten years before, spare on trees. Looking out across the old war-time airfield at Tangmere, over the scattered clumps of red brick and flint barns and houses that pass for villages, Simon could see a windmill capping a rise in the wall of chalk hills that backs the plain, the sun in its white sails. His friends, he knew, could think only of what news he would bring back from London.

It lay inside his battered briefcase, wrapped in tissues in a plastic carrier bag. Of one thing, Simon was certain: it was a rhino tooth. And he knew enough about prehistoric rhinos to know that during the long span of the ice ages, various species came and went. What he didn't know was how to tell them apart. Which was frustrating, as the implications for their work in the pits, if this tooth proved to be from one particular type of rhinoceros, were boggling: their site could be twice as old as everyone thought it was. Which was why Mark had bundled him off to see Andy Currant in London, that very afternoon.

How on earth had Greg seen it? The tooth looked exactly like a lump of flint. The box-scraper must have hit a skull, or perhaps a piece of upper jaw, and scattered fragments around in the dirt. They'd scoured the area, and found a bit of an adjacent tooth, with soil still attached; nothing more.

Simon grew up in Gloucestershire, near Tetbury. It was a landscape of deserted medieval settlements and ridge and furrow – fields from a forgotten way of farming. Near the village where he lived was a large, private estate with woods, ruined buildings, and a game keeper's decaying lodge. Just to the east, they kept digging up these fields to get at the gravel beneath: ancient beds from the upper Thames and its tributaries, feeding the demands of roads and construction, bequeathing a chequerboard of flooded pits.

He fell in with Arthur Witchell, a local farmer who found ancient flint tools on the rain washed surfaces of his land. Then, barely in his teens, he discovered the joys of excavating. It was a 20-mile cycle ride at weekends, slowly up to the top of the Cotswolds, then straight down to the site at Frocester Court, with a view across the Severn estuary. After that, he dug a lot in the school holidays. A Roman temple at Uley, not far from home; Wells Cathedral, across the border in Somerset; Carlisle, nearly in Scotland. And before he knew it, he was at the Institute of Archaeology in London: far from the ivy and rotting branches at the game keeper's lodge, but surrounded by fellow students who'd all, in their private ways, discovered the fascination of tracing their own routes to the past.

And then, of course, there was London itself. At the Institute, he'd got interested in a new concept that archaeologists were calling 'taphonomy'. In particular, there was an American anthropologist, Lewis Binford, who'd written a new book about how animal bones collect together into deposits, and then survive for archaeologists to find. Or rather, how they *don't* survive. How other animals, weather, rivers, geology, decay, even the archaeologists digging them up, all conspire to mess things about so that reading from the bones to the creatures they came from becomes a detective game of epic proportions: an intellectual puzzle to solve, past worlds of pristine tundras or huge, endless forests, inhabited by animals now more commonly seen in zoos than in the wild. If they weren't already extinct.

Binford's book was nothing if not controversial. When it came to criticizing the work of other archaeologists, its author relished his punches. But he wrote with conviction. It seemed obvious, at least to Binford, that to understand how deposits of bones had accumulated in the past, it was necessary to witness them forming in the present. So he had made friends with Inuit people in the far north. He had sat round fires and listened to hunters' tales; he had suffered the cold, crouching for hours watching wolf cubs through his telephoto lens; he had tracked caribou, and seen their guts ripped from their bellies in the fresh, white snow.

On one occasion, he had been setting up his camera to photograph a moose browsing amongst willows beside a creek, when he had noticed a dark shape in the viewfinder – an enormous grizzly bear.

With an explosive dash, the bear ran at the moose from the rear, and the moose began running; however, the bear overtook the moose in short order and hurled its full weight on the rear haunches while reaching forward with its front paws for the neck of the moose. As the weight of the bear buckled the rear legs of the moose, its head jerked up and back. At the same time the bear grabbed the neck and pulled backward. The moose and the bear crashed to the ground and the moose never moved again.

The bear had rested a little, before violently tearing the moose apart. Binford had watched until two in the morning, when the cold had driven him back to camp. The next day, wolves and ravens had moved in to finish off the carcass. Later he would talk to the Inuit about what he'd seen.

Simon was hooked.

The good thing about the Institute of Archaeology and London was their size. All those libraries, the museums, the visiting lecturers from around the world, the varied laboratories, teaching staff and hundreds of students: whatever your interest, you'd be pretty sure to find ways of following it up. So Simon attended courses about bones and making flint tools. At the Natural History Museum he discovered the biggest collection of old bones, anywhere.

In his third year he had to prepare a dissertation. He'd read about Kent's Cavern in Devon, from which one of the largest groups of ice age animal bones in Europe had been excavated in the nineteenth century, together with – notoriously – evidence for early humans. From the deepest layers had come apparent indications that people had been butchering cave bears. It seemed an ideal opportunity to pursue some of Binford's ideas about interpreting these ancient deposits.

Peter Andrews at the Natural History Museum – or, as it was then more properly known, the British Museum (Natural History) – was appointed to supervise his project. Antony Sutcliffe, Director of the Palaeontology Department, had done a bit of pioneering fieldwork himself, pursuing hyena in east Africa. These vicious hunters and scavengers, once common all over the old world, were four-footed refuse collectors. In an attempt better to understand fossil hyena dens, Tony went poking around crevices and burrows stuffed with left-over dinners. In one lair he found more than he'd bargained for: a human jaw and three skulls. Some local Maasai villagers suggested the hyena might have been dining at the nearby hospital cemetery, a theory which a quick visit to the hospital proved correct.

Andrews cautioned Simon against tackling Kent's Cavern: the site was a mess and its records difficult to make sense of.

Tony Sutcliffe had a better idea. The Museum had a unique collection of bones from a musk ox butchery site on Banks Island in Canada. A century ago, a ship looking for the doomed Franklin expedition (who had all died looking for a North West passage in the 1840s) had become trapped in the ice. Over subsequent years, Inuit had gradually stripped the wood from the boat, meanwhile leaving a growing heap of food remains that had, in time, found their way into the basement of the Natural History Museum. How had these bones survived all those Arctic winters? How had lichen growth affected the cutmarks left by the butchery process? How much could he tell from the bones alone about the way in which the oxen were prepared?

It was a good project. But most of all, it introduced Simon to the people and the collections at the Natural History Museum, where he was now to go with the rhino tooth.

Chapter 22

The Essential Rhino

Hundsheim rhino

It was a little over a century since the doors of the Natural History Museum first opened to the public on their own site (before which the collections had been bursting out of the corridors of the British Museum in Bloomsbury). Yet Alfred Waterhouse's building had a vitality about it, especially since, after generations of neglect, the terracotta facade had recently been cleaned.

Once through the entrance Simon strode out across the vast exhibition hall, making for a side tunnel off to the right. The décor in this particular passage of the Natural History Museum consists of framed fossils of giant fish-like creatures with long, toothed jaws and flippers. There's a pliosaur from Whitby, nine metres long. And a pregnant mother with the skeletons of three unborn young still inside her bony cage, her fourth actually half-way out of the birth canal. An eight-metre ichthyosaur from Lyme Regis, Dorsetshire, was figured (continues the heavily blocked nineteenth-century hand-painted note) in Hawkins' *Sea Dragons* of 1840. One watery monster after another, like huge black and white cells from the cartoon of Jurassic life.

Beyond the two doors into the Palaeontology Building at the end, stood Andy Currant. He already knew what Simon had in his briefcase – he had predicted as much in his short note for Mark's report published only six months before. What he had written, reproduced in tiny print, had been controversial, to say the least. The implications were too far-reaching for anyone to accept his argument – assuming they could spot it – without a lot of thought and further study. What it added up to was that the whole framework by which archaeologists and geologists understood the ice age in Britain – and from which it followed that the first ancestral humans had not reached these shores until about 300,000 years ago – was wrong.

We will look at these arguments in detail later. There is, at present, no magic clock for dating every ice age deposit and relating them to the long succession of cold and warm stages. Fixing Boxgrove is a matter of making correlations across Europe, and even beyond, with those few sites where dating has been possible. The best hope of making these connections lies in animal bones, and the constantly changing faunas they represent. Up to then, Currant's case rested on no more than a few vole teeth. Even Mark was taking a little convincing.

Andy grinned in anticipation at Simon. 'Come on boy, let's see what you've got there.'

The essential story about rhinos in Britain is that during the course of the last 600,000 or 700,000 years of the ice age, a succession of species came and went. First *Stephanorhinus hundsheimensis*, then *Stephanorhinus kirchbergensis* and *Stephanorhinus hemitoechus* and then, after *kirchbergensis* died out, just *Stephanorhinus hemitoechus*. During the very cold periods (these other rhinos were warmth-loving creatures) the famous woolly rhino, *Coelodonta antiquitatis*, carried the torch, but we're not concerned with them now.

Geologists and palaeontologists are all agreed that the first rhino, *Stephanorhinus hundsheimensis* (then known as *Dicerorhinus etruscus*) died out before a deeply cold period of the ice age that began around 480,000 years ago. This cold stage is known in Britain as the Anglian (named after East Anglia). It was also generally agreed, in 1986, that there were no humans in Britain until *after* the Anglian period. Which was why evidence for hominid activity had never been found in deposits yielding bones of *Dicerorhinus etruscus*.

After visiting Andy Currant, Simon knew about rhino teeth. Andy had taken him into the fossil collection, and pulled out tray after tray of bones and teeth, picking out this one to point out a feature, turning another in the fluorescent light to reveal its topography.

The specimen from the site was clean and dry, now, like a terribly mis-shapen snooker ball; cream, buff ivory coloured, with a grey, flinty chewing surface, it was heavy, even though the roots were missing. How on earth had Greg spotted it?

At 9 pm, Simon's taxi pulled up at the Anglesey Arms. As he entered, Mark looked up. Simon held out a little box with a clear plastic lid, and his whole face grinned. A 500,000 year, do-you-realize-what-this-means? now-let-them-argue grin.

All that time, looking for the buried land surface in the quarries, finding the animal bones and the flint artefacts that were so perfectly preserved, they'd been standing in trenches that were excisions into a world so hidden that even few geologists had been able to describe it. A world where archaeologists were not even sure that hominids had been. They'd been looking at a lost continent that was not 200 but 500,000 years old. What preserved that ancient land surface at Boxgrove? How could the discovery of a single rhino tooth so completely change things? How do geologists know that this creature became extinct 500,000 years ago? And why, before the tooth had been identified, did they believe the sands and gravels of the ancient raised beach in Sussex were of a different era? To answer these questions, we need to understand the ice age and why it happened. Indeed, we need to know why it's still not over.

PART FOUR
ICE AND THE FIRST HOMINIDS

Chapter 23

The Power of Snow

whooper swan

Midday sun softens and melts fresh powdery falls, the snow sinks, freezes and recrystallizes. Old snow piles up the weight, and deeper still the ever compacting firn turns to ice. As it flows, almost imperceptibly, like a dense liquid from the mountain ridged basin, the ice, frozen to the rock, plucks at the wall behind it. A deep crevasse opens at the head of the firn-field, a bergschrund through which angular fragments of rock reach the base of the ice. Even at birth the glacier has teeth.

Only the highest exposed peaks, nunataks, jagged islands of bedrock in a frozen sea, escape the tearing and rasping of the ice mass loaded with moraines. On steep bare slopes, freeze and thaw solifluction loosens softer materials and sludges them into the valleys.

Crawling away from the source of snow and down into warmer air, the glacier starts to break up. The ice melts and collapses in dirty, fissured blocks, releasing its rock load. Finer debris is carried on in the meltwater, weaving a network of ever-changing braided streams over the outwash-gravels and -sands. Icy winds blow dust from the drying ground.

If the ice fields are very large, a persistent glacial anticyclone will form, from which dry frost-winds blow across a periglacial zone of intense cold where, at depth, the ground is permanently frozen. Seasonal warming melts the surface of the permafrost, and the repeated thawing and refreezing crack and warp the deposits. These soft wet sludges can flow down slopes, building up many metres of broken rock in valley bottoms. Ice wedges prise into the ground, larger debris is sorted into surface stripes and polygons. Grasses and shrubs of the tundra twitch in the dust-laden winds, trapping the outwash silt and building great depths of loess far from the melting ice.

If circumstances change – the summer warms, the snowfalls thin – the snout of the glacier edges back up the mountain. Behind, it leaves a trail of semi-digested landscape: drumlins, low hills of boulder-clay or till gathered like pods of beached whales; rock basins that may become inland lochans, or coastal lochs or fjords; meandering ridges of gravel, eskers, left by streams that once flowed in torrents beneath the ice; protruding rocks worn smooth (*roches moutonnées*) or boulders seized and carried far from their source (erratics); and long scratches, striae, scoured into bedrock by boulders held fast in moving ice. And should it go completely, the glacier leaves a high circular cwm at the top of the rounded valley.

Thus like a tongue of ice grasping at a varied geology, the English language plunders highland Britain, Scandinavia and Alpine Europe, and even Greenland, for its glacial vocabulary. For the fact is that when thousands of years ago people in what is now England last told of these things, there was nothing remotely like English spoken anywhere on the planet.

Chapter 24

A Time of Ice

Norway lemming

The theory began with Swiss outdoorsmen early in the last century. When you live with glaciers, you know they are alive too. When your village is within earshot of the gunfire of cracking ice, you notice if the glacier is moving closer, crawling down the valley, slowly, over years, decades even, reaching for the houses and barns and the church. And if it should recede, you notice too the land it returns – bare, crushed and lifeless but, in time, more land for grazing animals. Educated men who travelled in this territory – miners, hunters, amateur naturalists – found that locals would confirm their intuitions. Once you knew how to read the signs, you could see where glaciers had extended much lower in the past. Very much lower.

On one of his expeditions into the landscape of mountains and ice, Jean Louis Rodolphe Agassiz suddenly saw the truth in his fellow naturalists' claims. But his vision was not just of times when some glaciers covered more land: it was of *a* time when glaciers *were* the land. At lectures in 1837 he handed out copies of Karl Schimper's latest poem, *Die Eiszeit*: The Ice Age was born.

Agassiz found a natural supporter in William Buckland. The Dean, famous for his promotion of the Flood as the agent for geological change, was yet troubled by doubts as to the ability of water alone to achieve everything he saw. In an Ice Age, the frozen water came armed with rocks like Creationist emery paper. Travelling Scotland with Agassiz, he could see the evidence all around.

'Here we shall find our first trace of glaciers,' said the Swiss scientist as their stage approached the Duke of Argyll's castle. And as they entered the valley, they actually trundled over an ancient terminal moraine.

᾿ Soon Buckland was off proselytizing, taking Charles Lyell in hand to search for more glaciers. 'On showing him a beautiful cluster of moraines within two miles of his father's house,' wrote Buckland to Agassiz, 'he instantly accepted it . . . Lyell has adopted your theory *in toto!!!*'

John McEnery, who was ill and dying in Torquay, probably never knew of Buckland's conversion.

Thus knowledge of glaciers came to Britain. Having covered the whole of Europe with ice as far south as the Mediterranean (which work by others soon showed to be excessive), Agassiz saw in ice what Buckland had found in water, a planetary catastrophe that isolated God's creation from a darker past. He was 'glacier mad', said Darwin.

Visualizing the impact of sheet ice in what is now a temperate world requires a powerful imagination – and measuring the effects scientifically is even harder. For it is not just a matter of climate. While Agassiz scanned for lost icebergs up the Amazon, others in Europe tackled the implications of an *Eiszeit*, a time of ice. Some of the key breakthroughs came in Scotland, where an active tradition of philosophy gazed on an ice-moulded world.

There is only so much water on Earth, so if the ice caps expand, the sea must fall. But the weight of permanent ice several kilometres thick would depress the land – a variable, localized event beside the global sea level change (we now see a further factor to be the lightening of land by erosion and the depression of the sea floor as it accumulates silt from adjacent continents). All this could clearly have something to do with those beaches raised high and dry above the Sussex shore.

Of profound significance for the pattern of hominid colonization in Europe was the theory that there was not just one 'Ice Age', but several. This was proposed by James Croll, who thought that variations in the Earth's orbit caused by gravitational pull from other planets could explain fluctuations in polar ice: when the orbit was particularly elongated, the sun's rays were less potent and the ice grew. He calculated that 'orbital eccentricity' varied in cycles. It followed that the Ice Age would have done the same. And in *The Great Ice Age and its Relation to the Antiquity of Man*, published in 1874, Archibald Geikie described plant and animal remains he had found in the sides of a railway cutting that confirmed Croll's thesis.

We still use Geikie's terms 'glacial' and 'interglacial' to describe the successive cold and warm periods. While most of us persist in thinking of 'an Ice Age', geologists use more precise language. We are technically in an interglacial today, and in time the ice caps will again grow: we live in 'the Ice Age', but we would hardly characterize our world in terms of the hackneyed imagery of snow and mammoths. The phrase has a limited, colloquial use, and it is only in this sense that it appears in this book.

These climatic changes on a scale not witnessed by humans for over ten millennia are responsible for preserving Boxgrove. The distinctive environmental features of each glacial and interglacial enable geologists and archaeologists to tell them apart and to say where Boxgrove belongs.

That's the theory. When Mark first dug at Boxgrove in 1982, it was really very difficult to say where it fitted in at all. But at least by the end of the first full season of excavation in 1985, they were able to understand how the deposits had formed and what was responsible for the remarkable preservation. It's time to return to the quarries.

Chapter 25

The Boxgrove Barometer

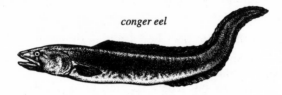

conger eel

It was Sir Mortimer Wheeler who really convinced archaeologists of the value of a good section, by which we mean the vertical wall of a trench dug down through different deposits. He did this partly by shaming some of his colleagues. 'Chaos', reads the caption to a photo he reproduced in 1954, illustrating a dig 'conducted by an archaeologist of considerable repute'. The plate shows a scene redolent of a gold rush pit after news of a strike; you cannot see the edges of the archaeological trenches for pick-wielding navvies and trails of dirt. Beneath this, Wheeler, not wanting to hide his light under a bushel, printed a photo taken on one of his own digs. Straight-backed men carry neat baskets of soil, manipulate tape measures and chat amiably beneath a parasol. The excavation is criss-crossed with vertical 'baulks', immaculately cleaned walls of deposit left in place between one small trench and another. There is a simple caption: 'Discipline'.

A handaxe found in a quarry can make a good ornament for the mantelpiece, but unless its context is known, where it came from and how the deposit was formed, its utility in terms of telling stories about the past is negligible. Sections are the key to understanding that context. Starting with the oldest at the bottom, successive deposits are displayed in a section in all their glory, where colours and textures can be compared, the way in which one layer changes into another can be scrutinized and samples can be taken for further analysis in the laboratory. They can be recorded with detailed technical drawings and photographs and, in some cases, left in the ground as references for the future. At Boxgrove the variety of sands and gravels, and the great depths of deposits allowed for some particularly spectacular and colourful sections. And neatly cleaned to plumb line straightness under Mark's tutelage, they certainly impressed the quarrymen.

Our present purpose is to gain a broad understanding of the geology, so we will begin with a generalized section, made by combining information from several exposures, particularly those seen in the sides of the Beach Section and the main trench in each of the two quarries. To make things clearer, we will split the drawing into three (figs 11–13).

One of the first things to do when viewing diagrams like these, just as with a plan, is to think about scale. In this case, the vertical and horizontal scales differ. This is necessary to compress onto a single page what would otherwise be a fold-out, without sacrificing the readability of the diagram. The whole section is nearly a kilometre long, the vertical drop from modern ground level in the northern third is around 20 metres (although there are few real sections that reach straight from top to bottom), and that the unbalanced ratio between vertical and horizontal distances means the angles of slope are grossly exaggerated.

We also need to know where a section is on the ground. This one is orientated north-south, but because it is a hypothetical view, it cannot be located precisely on a map. We can, however, note the position of the main trenches in each quarry and of the Beach Section, which provided the information for the deposits against the cliff, in fig 10. By doing so, we can appreciate how this large section has been compiled from evidence scattered across the area of study.

As layers pile up, the newest is always on top. It makes sense, then, to read sections from the bottom up, beginning at the beginning. The bottom line in the Eartham quarries is chalk rock (fig 11). This was formed many millions of years ago and is thus not itself relevant to understanding the ice age, but the process whereby it was planed away by the sea is. This is revealed in the platform, the gently sloping surface underneath all the later deposits, and at the northern end in the cliff, yet to be located in 1986. The raised beach itself is a sequence of pebble and coarse sand deposits that for obvious reasons is thicker near the cliff end of the section. The height of the gravels – known formally as the Slindon Gravels – suggests a sea about 40 metres above the present shore level (fig 11).

Covering the beach and the chalk is a thick (up to six metres) layer of

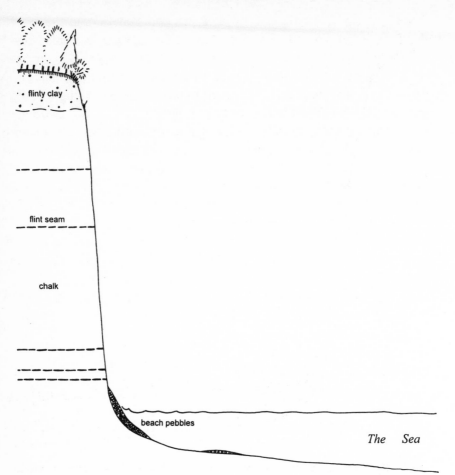

flinty clay

flint seam

chalk

beach pebbles

The   Sea

fig 11: The geology in the Boxgrove quarries is very complex, and picturing the landscape as it existed half a million years ago requires considerable imagination. It began with a sea cutting back a chalk cliff 75 to 100 metres high. Flint from the chalk and the clays above went into deposits of beach pebbles and shingle, which are mixed with chalk from cliff falls. A few heavily eroded fish bones have been found amongst blocks of chalk on the old sea bed, representing a flatfish, sardine/pilchard type fish and a large conger eel. These are all fish that feed in the intertidal zone. Because the land has risen since the creation of these beaches, they now lie at around 40 metres above present sea level. (Not to scale.)

fine, brownish yellow sand. The Slindon Sands (fig 12) are traditionally known as lug sand (perhaps so named by fishermen who had been digging for lug-worms in the low tide sands off Bognor or Selsey), and are an important commercial deposit. Whether or not our theory about the origin of the name for these sands is correct, they were undoubtedly deposited under a shallow sea. It is these sands that preserve the fossil burrows of worms and crustaceans noted by Shephard-Thorn and other earlier workers.

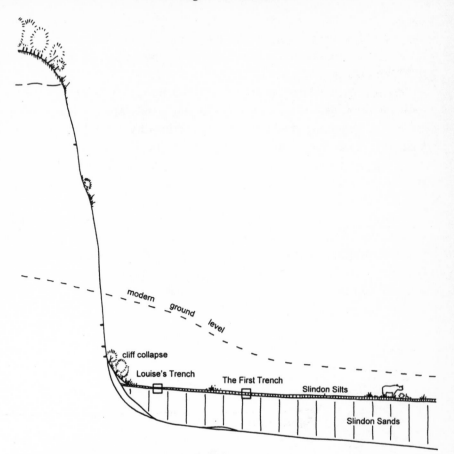

fig 12: By the time dry land began to appear at the foot of the cliffs, up to six metres of fine sand (now commercially valuable) had been left by the sea. These sands are covered in a metre of very fine silts, gently deposited in an intertidal lagoon. Most of the fish bones from Boxgrove come from the silts, and include both salmon or trout, which leave the sea to breed in freshwater, and eels and flatfish which swim out to sea to breed. Eventually a soil formed on the top of these silts, supporting a large grassy plain. Animal bones are well preserved in this soil, and represent a wide range of creatures, including lions, bears, hyenas, rhinos, a variety of water birds and amphibians and many rodents, not least beaver. Substantial herds of herbivores may have been responsible for keeping down the growth of large bushes or trees.

These silts contain some of the best preserved archaeology found anywhere in the world. Objects in the soil have sometimes been moved about a little by walking and burrowing animals and flowing water, but are still found near the place where they were dropped. Deeper in the silt, there has been very little disturbance at all, so that artefacts lie in precisely the positions they were left, half a million years ago.

Finer than the sands, the overlying Slindon Silts (fig 12) tell of the gradually falling sea, through an accumulation of about a metre of silts and muds in an estuary or marine lagoon. As we have seen, the top of the Slindon Silts was a dry land surface. It is here that flint artefacts and animal remains lying where they first fell have been found. We have marked the approximate positions of the two main trenches on this section (fig 12).

The end of the Slindon Silts is marked by a thin layer thought to indicate flooding, and a reversion of the landscape to marsh. The change is frequently made obvious in sections by a band of dark iron staining, which Mark called the 'Fe Layer' (fig 13). It is covered with up to one and a half metres of brickearth, a fine clay loam laid down in still or slow moving water. Bones in this brickearth come from animals that lived in a landscape of mixed woodland and open grassland, and include species we would now find in steppe or tundra, such as lemmings or arctic voles. We are seeing what for us would be a deterioration in climate: cooler weather, thinner vegetation and increased run-off when it rained. This is the start of an era of severe cold. At the poles, the ice caps are growing.

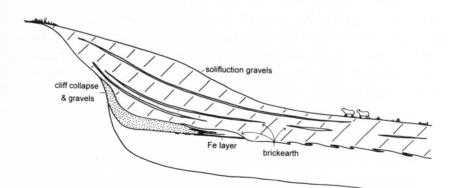

fig 13: The rich ecology of the wide coastal plain was cut short by deteriorating climate that ushered in the most severe period of glaciation seen in Britain, the Anglian. Evidence for this change is first seen at Boxgrove with a wettening of the land surface, as the grassy plain turned to marsh. In the miry conditions, a concentration of iron minerals was deposited in a thin layer of silt (the 'Fe layer'). In the following extreme cold, with thin or no vegetation cover and permanently frozen subsoil, the soft geology above the cliff rapidly broke up. In the summer thaws, quantities of debris fell over the collapsing cliff and buried the former plain. At the cliff base, the silts and sands were preserved. Two hundred metres or so further out, however, the gravels and mudflows destroyed the silts as they swept south (*compare* fig 12).

There are occasional thin layers of brickearth within the gravels, which suggest relatively brief episodes of warming climate. Flint artefacts in good condition have been found in these gravels. As yet, however, there has been no opportunity to investigate these finds in detail. Were hominids permanently present during the earlier part of the glacial period, or did they return north as the climate temporarily warmed?

Thereafter the geology moves. Chalk from the collapsing cliff and great washes of flint and chalk gravels smother the brickearth, and these in turn are buried beneath coarse solifluction gravels (fig 13). Near the cliff these are chalky, up to four metres thick, while further south the chalk has been dissolved and washed out to leave broken flint gravels in reddish silty clay, sometimes over ten metres deep. These deposits are classic features of a foothill periglacial zone, where intermittently thawing sludges moved slowly down-slope in an arctic environment. Some 300 metres south of the cliff the sludges took the older Slindon Silts and brickearth with them (as you will see by comparing fig 13 with fig 11: the 'Fe Layer' and the underlying Slindon Silts would originally have extended at least the length of the illustrated section). It was on the surface of the Slindon Silts, of course, that in warmer times plants grew in an environment favourable to land birds, mammals and hominids. All that survives of this landscape is an intermittent band, at most 100 or 200 metres wide, in the shadow of the old sea cliff.

It is as if there were a conspiracy to face one species of hominid with another, to effect that connection over hundreds of thousands of years. The chalk and the sea made the cliff which protected a little of the land surface from the ravages of the periglacial gravels; but without those same gravels, and the lug sands beneath everything, no one would have dug the quarries which exposed that land surface for archaeologists to see.

Chapter 26

Planets to Pollen Grains

wild horse

Most archaeologists interested in the palaeolithic, that ancient period deemed to cover every stone tool making creature on Earth until the world climate entered its present state over 10,000 years ago, are particularly intrigued by the stone tools. Although Mark's involvement with the Boxgrove quarries began in handaxe hunts, he never really shared this fascination with what the specialists call 'lithics'. And now, having dug up and meticulously recorded several hundred pieces of flint, it was not these that were at the front of his mind. The important thing had become resolving the geology.

The real challenges lay in the sands and silts, the flinty chalk sludges and the red clayey gravels. There was still disagreement over how these deposits had formed, and when. If you didn't know how old it all was, how could you relate the hominids who made the handaxes to what was going on anywhere else in the world? You couldn't even be sure which species had been there – were they neanderthals or something before them? And neither could you tell what the climate had been like, or what animals roamed the landscape, or what that landscape looked like. Were there hominids present only when the weather was warm, or had they managed to find a way of coping with extreme cold as well? If you couldn't answer questions like these, there really wasn't a lot of point in digging up more flints.

And the one key question remained, how old was the Boxgrove site itself? Traditionally there were three ways of tackling this.

Milutin Milankovitch, a native Serbian, was Professor of Applied

Mathematics at the University of Belgrade. He confirmed James Croll's old proposition (*see* Chapter 24) that the intersecting orbits of the planets affected how solar radiation fell onto their surfaces, and decided to explore the theory in detail. A German mathematician had recently calculated the required astronomical statistics to new degrees of comprehensiveness and precision. Planetary movements were sufficiently understood for it to be possible to 'predict' the relative positions of Earth and the other planets for huge spans of time into the future or back into the past. With this knowledge, Milankovitch could calculate the pattern of summer radiation at a series of latitudes in the northern hemisphere over the last 600 millennia. With pen and paper, he settled down to work at the maths.

When he published his first radiation curves in 1924, he compared them to what were then accepted as four great glaciations, separated from each other by three interglacials. Albrecht Penck and Eduard Brückner had produced a massive work, *Die Alpen im Eiszeitalter*, in which they had argued from the evidence of gravel terraces beside rivers in the Alps. They had named their cold periods after four of these rivers, starting in alphabetical order with the oldest: Günz, Mindel, Riss and Würm.

Milankovitch identified the Würm glaciation with three radiation lows at 25,000, 72,000 and 115,000 years ago. The Günz, Mindel and Riss each matched pairs of low radiation peaks; and a long interval of high radiation (on average, higher than present) in the middle of the graphs fitted the long warm period which Penck and Brückner had recognized in Alpine geology. In a mathematical tour de force, Milankovitch had shown how planetary movements could cause the ice ages; and he had supplied a chronology into the bargain.

Penck and Brückner's geological scheme, bolstered by Milankovitch's dating, remained popular throughout Europe in the 1940s and 1950s. But nowhere was it more promoted, and strengthened, than at the Department of Geochronology at the Institute of Archaeology in London, under the directorship of Frederick Zeuner.

One of its great attractions was that Zeuner and his colleagues could, if they so wished, completely ignore the archaeologists' attempts to provide their own dates for the ice age. 'It is hardly necessary to emphasize', wrote one geologist, 'that ... incessant wavering of [archaeological] judgement and opinion has for long been the despair of geologists.' What could possibly upset them so much?

The answer was stone tools. Archaeologists tried to use ancient

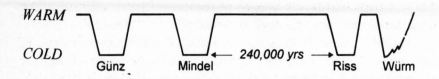

fig 14: The view of ice age Europe that held for most of this century was established 90 years ago by Albrecht Penck and Eduard Brückner. They identified four major cold periods, which they named after Alpine rivers. Milutin Milankovitch claimed that known historical variations in Earth orbit, affecting the quantity and quality of sunlight reaching the Earth's surface, provided a similar pattern. If he was right, the dates for the orbital perturbations could be transferred directly to the glacial stages. Frederick Zeuner, Director of the Department of Geochronology at the Institute of Archaeology in London, seized this as a chance to fix a time depth to ice age Europe. According to Milankovitch, for example, the warm period (or interglacial) between the Riss and Würm glaciations was about 60,000 years long, while the Mindel-Riss interglacial lasted nearly 250,000 years. (adapted from Zeuner)

stone tools in the same way that geologists used 'zone fossils'. Gabriel de Mortillet, Professor of Anthropology in Paris and later assistant director of the French national museum of antiquities, was the key promoter of this later-nineteenth-century idea. His basic principle was that the cruder a stone implement seemed to be, so the older it was. He divided tools into groups, which he equated with stages in time, giving each one a name derived from a place where representative flint tools had been found. As he and others tinkered with his first proposals, the hunting ground of Boucher de Perthes figured strongly, with such names as 'Abbevillean' and 'Acheulean'. If you found a handaxe of a certain shape, you could ascribe it to one of the stages and thus relate it chronologically to other finds, and, by implication, the deposits from which they were recovered. In an age of accelerating industrial 'progress' this was an idea that had obvious appeal in Britain as much as in France.

The first attempt to apply this argument to Sussex came in 1914, when Reginald Smith (later Keeper of British and Mediaeval Antiquities at the British Museum) proposed that a handaxe found in the raised beach at Black Rock was of 'St Acheul' date, and that consequently the overlying chalky deposit could be ascribed to the 'Le Moustier' period. Others followed suit, finding tools they recognized as 'Chellean', 'St Acheul I', 'St Acheul II', 'Mousterian' and 'Magdalenean' – each supposed to be a completely separate era reflected in artefact styles.

Almost at once, however, the archaeologists got into trouble.

In one case, by finding 'Acheulean' tools in both the upper and the lower raised beaches, they had to draw up an accommodating scheme that saw particular layers in each of the three deposits forming at the same time, stretching geological credulity.

At Slindon, although he had not actually been able to see any still in the ground, Joseph Fowler was convinced his handaxes, which were in a sharp and fresh condition, had come from the chalk debris. This gave Reginald Smith a dilemma, for the 'St Acheul II' implements, as he classified them, could not be contemporary with the 'Le Moustier' rubble. His solution was to suggest that a hominid had left them on the surface of the ancient beach just before the climate deteriorated, and they were promptly covered with freezing sludge.

Well, Frederick Zeuner had the answer to all this. 'PRIORITY OF GEOLOGICAL DATING' were the opening words of his book *The Pleistocene Period*, published in 1959. 'In order to rule out any chance of applying archaeological conceptions in the establishment of a Pleistocene chronology, no reference is made in the present book to the archaeological contents of the deposits.'

'Except', he conceded, 'incidentally'.

Relative dating, argued Zeuner, was a matter of geology and climatic change. Characteristic geomorphological deposits of cold and warm weathering could be studied where they lay one over the other. Terraces left by past seas on the coast, or inland up river valleys were to be related to each other by their matching heights above modern sea level (it had to be assumed that there had been no later movement of the land). Absolute chronology, on the other hand, relied on Milankovitch's studies of the perturbations of the Earth orbit.

By juggling an enormous amount of geological information, Zeuner reckoned to make a coherent story of the world scene. In Sussex he dated the highest fossil beach (*see* fig 6), then known as the Goodwood beach, to the Great Interglacial, the long warm period which Milankovitch said lasted some 240,000 years. The Aldingbourne beach represented a minor change in climate only slightly later than the higher sea level. The lowest beach, as seen at Selsey and at Brighton, followed the intervening Riss glaciation.

In the 1960s and 1970s, geologists were focusing on their local scenes. In Britain the ice age was no longer described in terms of Alpine rivers and global sea levels, nor the movements of planets, but by reference to a few villages and towns in East Anglia.

The idea was that the rise and fall of atmospheric temperature would be reflected in plants, which could be identified in pollen grains preserved by ancient peats and silts. It's worth looking at this in a little more detail, not only because the scheme dominated British thinking on the ice age until very recently (and thus, like the Günz-Mindel-Riss-Würm suite of glaciations, appears prominently in many books, and will undoubtedly do so for some time yet to come) but also because it gives us an opportunity to see what can happen in a landscape subjected to such drastic changes in climate. One of the classic studies was conducted at Selsey by the chief engineer of the British scheme, Richard West, working with his Cambridge University colleague Brian Sparks.

In May 1956, four schoolboys found the nearly complete skeleton of a rhinoceros near the lifeboat station on Selsey Bill (it was a *Stephanorhinus hemitoechus*, and we now think the deposit dates to around 200,000 years ago). The boys contacted the Natural History Museum in London. An excavation was mounted to study the site and recover more bones, and Sparks and West came down from Cambridge to look at the geology.

Over previous years the sea had taken away about 20 metres of land. The Lifeboat Inn could now boast, as an American real estate agent might describe it, unprecedented ocean vistas. Several good houses were at the bottom of the English Channel. But what interested the geologists was the gently sloping platform between the low tide mark and the current shore line. As the raised beach gravels and brickearth had been washed away, a former stream gulley, long filled with muds and silts, had been exposed: it was from this that the boys had pulled the rhino bones.

The fill of this channel had been permanently waterlogged, creating ideal conditions for the preservation of plant remains. In particular, West and Sparks were able to obtain a series of samples through the deposits that contained abundant pollen. All they had to do was take these samples back to Cambridge, identify the pollen grains under a microscope, and see how the vegetation in the area of the channel had changed during the time it was silting up. It was already believed that the Selsey deposits formed during the warm period before the last glaciation. What they hoped to see, then, was evidence for the gradual spread of trees as the climate warmed, the establishment of a permanently forested landscape, and finally a return to severe cold. Which is precisely what they found.

The oldest pollen, from deep in the channel, came from grasses and herbs, with a few birch and pine trees represented. Then broadleaved trees began to spread. Oak replaced first the birch, then the pine. Finally, with oak dominating a widespread forest cover, hazel started to increase and elm made a significant appearance.

At this point, the pollen sequence ended. Other remains showed why. The aquatic and marsh plants growing in the channel changed from freshwater loving species to estuarine. Suddenly all the shells came from brackish rather than freshwater molluscs. The sea level was rising – so the polar ice must have been shrinking.

Over these deposits were the beach shingle left by the rising sea, and the brickearth created by dust blowing about in an open tundra landscape. The shingle and brickearth had actually been churned together by permafrost action, as not so far away glaciers had again moved south.

So West and Sparks had been able to show in some detail how climatic changes between two glacial periods were reflected in geology and fossil pollen. We might say that it wasn't so much a case of sudden nuclear holocaust as of more gradual, but major global warming (or its converse).

Selsey was but one site in many that had been similarly studied by dozens of specialists: and there were patterns in the pollen. Sometimes certain trees arrived at different rates or in a different sequence; other sites might be characterized by the presence of a rare plant. Where geological deposits contained evidence for more than one interglacial, it was possible to see which flora came before which from the way in which one set of silts and clays lay over another. It was felt that deposits showing the same patterns were probably contemporary, a suspicion confirmed by other types of evidence, such as the comings and goings of various animals.

The numerous site studies of this type were all brought together in 1973 in a hugely detailed report published by the London Geological Society. Britain now had its own glacial scheme which, unsurprisingly, looked remarkably like Penck and Brückner's, with four major glaciations. Radiocarbon allowed calendar dates to be applied to some sites as old as the last glaciation, but before that, the sequence flapped like a concertina hung on the wall by one of its handles – Milankovitch's planetary explanation for the ice ages and the dates that went with that had fallen out of fashion. The Goodwood beach was ascribed to the 'Hoxnian' interglacial. The Selsey deposits and the raised beach at Brighton belonged to the 'Ipswichian'.

'No exact dates can be given', Mark had written in 1983 in his undergraduate dissertation, 'but generally a late Hoxnian, early Wolstonian period can be postulated' for the flint tools he had dug up in the Boxgrove pits. It was a pretty tentative argument, based

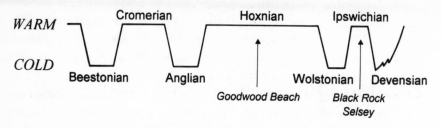

fig 15: A local ice age scheme for Britain had been worked out in detail by the 1970s. Glacials and interglacials were defined largely by variations in plants revealed by studies of fossil pollen. Although we show this scheme on the Penck and Brückner framework (*see* fig 14), in fact British geologists had by then come to discount the Milankovitch chronology and were unsure how to relate the British stages to those identified on continental Europe. The raised beaches at Black Rock and Selsey were ascribed to the Ipswichian interglacial, and the Goodwood Beach (as the deposits at Boxgrove were then known) to the preceding Hoxnian.

principally on the fact that the much lower beach at Brighton and Selsey had to be more recent (if the high beach was not older, the sea that made it would have removed all evidence for the others). If you assumed the Brighton beach belonged to the Ipswichian interglacial, then the Goodwood beach logically dated to the earlier one, the Hoxnian. And the evidence for the rapid onset of glacial conditions meant it would date from near the end of that long warm period. It was an argument first propounded by Frederick Zeuner, and no one had come up with a convincing reason to question it.

But in fact, someone had, nearly ten years before. It was just that, at the time, neither archaeologists nor geologists believed it.

Chapter 27

'Blasted Out in the Interests of Safety'

Bechstein's bat

The course of history is full of chance and accident, and no less so is the story of how we achieved present understanding of our most ancient past. You will remember how a young geologist identified a few animal bones found by Andrew Woodcock at the Boxgrove quarries in the early 1970s (Chapter 15). He had been given the bones by Roy Shephard-Thorn, who knew of Mike Bishop's interest in ice age vertebrates. The two of them went to Boxgrove, but Bishop never met Woodcock, and never saw any artefacts – thinking back now, he's not sure that he even knew there were any. At the time, he was in full flight studying a collection of bones from a cave in a limestone quarry in Somerset. That was something else: a site with quite exceptional animal remains, and the oldest evidence for humans in Britain, if not the whole of Europe. If more people had believed him, Westbury-sub-Mendip might once have been as famous as Boxgrove, and have contributed to a redating of the Sussex beaches even before Mark paid his first visit to the Eartham quarries. Instead, Bishop was banned from the pit by a nervous quarry company and the zone of richest deposits was blown into smithereens with dynamite. Nonetheless, his thinking lies at the root of our new picture of ice age time in Britain.

Mike Bishop was Curator of the Department of Geology at University College in London, a position that enabled him to pursue research for his PhD. He was extremely excited about Westbury. Like a huge slice of cake, the exposed infill of a formerly subterranean cave stood 30 metres high and 90 metres across against the back of the pit. Among the creatures whose bones had been washed into the cave (which had been occupied by families of bears) were a sabre-toothed cat, an extinct dhole (a kind of wild dog) and a jaguar. There were bones of a rhinoceros, then still known as *Dicerorhinus etruscus*, and so many vole specimens that he called one layer the Rodent Earth.

These fauna were hard evidence for something new, a completely unrecognized stage in the sequence of cold and warm periods in the ice age. It was a breakthrough, filling a huge yawning gap he was convinced existed between the traditional Cromerian stage and the Anglian (*see* fig 15). The voles *Pitymys gregaloides* and *Pliomys episcopalis* were both known to be pre-Hoxnian – in other words, their bones are never found in Hoxnian or more recent deposits; the rhino was Cromerian. So the assemblage seemed to date from the Cromerian warm period. *Arvicola terrestris cantiana*, a water vole, had evolved directly from another vole common in the Cromerian. The collection, then, had to be younger than one that would be found in a normal Cromerian deposit – to allow for the slow evolutionary change in this vole – yet because of the other animals that were known not to have survived the Anglian glaciation, it had also to be much older than the Hoxnian. This was the case for another warm period, possibly preceded by an unknown glaciation, between the Cromerian and the Anglian.

That was enough to make Westbury of international significance. *But at five different levels he also found small pieces of white, weathered flint.*

Flint was geologically totally out of place at Westbury, but Mike Bishop knew nothing about prehistoric artefacts. He showed some of his pieces to Kenneth Oakley at the Natural History Museum (a man who shot to fame in 1953 for his role in unmasking the Piltdown hoax), and barely had he got them out of the box than Oakley was saying 'Earliest Acheulean'. If they *were* artefacts, Mike knew, they held a very special message.

But the small, independent quarry company was worried about publicity, and the financial implications of possible accidents. Too much ballyhoo would bring too many visitors into a dangerous place, and perhaps put pressure on them to stop extracting limestone (never mind, thought Mike, that the deposits of interest were right on the edge of the area covered by their permit, and of no commercial use). Mike was stunned to find that he got very little backing from his peers. 'Don't upset the quarry, or all fieldwork in the county could be barred,' said one. Mike Bishop's reply was blunt: 'That's too bad, chum.'

He went to the press. He befriended Richard Leakey, who wrote him a letter of support, and took Mary Leakey to see the quarry. 'If this were in Kenya', she said, 'you'd have no trouble at all.' And early in September 1974 he sent a short paper to the journal *Nature*. Its title, 'Earliest record of man's presence in Britain', presaged the same publication's 'First European?' cover of a decade later.

Well, once the news was out, suddenly all the right people listened to Mike Bishop, were offering him congratulations on his work, were echoing his enthusiasm. But it was too late. He'd been outlawed from the quarry by insurance demands impossible to meet, and even as he dropped his *Nature* article in the mail, the fossil bearing deposits he wrote of (many of which he had failed to reach because of their inaccessibility) lay in ragged heaps on the quarry floor, 'blasted out in the interests of safety and . . . lost forever'. He'd been a one-man band at Westbury, and the thing was so damned big – the scale of the quarry, so many new things to deal with at once – that time was not on his side. He handed the site over to the Natural History Museum, and settled down to study and publish what he had himself been able to recover. This time, the Museum did not cavil.

Published only two years after the massive compilation of dating evidence for the British ice age based on pollen, Mike's proposals for a hitherto unknown warm period were largely ignored. If you couldn't see it in the pollen, geologists seemed to be saying, it didn't exist. The flints were a bonus: hitherto it had been universally agreed that humans had not reached Britain before the Anglian; indeed, remains of this date were very rare throughout Europe. But some archaeologists rejected these too, saying they were just bits of natural rock. In 1975, it seems, the world was not ready for Mike Bishop.

Chapter 28

Revelations from the Deep

mallard

As we have seen, Boxgrove was traditionally dated to the end of what was known as the Hoxnian interglacial, at around 200,000 years ago. The redating of Boxgrove, and with it the total shake-out of the earlier palaeolithic in Britain began for Mark with a single find in the quarries in 1986. This find was a rhino tooth: the tooth of an animal we now commonly associate with the African savannah, but not at all with the misty landscapes of the Sussex seashore. In similar contrast, the final breakthrough in understanding ice age climate came from the depths of a warm sea.

The well known process of radiocarbon dating, first developed at the University of Chicago, depends on measurements of the changing ratio between two carbon isotopes, one stable, one unstable. In the early 1950s, Cesare Emiliani, also at Chicago, decided he could use the ratio between two oxygen isotopes for a different purpose. With cores taken from the bed of the Caribbean, Emiliani was able to sample microscopic marine fossils (single-celled foraminifera) that had been deposited over the past 300,000 years. It was known that the two oxygen isotopes are absorbed in the living creatures' skeletons at different rates as water temperature varies. Oxygen trapped in the fossils should, reasoned Emiliani, reflect historical changes in ocean temperatures.

Emiliani's graphs showed what he claimed to be several cycles of cooling and warming climate: they fitted Milankovitch's astronomical curves quite well, but seemed to have less relevance to Penck and

Brückner's four glacial stages, by then well entrenched. As many as seven warm Stages, oddly numbered from the present, were separated in Emiliani's scheme by six evenly numbered cold Stages.

In fact it was another 20 years before Emiliani was proved right – even if, as Cambridge scientist Nick Shackleton showed, it was for the wrong reasons.

Shackleton had published his ideas in *Nature* in 1967. It was two years later, however, at a conference in Paris, that the impact of his research began to be felt. Before long, he would be working in an international project with nearly 100 other specialists. John Imbrie, another key player in this project to be, was in Paris to give a lecture on his own work. His talk, as he has described it himself, was late on a Friday afternoon.

'When Imbrie finally spoke, it was to an audience of two. Half of the audience understood no English. The other half was Nicholas Shackleton.'

Both workers, Imbrie from Brown University, New York, and Shackleton, from Cambridge University in England, had realized that Emiliani was not measuring ocean temperature. But this discovery enormously increased the significance of Emiliani's work. For the temperature of the sea varies locally, so can only be a rough guide to world climate. And according to Imbrie and Shackleton, the effect Emiliani had been describing was in fact a reflection of global, not local changes.

The main reason why the two oxygen isotopes varied in proportion to each other in foraminifera over longs spans of time, they said, was that these isotopes varied in the sea from which the microscopic creatures took their nutrients. And they varied in the sea because the climate changed. Evaporating water is relatively rich in oxygen-16 atoms. If the ice caps were growing, holding rain and snow which would otherwise flow back into the oceans, more oxygen-16 atoms were taken permanently from the sea; when the ice melted, the previously oxygen-18 rich water was diluted again. So a high ratio of oxygen-18 atoms in the marine cores indicated a relatively low sea level, reflecting an increased amount of water trapped in glaciers. Sea volume was global. Emiliani had inadvertently hit on a way of describing the ice ages by charting the ice.

By 1970, the technical resources were available for a massive attempt to sort out the old problems of ice age climate and chronology, which became the goal of the CLIMAP project. The pattern of long term freezing and thawing in the northern hemisphere could be resolved with more detailed analyses of deep sea cores (aided by refined techniques developed by Shackleton). Milankovitch's theory of the forces behind the climatic changes could be tested with new astronomical curves and sophisticated computer-driven statistics (at that time, astronomical theories were not popular; it was proving difficult to fit radiocarbon dated deposits to the old schemes). And, making it all worth the trouble, isotopic dating techniques could pin events down to a calendar.

This last became a matter of fixing a few key points that could be identified unequivocally in marine cores. Two of these points were what are known as 'magnetic reversals'. We think of magnetic north as a permanent feature, apart from minor wobbles of inconvenience to the map reader. However, for reasons that are not fully understood, magnetic direction sporadically flips over; there have been times in the past when, had we been there with our compasses, the needles would have pointed south. Some rocks are permanently magnetized when formed, so preserve a record of the flips, or 'reversals'. Potassium-argon analysis of lavas dated these occurrences:

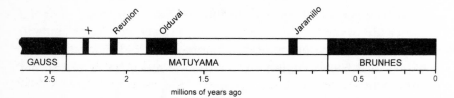

fig 16: Potassium argon dating of lavas that have preserved a record of the earth's magnetic field shows a sequence of 'normal' and 'reversed' polarities, by convention drawn as black and white respectively. Within the past 3,000,000 years, there have been two major epochs (or 'chrons') of normal polarity (we are currently in the Brunhes chron) and one of reversed. Significant normal events ('subchrons') within the Matuyama epoch are indicated. These magnetic changes have been used to date deep sea cores containing information about the size of global ice caps.

The first core to be identified that went deep enough to penetrate a magnetic reversal came from the Pacific Ocean, out to sea from island Papua New Guinea. Shackleton still refers to it as the Rosetta Stone of climate history. Neil Opdyke, of the Lamont-Doherty Geological Observatory at Columbia University, published the results of analysing this core, known as V28–238, with Shackleton in 1973. A decade later, nine authors from five institutions together described five deep sea cores from the Caribbean, and the Pacific, Atlantic and Indian Oceans. The longest core was nearly 36 metres; the oldest reached back some 900,000 years. All five cores showed precisely the same pattern. 'This empirical study of the marine isotopic record', concluded the scientists, 'leaves little room for doubt that variations in the geometry of the Earth's orbit are the main causes of the succession of late pleistocene ice ages.' Croll and Milankovitch had been right.

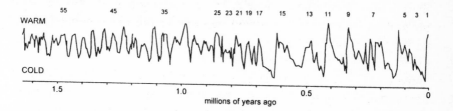

fig 17: Water evaporating from the oceans is relatively high in the light oxygen isotope ^{16}O. If land and polar ice accumulate, trapping precipitation, the seas become enriched in the heavy isotope ^{18}O. These changes are reflected in the composition of skeletons of microscopic foraminifera which fall to the ocean beds. Analysis of sediments in deep boreholes reveals the changing proportions of the two oxygen isotopes, which are a direct reflection of the size of global ice caps. In the graph (based on a mid-Atlantic borehole) the move from a higher $^{18}O:^{16}O$ ratio to a lower one can be read as a change from a cold to a warm climate. The changes are dated by reference to magnetic reversals identified in the deep sea sediments (*see* fig 16). There is a dramatic difference between the complex climatic fluctuations revealed by these curves, and the traditional view of the ice age in Europe (*see* figs 14–15). (adapted from Ruddiman et al/Bridgland)

So an explanation for the ice ages was finally agreed on (an explanation which, incidentally, allows the next major glaciation to be fixed with some accuracy to a comfortable, if nonetheless finite, 60,000 years from now – other things being equal). The deep sea core project achieved more than that, however. The old idea of four European glaciations had to be rejected; not only were there now something like twice that number in the equivalent period, but it was clear that the pattern of intermittent warming and cooling climate extended much further back than had been realized: in the past two and a half million years, there have been 50 such cycles.

Not the least interesting aspect of the new detail that became available, was the pattern of this climatic change. The isotopic curves are saw-toothed: they show a gradual build up of ice, followed by rapid melting. If this is a direct reflection of atmospheric temperature, then for most of the time when hominids are known to have been in Europe, the climate has been neither as warm as the present, nor as cold as it would have been during peak glaciations. The apparent predominance of 'intermediate' conditions was not suspected, and has important implications for our understanding of early hominid activity.

Finally, the beauty of all this lay in the fact that it was utterly independent of land geology. The dilemma of attempts to unravel glaciations from glacial deposits was that the very glaciers under study ploughed up the evidence for preceding climatic stages. Frederick Zeuner had asked for a dating program that was unfettered by archaeology: here was a detailed solution free of all ties to archaeology *or* geology.

Which, of course, is the great problem.

Chapter 29

The True Age of Boxgrove?

water vole

From a whisper in a wet field in the Cotswolds, through chit chat in ditches and streams, to a murmuring crowd with brief time to grow, the Thames reaches the sea less than 350 kilometres from its source. Mention the river to certain geologists and archaeologists, and their eyes will glow at the thought of Barnfield Pit at Swanscombe, now owned by the nation; it was Britain's first geological Nature Reserve. It was saved because of the exceptional deposits of sands and gravels that tell of part of the river's ancient history. It was also saved because of the remarkable interest of archaeological remains buried in those sands and gravels. And it was saved because, on three *separate* occasions between 1935 and 1955, parts of the same skull were found that was, until 19 November 1993, the oldest hominid fossil found in the kingdom.

Swanscombe is the great jewel of the necklace, but all along the Thames are old or new quarries, and records from building construction, roadworks and boreholes that contain the ingredients of its complex story. Over the past two decades this story has been almost completely rewritten. One of the leading figures in this work is David Bridgland, a former student of the City of London Polytechnic (now City University).

For most of this century, the Thames' terraces had been fitted into a sequence that reconciled two types of information: the results of matching their heights to hypothesized interglacial sea levels, and of arranging things so that the supposed typological ordering of flint tools was not violated. David Bridgland and his colleagues took a different approach. They looked at the deposits that actually made up the terraces – silts, sands and gravels – and found that in each major terrace there was a succession of three eras of deposition. At the bottom were gravels that had been washed down at times of extreme cold: waters from the spring melt would have poured over a thinly vegetated landscape, first cutting out a new river bed, then depositing their heavy load of eroded material from higher up the river. In the middle were fluvial deposits laid down by gentler waters during an interglacial (it is here that signs of hominid activity are sometimes found). Finally at the top of the terraces were more cold gravels signalling the start of the next glaciation.

All this erosion takes its toll. Over the millennia, the above sea land mass (in this case Britain) is little by little being washed away (by the Thames, into what is now the North Sea). The continental plate slowly adjusts, by rising where lightened, and subsiding where newly burdened on the sea bed. So each time the global sea level rises as a result of melting ice at the poles, the exposed land has in the meantime itself risen. The new interglacial shore line is slightly lower than the previous one. Along the coast of Sussex, and up the sides of the River Thames, water starts to cut out new cliffs. The result, over a succession of cold and warm periods, of falling and rising seas, is a stairway of terraces. As you climb the steps, you walk back through the ice age.

So how do we date these terraces? The starting point is the knowledge that the Thames as we know it today was created by the Anglian glaciation – it was already an old river then, but before this time, it flowed north and east of London through what is now Essex and southern Suffolk. The Anglian is the most severe cold period represented in British geology: the ice came further south than at any other time, covering the whole of Britain except the very bottom of England and Wales. In the process, the rivers Thames and Medway were pushed down to their present positions. The oldest glacial gravels in the lower Thames valley, then, have to be Anglian.

Nearer the present, it has for some time generally been agreed that the most recent interglacial, the Ipswichian (fig 15), is the equivalent of the last major episode of high global sea levels indicated by the oxygen curves, labelled OIS (Oxygen Isotope Stage) 5e. Counting back from the lowest and youngest Thames terrace to the highest, there is room for four interglacials: from Stage 5e to Stage 11 (warm periods, remember, are oddly numbered: *see* Chapter 28). The cold gravels at the bottom of the highest terrace would then date from Stage

12. And Stage 12 represents the largest growth of polar ice in the past 500,000 years or so, which is why it is commonly associated with the Anglian (by Shackleton amongst others). In other words, the terrace sequence of the Thames matches the oxygen isotope curve. We might say that geology and marine isotopes are perfectly in step (fig 18).

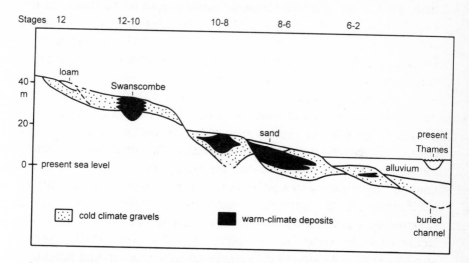

fig 18: A schematic section through the terraces beside the River Thames clearly shows the interleaving of gravels deposited by heavy waters during cold stages of the ice age and gentler river deposits formed in warm interglacials. Parts of a pre-neanderthal skull were found at Swanscombe. Boxgrove dates from Oxygen Isotope Stage 13, at which time the lower Thames flowed some way north of its present course, in a completely different valley system. It is hoped that future research on the coastal plain of Sussex will allow the description of a coastal sequence that mirrors this, but with more detail. (adapted from Bridgland)

Just as Mike Bishop argued for a new interglacial before the Anglian, other animal specialists had predicted more warm stages after this glaciation. Tony Sutcliffe had already written in the 1960s that animal bones separated a handful of British sites, all conventionally dated to the Ipswichian, into two groups. In 1989, armed with the Oxygen Isotope Stage evidence that pollen was underestimating the number of warm stages, Andy Currant brought all the evidence together, distinguishing a pre-Anglian/post Cromerian fauna (found at Westbury) from a post-Anglian fauna found at Swanscombe. As we saw (above and fig 18), Swanscombe can be dated geologically to OIS 11. Westbury could then only belong in OIS 13.

Recent work in several countries on the European continent confirms this new pattern. Famous amongst geologists are George Kukla's studies of wind-blown loess in Hungary and Czechoslovakia. Not only did he find evidence for these two 'new' interglacials, but he also saw that the cooling phase was much longer than the warming – a saw-tooth effect already observed in the oxygen isotope curves. With hindsight, it is easy to see why relying on pollen to identify and distinguish major climatic stages in Britain (Chapter 26) went wrong. It is simply that the differences in vegetation were not always sufficient for one interglacial to be discerned from another. Using pollen exclusively meant that the number of interglacials was underestimated.

You might think, having grappled with so much evidence, that this is starting to become a little pedantic. What does it really matter how we name interglacial periods?

But remember this is much more than nit-picking. This is arguing for two completely new interglacials in an era when hominids were present in Europe: two substantial chunks of time when earlier members of our own genus were part of landscapes that were each, in their little ways, unlike those of any other period – timespans in which animals from voles to rhinoceroses were evolving fast. It is the modern equivalent of a European expedition across the Atlantic five centuries ago. It is like the discovery of two entirely new continents that are as unknown to us as South America was to the first Spanish invaders.

But it is still more than that. There is a third 'continent', whose existence had been argued for by Mike Bishop a decade previously: that remote warm land before the Anglian glaciation that so few of his colleagues could countenance. Now it could be seen – the charts were being redrawn. And it could be dated, too, by its equation with OIS 13, to between 524,000 and 478,000 years ago: or, approximately, half a million years from the present.

---

fig 19: Over the past few hundred thousand years, several mammals have left Britain never to return or have become completely extinct. Others have evolved into different forms. When sediments at different sites preserve large numbers of animal bones, it is possible to propose that some of these deposits are contemporary with each other because the same suite of animal species is represented. There were significant changes in the mammal fauna during the severe Anglian glaciation, including at least seven extinctions. Before this two separate warm periods are suggested by the evolution of Savin's water vole (*Mimomys savini*) into the living species; work in progress suggests there may have been even more than two temperate stages between the cold Cromerian and Anglian, all of unknown duration. Immediately after the Anglian at least six species made their first appearances.

Boxgrove falls clearly with the group of sites characterised by several animals that did not survive the Anglian, with the evolved cantiana water vole. Every animal in the pre-Anglian column has been found at Boxgrove, except for Savin's giant deer. The Anglian is commonly associated with Oxygen Isotope Stage 12. (after Parfitt)

The True Age of Boxgrove?

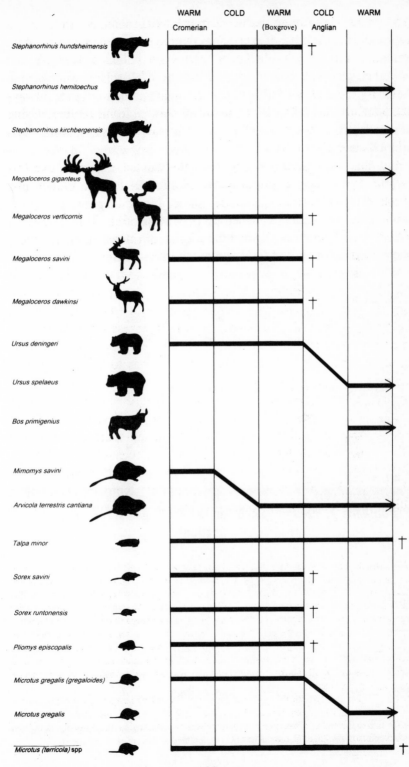

So, where does Boxgrove fit in? In the 1970s Mike Bishop identified amongst the small handful of bones that Andrew Woodcock gave him, remains of the water vole *Arvicola terrestris cantiana*. But there were no other species useful for dating, and by itself this vole is not much help. By the end of Mark's first full digging season in 1985, however, Andy Currant had again identified this vole at Boxgrove and, critically, the shrew *Sorex savini*. The two together pointed to an immediately pre-Anglian age, and Andy suggested, in very small print, that the traditional dating of the Sussex raised beaches was wrong. But it was when Gregory Priestley-Bell, sauntering back to work after his lunch break, spotted something white glinting in the sun amongst the dry gravels ruched up by wheels of heavy machines; and when Andy Currant confirmed the species of rhino that once held this tooth in its jaw: then, Mark was ready to be convinced (figs 19–20).

The Boxgrove story was about to begin.

Insectivores

Sorex runtonensis	an extinct shrew
Sorex savini	a large shrew

Rodents

Arvicola terrestris cantiana	a water vole
Pliomys episcopalis	an extinct vole
Microtus gregalis	
(*gregaloides* morph)	a narrow-skulled vole

Carnivores

Ursus deningeri	an extinct cave bear
? *Panthera gombaszoegensis*	an extinct large cat (provisional identification)

Perissodactyle

Stephanorhinus hundsheimensis (formerly *Dicerorhinus etruscus)*	an extinct rhino

Artiodactyles

Megaloceros dawkinsi	an extinct giant deer
Megaloceros cf *verticornis*	an extinct giant deer

fig 20: Up to the end of 1996, nine or ten animal species which only occur together in the warm period before the Anglian glaciation have been identified at Boxgrove (compare fig 19).

Chapter 30

'Dawn Stones' and the Quest for the First Europeans

spotted hyena

There was no questioning the evidence for hominid activity at Boxgrove. Here was nothing less than the best preserved British flint site from the whole of the ice age! From a dating perspective, the handaxes in particular had a crucial role to play.

For over a century, palaeolithic archaeology in Britain had been dogged by a rigid belief in stone-age technological progress. At first, so the theory went, hominids had been utterly incompetent knappers: their products were so poor, they were extremely difficult to tell apart from naturally broken stones. Later, they improved themselves to become moderately incompetent, and made rough flake tools. Finally, in a burst of savage creativity, they started to make handaxes, and achieved competence. The relative degrees of incompetence, archaeologists said, could be used to date the geological deposits in which the flint tools were found.

As we have seen, geologists were not always happy with the results. But they knew no more about knapping than did the archaeologists, so there was little scope for constructive dialogue. By the early 1980s, however, things were changing. Archaeologists had come to learn a great deal about stone technology (our putative ancestors, it turned out, were actually quite sophisticated in that department). We are only now beginning to understand how very wrong was this model of slowly improving primitive skills, not least as a result of experimental work being conducted at Boxgrove, as we shall see. But what really delivered the death blow to the 'zone fossil' approach to stone tools, the assumption that each type was restricted to a narrow range of time and so could be used to date deposits, was the realization that Boxgrove, a veritable market stall of superbly fashioned handaxes, was one of the oldest sites in the country. In the old view, axes like these should have been much more recent, because of their quality. This removed at a stroke archaeological objections to a radical new scheme for the ice age history of the River Thames (described above in Chapter 29) and released a number of long-known sites about which archaeologists had hitherto been highly guarded. The first lands occupied by hominids were on the move.

The most remarkable story of the recent redating of a British palaeolithic site, concerns animal bones and flint tools from a small chunk of landscape that was nudged out of place by the Anglian glacier. The results of excavations there were published in 1992, when it was stated that on the evidence of flora and fauna, geomorphology and archaeology, the collection was unequivocally pre-Anglian. The writers (then still doubtful as to the authenticity of the Westbury flints) knew of no other published sites in Britain of comparable date.

Artefacts were first discovered at High Lodge, near Mildenhall in Suffolk, by men digging clay for a brickworks in the 1860s. The agenda for the site was laid down in 1872, when John Evans described the finds in his encyclopaedic *Ancient Stone Implements*. At once it was apparent that 'sophisticated' scrapers were deeper down in the deposits than 'primitive' handaxes. Subsequent excavations then set out to prove that this was not the case.

First came Reginald Smith from the British Museum, in 1920. J. Marr dug down and found scrapers beneath handaxes. Smith said this was impossible, and the contradiction remained unexplained. Next was a large team of archaeologists, geologists and other specialists brought together by the British Museum under the direction of Gale Sieveking in the 1960s. They found scrapers beneath handaxes. Geologists said the site was pre-Anglian. The archaeologists said this was impossible, and the excavations remained unpublished. Finally, Jill Cook directed yet another excavation for the British Museum in 1988 (Greg Bell was on her team, taking a break from Boxgrove). The flintwork was studied by Nick Ashton, a key player in the new assessment of early stone technology. And at last the British Museum produced an attractive book in which all parties agreed that High Lodge was indeed very, very old.

It is interesting that this first reassessment to be fully published was of a site discovered so long ago. Indeed, several of the collections being investigated afresh already feature prominently in textbooks and museum displays. This is one good reason for summarizing the new chronology here, although some of the detailed evidence has yet to be published.

There are at least six places besides Boxgrove where traces of the first Europeans are now visible in Britain.

1) *Westbury-sub-Mendip, Somerset.* The importance of Bishop's finds has recently been underlined by new excavation and studies of animal bones by Peter Andrews and others of the Natural History Museum. There is no question that some of the flints are indeed prehistoric artefacts.

2) *Kent's Cavern, Devon.* Mike Bishop, now museum curator for the Torquay Natural History Society, has begun what promises to be a long project, re-excavating McEnery's finds and records from the museum shelves, as well as looking at more modern work conducted in the caves. Amongst the quantities of material are handaxes and flint flakes from a deep layer of breccia, with bones of animals that were extinct by the end of the Anglian glaciation, including two distinctive voles and a cave bear also found at Boxgrove. McEnery's sabre-toothed cat fangs (Chapter 8) are potentially of great significance: *Homotherium latidens* became extinct during the Anglian throughout Europe, and its presence should thus offer proof positive of the age of these finds. There is a possibility, however, that ancient hominids were themselves collecting these teeth, perhaps from carcasses already fossilized: but if that is shown to be the case, the teeth then acquire an altogether new interest as some of the oldest 'ornaments' from Europe.

3) *Waverley Wood Farm Pit, Warwickshire.* The geologist the late Professor Fred Shotton found a few handaxes and flakes near ancient river channels in this gravel quarry now used for landfill. The artefacts are especially interesting for being made from andesite and quartzite rather than flint – anything other than flint for palaeolithic tools is still rare, and the extent to which this reflects a propensity for modern collectors only to look for flint tools is an open question. Amino acid analysis of mollusc shells suggests OIS 15 for this site, which would make it the oldest known in Britain. However, substantially researched

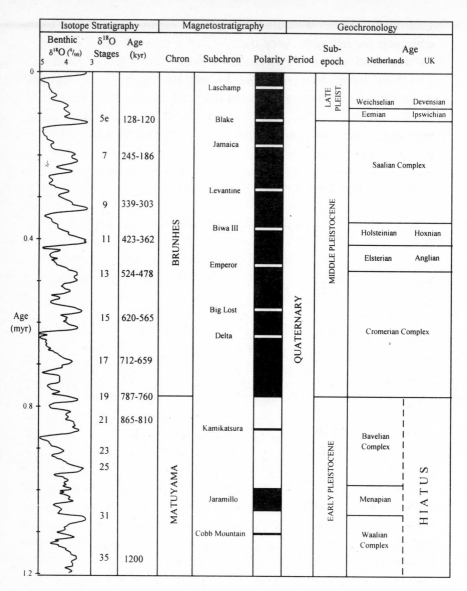

Isotope Stratigraphy			Magnetostratigraphy			Geochronology			
Benthic δ¹⁸O (⁰/₀₀)	δ¹⁸O Stages	Age (kyr)	Chron	Subchron	Polarity	Period	Sub-epoch	Age Netherlands	UK

fig 21: In this diagram all the key dating schemes for the past 1,000,000 years of the ice age are brought together. On the left is the Oxygen Isotope sequence, with the warm (odd numbered) Stages indicated. The calendar dates (in thousands of years before the present) are derived from 'magnetic reversals' identified in the deep sea cores from which the isotope curve has been constructed. These reversals (centre columns) are independently dated. By convention, 'normal polarity', when magnetic north is parallel to map north, is shown shaded and 'reversed polarity' (magnetic 'north' is to the south) shown white. The 'chrons' are major episodes (the Brunhes chron, for example, is an era of normal polarity) and the 'subchrons' are short term fluctuations within the chrons. The 'Quaternary' is an old term for the division of geological time that roughly coincides with the ice age. The former named stages of the ice age in Britain (far right) cannot be matched precisely with the Oxygen Isotope Stages.

geology and fauna (including *Arvicola terrestris cantiana*) point more convincingly to a date near the start of the Anglian glaciation.

4) *Wivenhoe, Essex.* Two small flint flakes were recently found by David Bridgland in this gravel pit, during geological sampling of strata that are unquestionably pre-Anglian.

5) *Warren Hill, Suffolk.* This area is well known to flint collectors, who have recovered more handaxes from the gravels than from anywhere else in Britain. Current geological work by David Bridgland and Simon Lewis suggests these sediments date mainly from OIS 13.

6) *High Lodge, Suffolk.* This site, already discussed, has produced a good collection of stratified flint tools and waste, but nothing approaching the quality of the material from Boxgrove.

This may not seem a weighty catalogue, but you must remember how recently archaeologists were unprepared to countenance the presence of hominids in Britain at all at this early time. Although there are hundreds of thousands of handaxes in museums, there are very few places where such remains are found in contexts good enough to survive critical dating analysis. Boxgrove itself stands out for the unique preservation of evidence: most other sites are little more than loose collections of tools. Anyone pursuing their interest by further reading, will come across palaeolithic evidence of more recent age. Swanscombe and its skull, and Clacton (famed, amongst other things, for the discovery of part of a wooden spear, about which we will hear more later) are now seen to date from as much as 400,000 years ago. John Frere has been proved right yet again, in his description of handaxes from Hoxne in Suffolk as dating from 'a very remote period indeed; even beyond that of the present world' (Chapter 4): Hoxne is another well known site now seen to be older than traditionally thought (separated by three major cold periods from the present, rather than two). And the rhinoceros channel at Selsey (Chapter 26) is now placed in the warm interval that preceded the Ipswichian one.

If, then, it is possible for geologists and archaeologists to redate so many discoveries, who is to say, you might ask, that the same thing could not happen again? Perhaps there are stone tools and hominid fossils out there still older than Boxgrove's, waiting to be found?

From a geological point of view, the correspondence of the new glacial zoning scheme with the oxygen isotope stages makes drastic reappraisal improbable. It is likely that as more detailed evidence accrues, the six major cold phases and the warm intervals separating them will themselves be found to contain many smaller episodes of climatic fluctuation. But this would not affect the broad outlines of the scheme described here. The most interesting developments will undoubtedly be with completely new sites, studied from scratch with modern techniques, as has occurred at Boxgrove.

On the other hand, it would plainly be wrong to state *a priori* that no older flints or fossils will ever turn up. However, there is a persuasive case to be made that this is in fact unlikely to happen. The evidence comes from the huge collections amassed by amateurs over the past century or so. The case has been put by the Dutch archaeologist, Wil Roebroeks, enthusiastic Professor at the Faculty of Pre- and Protohistory at the University of Leiden. If you feel we have maligned the great British flint collector, now is the time of their triumph.

At the end of his momentous address to the Society of Antiquaries in Burlington Gardens in June 1859 (Chapter 10), John Evans exhorted his audience to follow Boucher de Perthes' example. Frere had reported in 1797 that quarrymen at Hoxne used handaxes to fill ruts in the road (Evans and Prestwich had nipped up to Suffolk the year before to pocket some confirmatory evidence). But there were gravels everywhere, and who knew what they contained? Evans mapped out the territory: 'the banks of the Thames, the eastern coast of England, the coast of western Sussex, the valleys . . . of many other rivers, in fact . . . nearly every part of England'.

'Almost everyone must be acquainted with some such locality', he added. 'There let him search also for flint implements such as these I have described'.

These were exciting times. We have seen how the first handaxes were found on the coasts of Sussex and Hampshire in the 1870s (Chapter 14). Collectors scoured southern Britain, and, at a time of great public and private construction using gang labour, many of the palaeolithic sites which are so important today were discovered. Thanks to Boucher de Perthes and the British handaxe brotherhood of 1859, they knew what they were looking for.

Or did they? Just as they could only guess the age of the implements, it was certain that no one remembered how to make them. Some antiquarians knew about skilled stoneworkers in remote parts of the world, and could study reports of their craft. A few (John Evans among them) were prepared to learn from their compatriots, distinctly lower class men who maintained a rare and unique technology in the cause of gun-flints and architectural decorations. But most relied only on their instincts. What, in late Victorian Britain, could a savage forebear have to teach an educated gentleman? These were primitive tools, and everything about them was self evident.

The dilemma was built into their model of the past. The further back in time you went, the more uncouth were the early Europeans, and the less accomplished would have been their stone tools. The Dutchman Eugène Dubois claimed to have found fossils in Java in the early 1890s dating from the transition from apes to humans. If the Missing Link himself was yet elusive in Essex, his tools were to be found in abundance: their great antiquity was attested to by the fact that they were so primitive, you could hardly tell they were tools at all.

There was a word for these flints: 'eoliths', or dawn stones. Their makers were 'pre-palaeolithic', and, it seemed, their age was limited only by the age of the gravels which preserved the tools – in East Anglia probably millions of years.

Among the supporters of these ultimate antiquities were Joseph Prestwich and the explorer-naturalist, Sir Alfred Wallace. In 1895 there was an exhibition of eoliths at the Royal Society in London. Influential collectors tended to be eccentric and colourful characters. One such was James Reid Moir, unveiler of 'pre-Crag man' and his 'rostro-carinate' tools (an impressive term coined to label things that were shaped a little like flint bird-beaks), which Moir found on the bleak Norfolk coast, 'where it is possible to walk for hours amidst beautiful surroundings and to avoid seeing any signs of civilization so apparent at most seaside resorts'. Another was Benjamin Harrison, a village grocer in Kent. The eolithic movement was at its height in the first two decades of this century, and Sir Ray Lankester, retired Director of the Natural History Museum, was a powerful ally. Dr Marie Stopes, known better for her promotion of family planning, produced a human portrait scratched onto an antique shell (this 'crushing blow to Scripture' had been found by a 'red-hot atheist', who was promptly converted at a Revival Meeting, and would have destroyed the evidence but for the intervention of Stopes' father). The stone tools found at Piltdown were, naturally, eoliths.

John Evans rejected these dawn stones. But it was not until well into this century that majority opinion sided with him. Sceptics had shown by a variety of ingenious experiments that perfect eoliths could be made by entirely natural processes, of which the forces of rivers and glaciers and the sheer weight of gravels in deep deposits were prime examples. Basic principles were established for identifying proven artefacts. There had to be signs of knowledge and skill – a knapper's

techniques (however 'primitive'), determined by the physical properties of stone, leave their distinctive mark on both tools and waste
products, while glaciers are not so fussed; the most persuasive
artefacts were in fresh condition, not heavily broken up by waves or
falling rocks; and, in cases where there were genuine reasons for
suspecting the presence of simple, crude tools, it was important not to
make the mistake of picking out one object that happened to look
artificial, and ignoring the millions that did not.

The moment these critical principles were applied to eoliths, the
case for their being shaped by early Man fell apart. If there really were
stone artefacts in million-year-old gravels in Britain, those assiduous
collectors, under strong pressure to justify their claims, would have
found them. So the great achievement of the eolith proponents, says
Roebroeks, was to find nothing.

The point was reinforced in autumn 1995, when the last remains of
a wonderfully preserved elephant skeleton were raised from the
Norfolk coast, watched by a bevy of journalists and photographers (the
dig was partially funded by the only excavation grant from the UK
National Lottery in its first year). The bones lay in silt of the 'West
Runton Freshwater Bed', dating from up to one and a half million
years ago. Eolithic Man is unlikely to have missed a good mammoth,
weighing in somewhere between a modern elephant and a large
dinosaur. But where were the rough stone tools? Where the signs of
butchery? Instead, the only diners at this massive mound of flesh were
spotted hyenas, who left souvenirs – one now perches behind glass in
Norwich Museum, looking every bit as fresh as the day it was
dropped. In their inimitable way the hyenas add their own comment to
the eolithic controversy.

Until around 450,000 years ago, Britain was but a north west
extension of the European land mass: there was no sea channel to
prevent access by hominids. So if the labours of English collectors
appear to have proved the absence of stone tool makers much before
then, this might imply there were none elsewhere in northern Europe
at this time. What is the evidence for this?

It turns out that the later-nineteenth-century search for the oldest
and most primitive stone tools was not restricted to Britain, but
occurred all over Europe. Some of the first claims for 'Tertiary Man',
early hominids in that remote geological epoch where conventionally
they had been thought not to exist, came from France in the 1860s; but
sceptics said the engraved bones and stones had only been chewed by
beavers. Eoliths displayed at archaeological congresses in Paris,

Brussels and Budapest created much interest and controversy. Two-million-year-old flints were unearthed in Spain and Italy.

But, as in Britain, none of these claims survived critical scrutiny. Some 'tools' were seen to be flints broken under the pressure of sliding geological strata. In a famous project Marcellin Boule showed in 1905 that he could make exemplary eoliths in a cement mixer. Collectors swarmed the Somme gravels made famous by Boucher de Perthes, yet found no artefacts in deposits that we would now say were older than 500,000 years.

Nonetheless, the old ghosts linger on. Over the past decade there have been several European archaeological conferences and books featuring words like 'Earliest', 'Erste' and 'Premier'. Whilst fossils from Africa draw the media, the search for elusive ancestors in Europe continues unabated. It was to bring together some key protagonists of this quest (with their disputed finds) that a European Union funded workshop was held in Tautavel, France, in November 1993. The meeting was called by a committee whose members ranged far: Sweden, Russia, Britain, the Netherlands, Germany, France, Portugal, Spain and Italy. Papers were circulated in advance, and people brought along their photos and their stones. Karel Valoch presented his evidence for two-million-year-old tools from Moravia; Henri de Lumley described similar material from le Vallonet in southern France; Mark Roberts (taking a brief break from Boxgrove, where Roger Pedersen was finishing off some geological test pits) showed slides of the excavations.

Claims for very ancient sites had been published before, but for several of the participants, it was their first chance to examine the actual finds. It was a shock. While you had to reserve judgement on something you had not seen, you could not ignore lumps of rock that were plainly natural. Discussion ranged from embarrassed mumbling to heated argument; there were exciting evenings at the inn. Wil Roebroeks later said the meeting was 'very lively', with debate 'occasionally reaching critical peaks'. 'I've seen some upheaval in my life', said St Petersburg archaeologist Vassilij Ljubin, born in the year of the Bolshevik revolution: 'but never before have I witnessed a *perestrojka paleolita.*' Some of Mark's comments were unprintable.

One of the most interesting Tautavel papers was by Wil Roebroeks and his colleague at Leiden, palaeontologist Thijs van Kolfschoten.

They reviewed the entire field, and concluded that there was no compelling reason to believe hominids had successfully colonized Europe before half a million years ago. Rather, said van Kolfschoten, in central and north west Europe the earliest well documented sites were all of the *Arvicola terrestris cantiana* era – which we have ascribed to the end of Oxygen Isotope Stage 13 (fig 21). There were a few finds in Spain and Italy that could be older, but as yet the evidence for this was equivocal. In fact, there was a striking difference in the record before and after 500,000 years ago, which is best described in the Dutch researchers' own diagram (fig 22):

Before	After
not one hominid bone	hominid remains common
many finds of animal bones with no stone tools or evidence for butchery	animal bones often associated with tools or showing cutmarks
contested 'eoliths'	unquestioned stone tools of types recognized throughout Europe and Africa
handfuls of supposed artefacts selected from huge collections of natural stones	large collections of artefacts, frequently in excellent condition
random stones that do not fit together	flakes can often be fitted back together, showing incontrovertible signs of having been intentionally made
objects found in coarse, disturbed matrix	discoveries in fine, undisturbed contexts

fig 22: There is a clear distinction between supposed evidence for hominids in Europe before and after 500,000 years ago. (adapted from Roebroeks and van Kolfschoten)

There are sites all over Europe, dating to what we would describe as OIS 13, that fit the 'After' criteria (fig 23). Nothing older yet does. Fifteen years ago, Robin Dennell, a British prehistorian, described the evidence for hominids in Europe before half a million years ago as 'frankly atrocious'. It seems this has not changed. It is interesting to reflect that material from Africa, well dated to two million years ago and earlier, is often of a quality that would fit into the right hand column of this diagram.

There was overwhelming agreement among the Tautavel group that Roebroeks and van Kolfschoten were correct. Of course, new evidence could easily change the picture – but it would have to be convincing. At that moment, the idea of what archaeologists call 'the short chronology' made more sense. It also removed a serious problem that proponents of a 'long chronology' had to explain: why did hominids leave Africa (no one is suggesting Europeans evolved from apes locally, as the evidence for evolution in Africa extends further back than even the wildest claims for old stone tools in Europe) as highly skilled stone knappers, forget everything for hundreds of thousands of

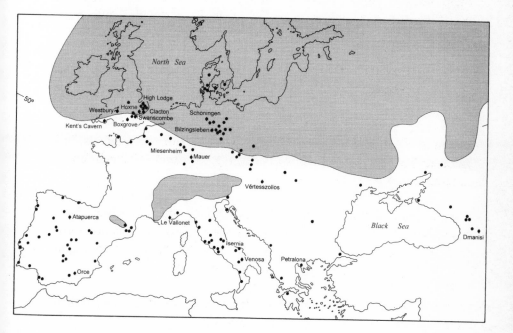

fig 23: Evidences for the first Europeans are notoriously difficult to date, and in many cases there is debate over whether claimed artefacts are indeed really artefacts at all. All proposed sites are marked on this map, regardless of any disputes as to their significance, and some of the better known are named (*compare* fig 4). (data from Roebroeks & van Kolfschoten, Tautavel Workshop)

years, then suddenly start to make exactly what their distant ancestors had been producing? And there's another problem. If the handaxes were as important to the survival of the hominids as they appear to have been, how is it that the first colonizers of Europe, of all hominids, managed without them? Placing Boxgrove at the start of the sequence solves all this. At what on the 'short' argument would be the earliest well preserved and substantially excavated site in Europe, there are very fine handaxes.

Of course, in the autumn of 1985, when Mark sat at a desk in London writing about the first long season at Boxgrove, much of all this was yet to come. But in a year's time, when the report was going to press and Boxgrove digger Greg Bell found the rhino tooth, the way ahead was clear. They already understood the geology of the quarries, and why the land surface was so well preserved. They knew then that they were excavating evidence for some of the first hominids in Europe.

There was just one question. Who, or what, on earth were they?

PART FIVE
IN SEARCH OF INTELLIGENCE:
1985–1992

Chapter 31

The Missing Intellectual Link

beaver

To underline the stupidity, brutishness and sheer depravity of a situation or a person, we make comparisons with the stone age, or perhaps with greater linguistic refinement to the palaeolithic or neolithic, or the only named stone age 'people' most of us can come up with: the neanderthals.

Few of us would pretend to know much about the archaeology of human origins. The old cartoon showing a sequence of ape-like creatures improving bit by bit – learning to walk properly, to stand upright and to greet the world head on – is ingrained in our psyches. Louis Leakey titled a well known book about his early search for hominid fossils in Africa *Adam's Ancestors*. But we do not imagine our ancestors safely grazing in Eden; they lumber about in a world of bleak misery. They are us *after* our fall. We blame them for not behaving like us, for not looking like us. And, especially, for not thinking like us.

But how on earth do we know that? Are we just making it up? And if so, can there be any alternative approach? What right do we have to dismiss these creatures for being what we make them out to have been?

Neanderthal anatomy differs from that of a modern human in ways that can be construed to indicate an inferior intellect: clearly human-like, yet short and squat in stature, with flat foreheads and no chins, neanderthals might look like caricatures of idiocy. As one writer put it in 1895: 'a weak chin generally denotes a weak . . . race or individual'.

This claim – and the hint that as possessors of strong chins, the British were born to rule – is quoted by Chris Stringer and Clive Gamble in their recent study of neanderthals, where they describe with copious illustration how these creatures have been represented so frequently as bestial. The first neanderthal skeleton to be recognized was found in Germany in 1856 (in a cave in the Neander valley, or – in archaic spelling – thal, near Düsseldorf, hence the name). This was not the best time for such creatures to make their début. Drunk on imperial power and conquest, shaken by theories that demoted humans from divine-blessed omnipotence to an animal ancestry, inspired by snowballing industrialization and greedy for land occupied by other, little understood peoples in dark corners of the world, later-nineteenth-century Europeans were peculiarly ill-placed to make sober assessments of an extinct and, undoubtedly, primitive would-be ancestor. The tragedy was that many of the fossils that inadvertently found themselves in the limelight were actually still alive.

'What is the right of the huntsman to the forest of a thousand miles over which he has accidentally ranged in quest of prey?' asked American President John Quincy Adams. 'This great continent', replied President Theodore Roosevelt after the deed was done, 'could not have been kept as nothing but a game preserve for squalid savages.' This is an attitude that some feel still lives. In 1975 uranium was extracted from the hunting and fishing territories of the Chipewyan Indians of northern Saskatchewan, Canada. '. . . the companies think we're animals in the north', said Terri Daniels, an administrator for an affected Métis community. 'They don't ask the animals for permission, so why would they ask us?'

In the last century, native Europeans or their descendants in north America and elsewhere around the world commonly spoke of living and ancient peoples in the same breath. Classifying the living as primitive or degenerate made it easier to act as if they did not matter, to seize their lands and properties, and deliberately or indirectly to reduce their numbers. If Australian aborigines were somehow equivalent to ancient hunters in Europe, it was only a matter of time before the former, too, became extinct and ceded to higher races. This was the natural path of history.

A fall from grace in the Garden of Eden sat ill beside later-nineteenth-century Europeans' view that they were destined to excel. How much easier it was to proclaim their achievements when, thanks to Charles Darwin and the first fossil hunters – John McEnery, Boucher de Perthes, John Evans and the rest – new science was arguing for an extended prehistory of savagery: see how different *we* are. Popular acceptance of a great age for human fossils launched a quest for the Missing Link, the skeletal remains of creatures to bridge the gap between the modern European and the gorilla (the Far East was favoured by early explorers). No one could dig up the minds of these lost ancestors, because, of course, it was only the bones that survived. But that didn't matter, for there was no need: around the globe was living evidence for those primitive thoughts. The physiques of these backward people may have looked close to that of a modern European but their mentalities were retarded. The whole story was there, in the present. When it came to intellects, nothing was Missing.

'It is not very flattering to our own powers of intelligence,' wrote William Sollas, bemoaning the annihilation of native Tasmanians by Europeans, 'to find that we allowed this supremely interesting people, the last representatives of one of the earliest stages of human culture, to perish without having made any serious effort to ascertain all that could be known about it.' Sollas was a Professor at Oxford University. In *Ancient Hunters and their Modern Representatives*, published in 1911, he proposed using living peoples as a guide to the makers of prehistoric artefacts – 'a saving procedure', he wrote, 'in a subject where fantasy is only too likely to play a leading part'. If the Tasmanians had all died, there were still enough Australian aborigines around to spot them as 'the Mousterians of the Antipodes' – culturally and intellectually equivalent to the neanderthals. Back in Europe, he found 'no reasonable doubt' that one particular ancient skeleton represented 'the remains of a veritable Eskimo' who lived in southern France during the ice age.

'What perhaps is most impressive in each of the cases we have discussed', continued Sollas, 'is that the dispossession by a new-comer of a race already in occupation of the soil has marked an upward step in the intellectual progress of mankind. It is not priority of occupation, but the power to utilise, which establishes a claim to the land.' Such arguments gave Sir John Lubbock grounds for optimism. In his *Origin of Civilisation and Primitive Condition of Man* (1870) he concluded that 'various races have independently raised themselves . . . We shall not be the less inclined to adopt [these views] on account of the cheering prospects which they hold out for the future.'

Not everyone agreed. The Duke of Argyll, criticizing Lubbock in

1868, said modern savagery was 'the result of corruption'. Take the Inuit in northern Canada. 'To civilized man', wrote the Duke, 'it is hardly possible to conceive a life so wretched, and in many respects so brutal', as that led by the Inuit race. They owed their impoverished existence to having been driven to one of the furthest extremities of the globe by other peoples, where they lost their former skills of civilization.

What particularly impressed early writers when it came to making comparisons between ancient and living peoples, were their shared simple technologies and lifestyles. Modern African or Australian hunters and the first Europeans could hardly be more distant from each other in time and space. Yet so remote are those earliest hominids, if we are to understand them at all, we should surely learn something from those living people who lead the most comparable lives. Can we take a more dispassionate look at some of our contemporaries to gain an insight into the minds and behaviour of our ancestors?

Modern hunter-gatherers have been hot topics in anthropology since a conference held in Chicago in 1966. Of course a lot of that interest is in recent history and present lives, but there is always a strong representation of the notion that these people might have something to tell us about very early hominids. Opening the book that followed the immensely influential conference they organized over thirty years ago, Richard Lee and Irven DeVore wrote: 'Cultural Man has been on earth for some 2,000,000 years; for over 99 per cent of this period he has lived as a hunter-gatherer.' The 'hunting way of life', they continued, 'has been the most successful and persistent adaptation man has ever achieved.' (The conference actually considered a proposition that would have explicitly defined 'hunters' as those people who lived in the era of the ice ages, but realized that this would then have meant there were none for anthropologists to study.)

This was a far cry from the self-righteous dismissals that these remote peoples received at the pens of an earlier generation of Europeans. Lee and DeVore were writing at a time of new fears of ecological disaster, combined with youthful optimism for a future of peace and harmony. If 'nuclear annihilation and the population explosion' didn't finish everything, there was still a chance to establish 'a sane and workable world order'. Perhaps hunter-gatherers, ran the clear sub-text, got it right.

Lee had spent 15 months with !Kung Bushmen in the Kalahari Desert of Botswana. Even in this land inflicted with drought every two or three years, the !Kung regularly ate well with seemingly little effort. At one camp he studied, adults spent no more than two or three days a week getting food. A woman provided for her family on one day, and could spend the next two 'resting in camp, doing embroidery, visiting other camps, or entertaining visitors'. If a man had a run of bad luck hunting, he might give up for a month or so, and instead fill his time 'visiting, entertaining, and especially dancing'. In the Tanzanian dry season, reported another speaker, Hadza men would spend more time gambling than hunting. Marshall Sahlins summed it up by describing hunter-gatherers as 'the original affluent society'.

There were more surprises. Most modern hunters actually hunted very little. Outside the arctic and subarctic, reported Lee, whatever people *said* they did, most food came from fishing and gathering. In fact there was a broad relationship with latitude. Near the equator, plant foods were most important, near the poles mammals, and in between a mixture that included fishing as well as both plants and mammals. What's more, the gathering was done by women and not men. 'For all their talk about this or that kangaroo they once killed', said an anthropologist of some Australian aborigines, 'the men contribute relatively little to the subsistence of the group.'

The Chicago conference was called *Man the Hunter*. There is no doubt about it; theories put up to explain the evolution of humans were sometimes extraordinarily sexist, and needed exposing. It wasn't just that our remote ancestors were supposed to be bloodthirsty hunters. Descriptions of males rampaging the landscape while females stayed at home with the young and the washing up were common. All early females were monogamous, wrote one male American anthropologist, and 'continually sexually receptive'. A female American anthropologist put the origins of standing on two feet down to a thitherto neglected detail of male anatomy: 'sexual selection was more significant for male bipedalism since their penises (especially when "upright") could be noted more readily when they walked bipedally'. We have yet to see this theory portrayed in a museum diorama.

Inevitably a book appeared with the title *Woman the Gatherer*. Adrienne Zihlman suggested that the first distinctively human behaviour was food gathering, an activity at which women had been shown to be central. Only much later, and on the back of a stable gathering economy, did men escape for a little hunting. Frances Dahlberg emphasized how anthropologists saw everything through male eyes. Taking the female view into account opened up yet more lifestyles, more world views. It wasn't only men who hunted; there might be divisions of labour, but these didn't have to be along sexual lines; contrary to male claims, childbearing and child care seemed to be small hindrance for women foragers.

But for some there were problems with the feminist approach, too. Catherine Berndt had been working with Australian aborigines for 40 years when *Woman the Gatherer* appeared in 1981. She objected to a theory put forward by Eleanor Leacock, that originally all women were autonomous members of egalitarian societies. If anthropologists reported otherwise, said Leacock, this was because they were blinded by their male-dominated vision, or because the communities had been corrupted by contact with imperial powers. But how do we know what aboriginal culture was like before the coming of Europeans, asked Berndt? 'The answer is that we don't and can't know. We can only surmise.'

In sum, we may know much more about recent hunting and gathering peoples than we did a century ago, and we may have a wider range of ideas and opinions about their achievements. But we are still looking for ourselves in the shadows of these fast vanishing lifestyles. We still have our agendas.

Suppose we could nonetheless claim an 'objective' understanding of people who live off the wild. Would that really assist us with what was happening a million or more years ago? Could we then get closer to our remotest ancestors? The answer has to be no, except in the trivial sense that knowledge of modern foragers does at least guard us against making too facile assumptions about what is 'possible' or 'likely'. The fact is that it would only help us if we assumed the very thing we were most concerned to find out. We would have to take the humanity of early hominids for granted.

There is a book by Margaret Doyle called *The A–Z of Non-Sexist Language*. Many who write about hominids today would find this a useful text to have beside their keyboards, as they struggle to avoid old 'Man the Hunter' clichés. Not so long ago, people published such titles as *Early Man*. Now we have *The Origin of Humankind*. Yet these word games miss the point. 'Human' is no better than 'Man' when it comes to fossils that are millions of years old. How can we talk glibly of early humans when all we have is a few piles of bones and stones? How did these creatures behave, how did they think, feed, breed and die? Isn't that the greatest question of them all: *when did they become human?* At what point can we justifiably start to talk about 'men' and 'women'? Until we can confidently answer that – and indeed, perhaps *after* we have answered it, too – it is surely wrong to refer to early hominids as human in any language. Better to follow Doyle, with phrases such as 'abominable snow creature'.

So Lee and DeVore were unintentionally misleading when they wrote: 'Cultural Man has been on earth for some 2,000,000 years; for over 99 per cent of this period he has lived as a hunter-gatherer.' 'Hunter-gatherer' is a human entity. We cannot assume early hominids behaved in any way still to be seen among modern peoples – that is what, as archaeologists, we are trying to find out. It is better to think of their lifestyle as a recent phenomenon. Hunter-gatherers 'along with modern agriculturalists ... are an evolutionarily-derived form', says anthropologist Robert Foley, 'that appeared towards the end of the pleistocene [around 10,000 years ago] as a response to changing resource conditions'. They are of endless fascination for us. But they are not the remote past in the prese nt.

There have to be other ways to interrogate our ancestors, ways that allow us not only to postulate the former existence of types of intelligence no longer to be seen, but also to identify them. We are on a new quest where archaeology is essential if there is to be a chance of success: the search for the Missing Intellectual Link.

Chapter 32

First Thoughts on Flint Knapping

Mosbach wolf

The report on the first year's digging at Boxgrove was ready in 1985. Work on the flint artefacts had progressed sufficiently only for Mark and American flint knapper Chris Bergman to say a little about the main trench in the East Quarry – the one that began with Mark and his student friends unearthing a handaxe at Christmas 1982 – which was still under excavation. Nonetheless, it was already apparent that they had something exceptional.

Within the 200 square metres of the hole was a pair of clearly distinct spreads of knapping debris. Many pieces had already been fitted back together (a slow, laborious task: think of reassembling the crockery from a container of precious china dropped at the dockside, without knowing whether or not there were actually any complete cups or plates to begin with). Two of the handaxes were associated with the meticulously plotted debris. The flints were stained orange by the iron minerals washing through the silts, but were otherwise fresh and sharp.

The near pristine condition of the flakes, the discrete scatters and the frequent refits made it seem that there had been little if any disturbance since the knapping took place. Here was an almost unique opportunity to look at the making of acheulean handaxes – what sort of flint was used, where it came from, the skills and tools applied to create the handaxes and what happened to them once made. And this was just one hole. There was a huge quarry out there.

And then there were the bones. To get the flintwork was prize enough, but to have such a rich diversity of animal remains as well seemed almost greedy. Creatures ranging from bear, wolf and beaver, through birds and fish to moles, lemmings and mice had been identified. At this stage, there was no reason to think that the presence of any of these animals was related to the hominids who made the flint tools. They could all have died naturally, and been naturally incorporated into the silts. Further work would throw more light on this.

If Mark had some exceptional flintwork to write about in 1985, as the years passed the first collections from the Eartham quarries became but part of a unique record of early hominids in Europe doing things with flint – although of course there were still no remains of the hominids themselves. This record piled up in bags and boxes in the barn offices and stores, on rolls of paper plans, in notebooks full of coordinates and angles of repose (measured with a hiking compass), and in thousands of detailed photographs. At the end of 1988 most of the finds were moved to a British Museum store in Shoreditch. That was how the 'spoils' – or the costs and responsibilities, depending on how you look at it – were divided up: the Natural History Museum was to get the bones, the British Museum the artefacts; the local museum at Chichester, already custodian for the first precious finds made by Andrew Woodcock, would be given flintwork from unstratified contexts, ideal for displays. Up in London there was space to work on the flints: laying them out on big tables, studying every piece, trying to fit flakes together and maybe read the minds of the creatures that left all this debris.

The British Museum had recognized the importance of this imminent addition to their vast collections by mounting a small Boxgrove exhibition over the summer of 1987, on the occasion of the Institute of Archaeology's 50th anniversary (the Museum and the Institute are only a few blocks apart). Some flints and bones were mounted in little glass cases, with explanations of knapping and photos of a modern flint worker.

The material was unique for a combination of three reasons. In the first case it was very old. Nowhere else in Europe had such a large collection of knapping waste and tools been excavated that dated from half a million years ago. Evidence of any kind of that age was very rare. What was really special, however, was the condition of it all.

Most – not just the odd scatter of flakes, but a huge quantity – *most* of these pieces were fresh, sharp, still close to or even in the same places they had first been dropped. Variations in preservation were not questions of the impact of large rivers or glaciers churning up slices of landscape (the more typical situation for ice age archaeology), but of shallow water washing over flakes, or of animals – or perhaps of hominids themselves – kicking things about as they wandered across the estuary and the grassy plain.

There was only one other place where anything comparable from this era of early European hominids had been found and recorded to modern standards. This was at Maastricht-Belvédère in the Netherlands, excavated by Wil Roebroeks over ten years, starting about the same time that the student Mark descended into the Eartham quarries (the first part of the Belvédère project was Roebroeks' doctoral dissertation, to be completed in 1989). But Belvédère was half the age of Boxgrove, and animal bones were not as well preserved – a crucial distinction that would contribute enormously to the importance of Boxgrove.

To cap all this, the huge size of the preserved land surface created the opportunity to see a variety of different activities conducted at different times and places. There was really nothing quite like it from anywhere else, from the tip of southern Africa to the most northerly part of occupied Europe.

In the six seasons of excavation since Mark and his friends sank that line of small pits in December 1982, the holes had multiplied. The pit beside the place where Tony Tynan and Richard Champion found the first handaxe had grown to a large trench, at last finished in 1987. Four of the geological test pits in the same East Quarry had also become major excavations in their own rights. A new area had been opened in 1987 as a potential large site, but it had not been productive and was abandoned the same year (fig 24).

Across the track and beyond the barns in the West Quarry, at the main site ('Louise's Trench', about which we will hear more later), where excavation was so slow because of the extraordinary quality of the preservation of flint scatters which demanded recording techniques to match, the last flints were removed at the end of 1988. A large L-shaped area had been opened on the north edge of the quarry the year before, to experiment with a faster, less intensive excavation technique. It seemed to work. 'The L-Shape' in the West Quarry was productive of both flintwork and fauna (although the bones were poorly preserved). But the summer of 1987 was very wet, and progress was held back by the frequent interruptions. They decided to leave the L-Shape at the end of 1988 as well.

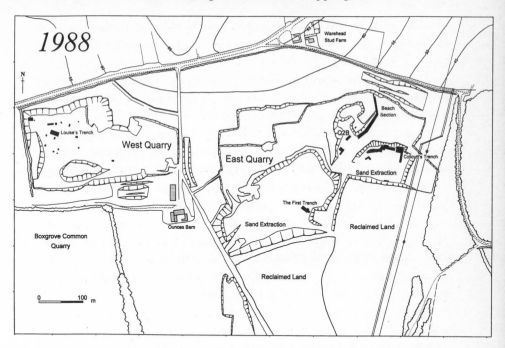

fig 24: By 1988 the silt ponds to the south of the East Quarry had been refilled. Archaeological excavation had finished in the First Trench, but was continuing in the main trench in the West Quarry. Two very large trenches, excavated with heavy machinery, had been dug to explore the geology. In the long Beach Section, the base of the old chalk sea cliff was finally located, and in Simon Colcutt's Trench a deep section was obtained through the complex of marine sands.

Besides these larger trenches, the ground was spattered with small test pits, placed to explore opportunities for excavation wherever there might be a danger of the deposits being quarried away, and where the overlying gravels and brickearth had been removed, making the preserved land surface accessible. Every trench, every hole, every wander across the quarries after work or back after a lunch break at the barns, produced more finds; every specialist who visited the excavation left with bags of material for their laboratory. Future analysis and research were accumulating like silt behind the dams in the settling pits.

But out in the Boxgrove quarries in 1986, with the first major report behind them, it was not academic study that was on anyone's mind.

Just over a century before, amateur anthropologist and artist Worthington G. Smith was walking home to Dunstable, Bedfordshire, one evening in March. He'd been looking for palaeolithic flint tools in brick pits, without success. In the village of Caddington, he hesitated, uncertain whether to continue straight home over the fields, or pay a visit to a clay pit he'd seen many times before. Keen collector that he was, he went to the pit.

'Some digging ... close to the brickmakers' cottages, had been done since my last visit, and the moment I entered the excavation I saw many flakes in the newly disturbed brick-earth ... So exceedingly sharp and thin were these flakes, that I cut my fingers with their edges in removing them in the dusk ...' Early the next morning he was interviewing the workmen. They already knew about the 'keen-edged splinters of flint': they dreaded coming across the seam which contained them, as it would leave their hands lacerated.

Worthington Smith was an unusually perceptive flint collector, gifted with a vivid imagination ('Did any early members of the human family commit suicide? Probably they did; the feeble, the dying ... would ... cut their throats with large and keen-edged knives of flint'). At Caddington he had found an ancient land surface analogous to that at Boxgrove, and the flints he retrieved from the brick pit (which are now in the British Museum) were exceptional by any standards.

Only a few days after his discovery, early in April 1890, Smith noticed that two small flakes could be fitted back together. This told him that he had 'really lighted upon the actual spot at Caddington where implements had been manufactured in palaeolithic times'. 'Conjoining flakes', as he called them, would only be found close together if they were still at the place where they fell when struck off by the knapper. He looked for more refits, and finding them, devised a system whereby he could systematically scan all of the thousands of pieces he eventually recovered from the pit. In his residence, he filled two rooms with tables on which he laid out his finer flakes, and in the brickfields he found some grassy patches where he arranged his coarser finds. There they lay for over three years, where they could be 'examined and re-examined ... almost daily'. The fruit of this concentrated effort was more than 500 'reattachments'. As Smith realized, none of these would have been possible if the flint debris had been significantly disturbed since it was first made by his remote ancestors shaping stone tools.

Worthington Smith's pioneering work is little heard of these days, known only to a clique of dedicated flint-knapping archaeologists. Boxgrove may help to change that. In 1984, one of the London students on Mark's summer dig did know about Smith's flakes, and was already developing his own skills as a flintworker. What he saw coming out of the silt as they followed up the discovery of that first handaxe the week before Christmas, reminded him of Smith's finds in Bedfordshire. The next year, in his undergraduate dissertation, Francis Wenban-Smith compared the results of his knapping experiments with the Boxgrove flints – the best to be recovered, he felt, since Caddington brickmakers were cutting their fingers on those exceedingly sharp splinters. The results of this comparison were at once exciting and disappointing.

The schoolboy Wenban-Smith had been fascinated by the refitting flints on a hunter-gatherer dig in Yorkshire (a mere 10,000 years old, those) and was already a competent knapper when he came to do his degree at the Institute of Archaeology in London. With Mark Newcomer at the helm, a lot of knapping went on in those days at the Institute. It was still a fairly new and minority interest in Britain, even within that small world of archaeological lithic specialists, where most practitioners were more concerned with looking at finished tools than thinking about how they were made (it was very different in North America, where knapping was all the rage: it was no coincidence that Newcomer was a transAtlantic). People like John McNabb (another Boxgrove digger), Chris Bergman, Phil Harding, Mark Newcomer and Frank would gather flint from all over (the best came from Norfolk) and hammer away, perfecting their skills, swapping ideas, trying to outdo one another on an esoteric point of technique.

For his dissertation, Francis asked what could be expected if archaeologists were to dig up perfectly preserved flint debris left after making a handaxe? He set up trials reminiscent of Dean Buckland's studies of a hyena. But while Billy chomped bones pacing a cage in Oxford, Francis sat on white-sheet covered concrete in a London basement, and made flint tools. He was his own experiment. Depending on how close to the ground he sat, he found he created more or less concentrated spreads of flakes and chips that radiated out in the direction he was facing. Newcomer had tried something similar already, sitting mostly on stools and chairs: but Francis sat on the ground amidst all the razor sharp flakes. In the only published reference he could find, traditional stoneworkers (in Australia) were described thus sitting cross-legged or kneeling (*see* fig 25).

By the end of July 1986 they had finished 50 square metres of what we will call the First Handaxe Trench, plotting tens of thousands of pieces of flint, taking several months to excavate a layer of silt less than ten centimetres thick. In one part of the trench there seemed to be a concentration of fine flakes. A second such focus had some bigger

161

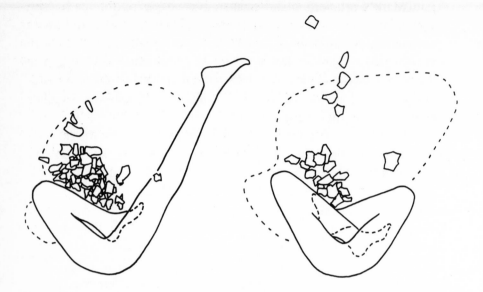

fig 25: For his undergraduate dissertation, Francis Wenban-Smith thought about how the flint knapping debris that was being excavated at Boxgrove had accumulated. He made handaxes similar to those found in the dig to see what happened to the waste flint. In these two diagrams, he has plotted flakes larger than 5 centimetres across; the dashed lines enclose the main spread of smaller chips and dust. He supported the heavy flint nodule on his left leg, and worked it with his right hand. Most of the larger flakes fell to the ground against his left leg, and the rest of the debris made a fan shaped pattern, rather than a random spread around him.

flakes, indicating that coarser work had been carried out there too. But when they came to refit the debris, so many bits were missing they realized they only had part of this spread, and extended the trench in one corner.

All this was done underneath a horticultural tunnel: in the summer warmth, it proved its design, as the atmosphere inside became positively tropical. To keep the ground moist so they could see the most delicate changes in colour and texture, it was regularly dampened with water using a garden weed-killer spray bottle. At the end of the day, it was given a good soaking, and covered with plastic sheets. Diggers gently picking away at the silt on their hands and knees would feel ice cold drops of condensation on their backs. It was of course a perfect environment for tomatoes: and indeed in a photo published by the *Observer* early that autumn, some fine tomato plants could be seen at the back of a shelter, behind the gently undulating surface with its 50 centimetre grid of white string.

In his first report on these two flint scatters, prepared just in time to

join Mark's article, Chris Bergman had suggested that each represented the site where a handaxe had been made. Continuing
excavations showed the flakes were rather dispersed, however, and
even if Chris made an axe standing up, his debris fell into a spread
more concentrated than the two from the First Handaxe Trench.
Perhaps, he now suggested, a little surface water had moved things
about. Francis had written much the same thing in his 1985
dissertation. His own scatters were far more restricted than those in the
Boxgrove trench, which might have been subjected to 'the scuffing of
Palaeolithic feet'.

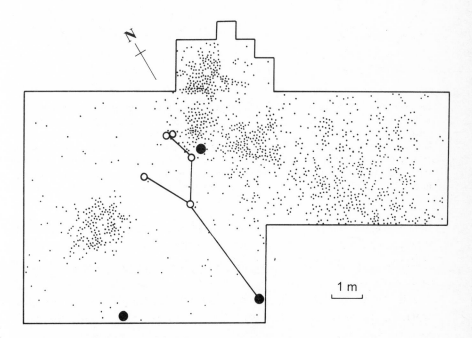

fig 26: The main archaeological trench in the East Quarry, begun in 1984, was finished in 1987.
All the flint artefacts greater than 2 centimetres across are plotted in this plan. They mostly derive
from finishing handaxes; the axes must have been roughed out somewhere else, perhaps nearer the
source of fresh flint at the cliff 300 metres to the north. Three handaxes were found (large black
circles), onto one of which five sharpening ('tranchet') flakes could be refitted (open circles). Many
more flakes in the scatters could be fitted back to each other again. This refitting indicates that the
debris has been little disturbed since it fell to the ground. However, the distances between many of
the fitting flakes are greater than would be expected if there had been no disturbance at all. There
are no small, dense scatters that Francis Wenban-Smith had shown are left by someone sitting on
the ground to make an axe (*see* fig 25). It seems that these flakes had been kicked about by animals
and moved a little by surface water. Nonetheless, this material was then the most complete group of
refitting flakes from making handaxes found anywhere in Europe. (adapted from Bergman,
Roberts, Collcutt & Barlow)

So though it was clear there had been no major disturbance – the refitting flakes proved that – yet there was something about the excavated flints that was not perfectly right. The same pattern was occurring in the main trench of the West Quarry: very fresh flintwork that could be fitted together, but remained too scattered, so that two flakes representing successive hammer blows might lie five or more metres apart. There was no denying it was a little frustrating, to have reached that close and still not to have arrived.

They didn't have to wait long for something different.

Chapter 33

Intelligent Chimpanzees

squirrel

A sailor returning to Paris from Borneo with a captive orangutan had one night surprised the creature as it attempted to shave itself with the man's razor. The orangutan fled through an open window, roamed the dark city streets until it saw a light, climbed the wall and entered a lady's bedroom. The lady, understandably misinterpreting the animal's attempts to shave her, panicked, the orangutan followed suit, accidentally severed the lady's head and sank its teeth into her daughter's throat. Thus occurred, according to Edgar Allen Poe, the mysterious murders in the Rue Morgue.

This seems to be the first description, albeit fictional, of one species of primate learning from another the use of a tool. The more remarkable achievement, of a man teaching an ape actually to *make* the tool, occurred more recently, in March 1971, in Bristol Zoo in England. Richard Wright, an archaeologist with an interest in stone tools who subsequently made his career in Australia, managed to train Abang, a five-and-a-half-year-old male orangutan, to knock a flake off a lump of flint (procured from a quarry in Wiltshire), then use the flake to cut a cord that opened a box of food.

The experiment was brief and informal ('It is impossible', noted the archaeologist, 'to write notes when in the same cage as an ape'). He would rather have worked with a chimpanzee or gorilla, but 'matters of housing and pregnancy' forced Wright to try his skills on Abang. Nonetheless, it was a momentous occasion. An ape of presumed lower abilities than the earliest proposed humans had made and used a stone tool. And it was all filmed by the BBC.

'Man', said Dr Boswell, misquoting Benjamin Franklin, is 'a tool-making animal.' This was a popular philosophical point of view: making tools, it was felt, required intellectual capacities that were uniquely human. But for archaeologists, there was also a practical aspect. Stone tools survived in the ground, giving the presence of something as ephemeral as 'humanity' lasting physical form. Thus the famously titled booklet, *Man the Toolmaker*, published by the British Museum (Natural History) in 1959, is actually not about 'Man' at all – it's about flints.

Wright's experiment in Bristol Zoo was not just a playful attempt to show that this logic might be flawed. It was itself prompted by the well publicized discovery by Jane Goodall, a student from Cambridge, England, working in 1960 in what is now Tanzania, that it was utterly wrong.

We are familiar with chimpanzees as entertainers, and it is well known that laboratory apes have been taught skills that include rudimentary use of visual symbols or 'language'. The really significant research, however, is being conducted in the forests and savannas of west and central Africa, in patient long-term studies of chimpanzees in their own habitats. It is now impossible properly to approach the question of early hominid behaviour without considering this work.

The early reports from Jane Goodall that caught the attention of anthropologists described chimps systematically making small tools of grass or twigs and using them to poke into termite mounds – much as a mechanic uses a dipstick to check a car's engine oil – to extract the edible insects. But it is not just the way in which they make and use tools that is of interest (although we shall shortly return to this): it is the whole nature of chimpanzee society and behaviour.

Pan troglodytes, the common chimpanzee, is an intelligent, sensitive creature. Individuals have distinct personalities, and show self-awareness; they play; they have a need for physical contact, patting, kissing, holding hands, greeting each other in a variety of gestures and embraces; they have a rich knowledge of the world around them, extending, it seems, to the medicinal qualities of some plants; they hunt small animals for meat, and occasionally scavenge larger carcasses from other predators; males kill other chimps as a means of maintaining troop power and identity; in their food gathering activities, they show sophisticated planning and strong powers of

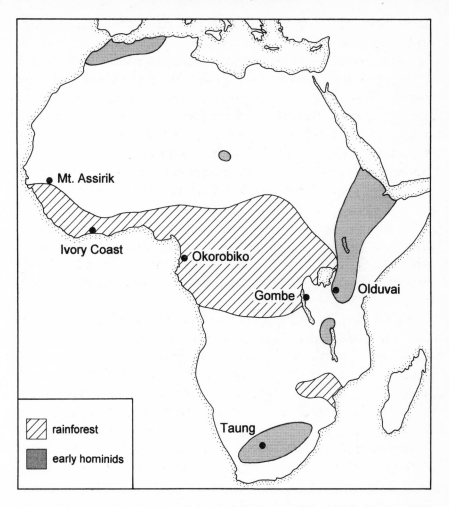

fig 27: The earlier extent of rainforest in central Africa is probably a broad indication of the maximum occurrence of chimpanzees and bonobos; the locations of some modern studies of these animals are marked. Early hominid fossils are found principally in two areas in east and southern Africa. It is not known how much this restricted distribution is a genuine reflection of where these creatures lived, and how much of geological deposits that preserve fossils.

memory; they travel along regular paths, frequent favourite resting spots and sometimes stay for extended periods at restricted sleeping sites. All this has emerged only in the past few decades, even as their habitat and their livelihood come increasingly under threat.

The most extraordinary instance of chimpanzee tool use – cracking nuts – was first reported in 1843 (just a year after John McEnery's collection was auctioned in Torquay: *see* Chapter 8), but no one was ready for such a thing then. Instead, we owe our knowledge of nut-cracking largely to Christophe Boesch, a Swiss biologist, his wife Hedwige and their colleagues who have been studying chimps in the Taï forest and other areas of the Ivory Coast and Liberia since 1979 (*see* fig 28).

fig 28: Chimpanzee using a log as an anvil to crush a nut with a stone, on the Bassa Islands, Liberia. (after photo by Hannah)

For three or four months a year, when the nuts are in season, they are a major food source. A chimpanzee will typically spend over two hours *every day* cracking nuts, so that the forest echoes to the din of hollow hammering, as stones or broken branches are brought down on nuts carefully wedged in tree roots. They know exactly where to find nuts – which trees will be ready when – and still more remarkably, can memorize as many as five sites at which they have previously hidden valuable stone hammers, knowing which is the nearest to the tree they wish to harvest, even if that stone is over 200 metres from the tree (in a different context, Goodall saw chimps carry termiting sticks from mound to mound for more than 800 metres).

Cracking nuts is not easy. In fact, it is a skill only fully acquired by adults, so that for the first eight years of its life, a chimp relies on its mother to share nuts and to pass on the craft. And this is where things start to get really interesting. Because if a mother has to teach its young to make and use tools – and they have been seen doing just that – it follows that tool-making could have been a serendipitous invention by one animal (perhaps female), who passed it on to others in her family, who shared it with other families – *but not necessarily all families* – some of whom might have subsequently lost the skill. Which sounds remarkably like many anthropologists' definition of culture (being everything we owe to our membership of a society, as opposed to our instincts) which is, of course, a uniquely human attribute.

And this is precisely what Boesch and his co-workers found in the forests of the Ivory Coast.

They looked for evidence of nut-cracking at two dozen chimpanzee locations where the conditions (availability of hammers and anvils, and similar environments, including the presence of nut trees) suggested that this activity would likely occur. In fact, it was only present near the border with Liberia (where nut-cracking has also been observed), or more particularly west of the River Sassandra. During the temperate ice ages, when the African climate was significantly drier than present, the forest shrank into isolated refuges; where the Sassandra now flows became a desert corridor. Boesch suggests that nut-cracking appeared in the western refuge (and a diminished forest is good enough reason for new ways of obtaining food to evolve and stick) around 17,000 years ago. The practice spread with the expanding forest as the climate got wetter, but stopped at the Sassandra, which by then was too wide for chimpanzees to cross.

Another team of researchers, led by Bill McGrew, now at Miami University, Ohio, found further behaviour that they, like Boesch, refer to as 'truly cultural'. In this case, they looked at the sticks and stalks used for termite fishing. (As an aside, it should be said that tool use is not restricted to cracking nuts and catching termites, but is also applied to activities such as drinking water, cleaning body or teeth and fighting and displaying. 'Cultural' differences have been claimed for some of these cases as well, such as the varied use of fly whisks or of crumpled leaf sponges).

McGrew considered three groups of chimpanzees: at Mount Assirik in Senegal (where he began research in 1976 when at the University of Stirling in Scotland), at Goodall's chimps in the Gombe reserve in Tanzania and at Okorobiko in the Republic of Equatorial Guinea. The most obvious difference is that the Okorobiko sticks are longer and thicker than the others. However, this is related to the way the chimps there catch termites, in turn a function of the effect a different climate has on the structure of Okorobiko termite nests. The chimps use their sticks to break open the mounds, before scooping out termites with their hands; at Gombe and Mount Assirik, finer tools are preferred for the more delicate task of fishing through small holes (fig 29). A majority of sticks used at Gombe are made from grass stems, while this material is rarely used at Mount Assirik. But climate can explain this too: a longer dry season in Senegal means that less grass is available in the termiting season because of more thorough ground fires. (Nonetheless, a Gombe chimp transported to Mount Assirik would presumably have to learn how to manage without grass.)

fig 29: Gombe chimp using grass stem to fish for termites. (after photo by McGrew)

However, there remained several aspects of termiting amongst the three chimp populations that McGrew and his colleagues could not explain by reference to varied environments. A third of tools at Mount Assirik are made with leaf stalks, and one in five at Gombe with bark, but these respective materials, although equally available, are never used at the other location. At Okorobiko and Gombe, chimpanzees commonly use both ends of their sticks; at Mount Assirik they throw them away after using one end. The great majority of twigs used at

Mount Assirik are peeled of bark; at Gombe, twigs are always used with the bark still on.

This may not sound particularly impressive as a claim for chimpanzee 'culture'. But you must remember that only a few decades ago, such behaviour was not only unknown, but generally dismissed as impossible for any creatures other than humans. And there is a further twist to the tale. All this time we have been considering the common chimpanzee, *Pan troglodytes*. But there is another chimp species, *Pan paniscus*, or the bonobo, found in a restricted area of central Africa. And bonobos behave altogether differently again.

While common chimpanzees live in groups of about 50 dominated by males, establishing their authority through aggressive displays, bonobo society revolves around females, who form the core in troops twice the size. Male chimpanzees occasionally kill other chimpanzees; bonobos mediate relationships with sex. In fact, in a sophisticated repertoire of calls and gestures, at least 20 are thought to signal a readiness to copulate. Unlike chimpanzees, bonobos, who live in trees, when on the ground regularly walk upright on two legs. Given this last observation, it is all the more remarkable that, at least to date, bonobos have never been observed to make or use tools.

The relevance of all this to Boxgrove – we thought you might be wondering! – becomes apparent immediately we think back to our opening discussion (in Chapter 2) of archaeologists' ideas about hunting, meat-eating and early hominid behaviour. On the one hand are descriptions of early humans as bloodthirsty and brutish killers (Dart, Ardrey); as 'the most marginal of scavengers', with no ability to plan, cooperate in groups or map out fixed paths and activity loci (Binford); and as clever scavengers with 'home bases' (Isaac). Chimpanzees, on the other hand, while spending a great deal of time eating (mostly plants), rarely engage in any activity that does not have a social component, whether this means teaching each other tricks, sharing food, confirming status relationships or just playing together. Furthermore, they are capable of elaborate planning, have good memories and, in some cases, pass on regional traditions of making and using tools. In short, chimpanzees emerge as more 'human' than our immediate ancestors. Only Isaac's hominids seem capable of holding their own against a troop of apes.

The importance of chimpanzees to understanding early hominids is further apparent when we look at genetic similarities. We share 98.4% of our genes with the two chimp species, our closest animal relatives. It is estimated that this difference would have taken something between five and eight million years to develop (bonobos differ from common chimpanzees by only 0.7%, representing about three million years of separation). In evolutionary terms, we are extremely closely related. Indeed, Jared Diamond, in *The Rise and Fall of the Third Chimpanzee* – that's us – suggests that if chimps were to learn biology, they would classify all three of us as species of a single genus, which we might call *Pan* or *Homo* according to taste. It seems when the Oubi of the Ivory Coast told how humans and chimpanzees descended from two brothers, they may have been onto something. The good-looking brother sired humans: the second brother was the intelligent one.

Finally, if, as seems likely, modern humans have diverged more from our common ancestor than have the two chimpanzee species, then the very earliest hominids – say around four and a half million years ago, well before the time when the two chimps separated – are likely to be closer genetically to chimps than they are to us.

Chapter 34

More Flints and a Unique Find

European eagle owl

Mark and Jane Murray had met in 1984. Jane's sister, Josie, was an early volunteer at Boxgrove, and when Jane left her job in the City of London to pursue archaeology, she went down to Sussex for some experience of digging. In June 1985, Mark and Jane were married; Tony Tynan was best man.

While the newlyweds were away on honeymoon, torrential rain called for action to prevent the delicate trench in the West Quarry from flooding. The team dug drainage gullies around the shelter (by then they had bought another two horticultural tunnels), and a deep sump to the south. Slowly down through the land surface, looking out for artefacts, then shovel out half a metre of silt, known to be sterile of archaeology. But they were brought up by a sudden 'clunk', as the spade hit something hard: they had found worked flints at a lower level for the first time, and subsequent investigation revealed animal bones as well. This was a shock, and Mark was as surprised by it as the rest of them when he got back. The artefacts had to be older than anything found before (by how much they couldn't tell – decades, perhaps centuries); there might be a whole new site at this low level. The discovery changed their excavation strategy in the West Quarry. Instead of digging out the land surface and then moving elsewhere, they continued going down where they were.

It so happened that the Supervisor of this trench, Louise Austin, had prior experience of excavating well preserved flintwork on a large scale. She had graduated from the Institute in 1984 with a dissertation on late palaeolithic huts, and with Mark Newcomer's help she had worked at Pincevent in northern France, a meticulously excavated camp of modern humans dating from near the end of the ice age. Louise had joined the Boxgrove team in that first cold winter a few months before her graduation (and would stay with the project until the end of 1989). At Boxgrove, her greatest effort was directed at that trench in the West Quarry.

The flintwork in the top of Louise's Trench was similar to that in the First Handaxe Trench in the East Quarry – fresh, refitting flakes that were yet slightly disturbed. What distinguished Louise's Trench from the start was the quantity of animal bone. It was very well preserved, and frequently from such small animals (voles were common) that it was too delicate to be excavated outside (even with their plasterer's leaves and wooden modelling tools). Such remains had to be lifted in blocks of silt for later dissection with the aid of a binocular microscope.

But progress was slowed even more by the sheer density of flint debris that appeared as the trench level descended into the deep silt. Normally they would pin out little flags to mark flints for measuring in (anything more than two centimetres across was given treatment that a Roman archaeologist would accord a gold coin), and the surface would become covered in the flags, like a model battlefield. This silt was different. Instead of a general scatter of flakes, with areas of slightly richer concentrations, flint was either very scarce, or so common that you couldn't get the pin of the flag through. This was exactly what knappers like Mark Newcomer, Chris Bergman and Francis Wenban-Smith had predicted of a surface with no disturbance at all. After her experience at Pincevent, Louise knew what to do.

They finished the upper level early in 1986, having recovered numerous flint flakes, six handaxes and some 2000 bones and bone fragments. Continuing down, the first concentrated heap of flint was signalled by quantities of very fine spalls in the silt above. Louise divided the grid into smaller squares, and the silt that had been scraped off each square was sieved to recover this minuscule evidence. The working surface was kept horizontal, and silt prised away from around the flint flakes. Photographs were then taken looking down vertically, and prints made at about half actual size: four or five covered the first flint scatter. Then one by one, flints over a centimetre across (or about as wide as the nail on your little finger) were removed. They were entered on a 'finds sheet' (recording orientation, dip from the horizontal and which way up they lay) and slipped into a numbered polythene bag, and then the number was written onto the same piece as it appeared in the photo. Once all the exposed flakes and chips had been lifted in this way, and the residue bagged for later sieving, a little more silt was scraped out, another series of photos taken and the procedure started again. It was not a job to rush.

There were three of these dense concentrations of flint in Louise's Trench, and the last tiny spall was not removed until the third summer in 1988. But it was the first spread that was the most spectacular. One thousand seven hundred and fifteen pieces of flint were individually recorded and thousands of chips less than 5mm across recovered by sieving: there was even flint dust between the chips. Mark and Chris Bergman were able to describe it briefly to a conference in Amiens, not far from Boucher de Perthes' discoveries in the last century (Chapter 10), in December 1986. Their suspicions that it might be unique were confirmed: none of the archaeologists present had seen anything like it.

One of the diggers at Boxgrove, however, had: indeed the year before, he had created something almost identical for his undergraduate dissertation. Francis Wenban-Smith, who at the time was working over in the East Quarry, knew what Louise had found.

When he sat on his white sheet to make handaxes, one position he had taken up was with his left leg folded under and his right extended straight. Francis was right handed, so he had held the axe in his left hand over his left leg, and his hammer in his right. As he knapped out the axe, flakes and chips flew out across the arc between his two legs, or fell more or less straight to the ground. Many of the pieces that fell glanced off his left leg and gathered on the inside.

Louise's scatter was a triangle of fine debris that gradually thinned out in one direction, but came to an abrupt halt on the other two sides. On the right side there was an especially thick accumulation of flakes – some of them were actually standing vertically in the sediment, just as, half a million years ago, they'd sliced through the air after being struck from an axe and stuck in the ground. This suggested that the flint being worked was held over the right leg. The whole thing covered an area of less than a quarter of a square metre, and beyond its boundaries there was nothing but clean silt: except that about 20 centimetres to the right were some larger sized flakes that looked as if they had been deliberately selected, carefully picked out, as they were struck, from the morass of razor sharp slivers and dust (later they were able to refit these flakes to pieces inside the scatter). In every respect, it was what Francis had recorded when he sat and knapped on the floor – except for one thing. The heaping of flakes towards the right side of the triangle indicated that Francis' forebear of half a million years ago was left-handed.

Later, in the echoing spacious warehouse that was the British Museum store in London, Louise managed to refit two thirds of the pieces, and in doing so uncovered the story behind the scatter. Somewhere beyond the excavated area (perhaps near the cliff at the flint source) a knapper had decided to rough out a handaxe. But before it was done, one end of the axe snapped off in an exasperating accident that can creep up on the most skilled modern flintworker if their attention drifts. The larger part of this rough was then carried to a spot about 100 metres from the cliff, where the knapper sat down, worked it into a fine tool (which must have been smaller than the one originally intended), leaving a tidy heap of waste, and took the tool with them for use somewhere else.

Meanwhile, back in the quarries, they were striving to comprehend the details of the geological succession: to tell the complete story of how the sea built up the beach, how the subsequent lagoon dried out and how the sludges and gravels began to accumulate under a changed climate of severe cold. In May 1987, Mark hosted the second Boxgrove seminar. They'd dug the holes. Now it was time to fill them with specialists to see what they would make of it all.

Mark posted 40 invitations to the seminar, and everyone who could turned up: although little had been formally published since the first report, word had spread about the remarkable finds. Nick Brooks, a local farmer, brought a tractor and trailer furnished with straw bales and drove the visitors from one excavation to another. (Later Mark and Jane moved from the barns into one of his cottages: their daughter Harriet was born in London three weeks before the seminar.) At every trench they piled out in their wellies and muddy shoes, gripping their waterproof coats, Mark sporting a cloth cap and green jacket, and listened to members of the excavation team and each other as they described what they could see and what they thought it meant.

There was a large geological pit dug for Simon Collcutt in the East Quarry. In the West Quarry they had just begun machine stripping the top off the L-Shape. Under the shelter over Louise's Trench, Mark explained how they were digging out the finely preserved flintwork. Back in the large hay barn they had wine and food (with borrowed furniture) and the opportunity, with electricity laid on for a slide projector, to talk about the geology in more detail.

176

The seminar was a memorable success. A nervous Simon Parfitt gave his first public talk; Francis baffled everyone with overhead projections of his knapping experiments; Andy Currant talked about voles (to be stopped dead by a Cambridge University scientist, who rose to object to his interpretation of ice age time). One outcome was that two new specialists joined the project: the geological investigation had become a substantial undertaking in its own right.

Later that season, Collcutt, a free-lance geologist working on English Heritage contracts, deepened the pit that went down through the yellow beach sands, and hit the chalk rock beneath. He found a couple of small flint flakes in the sands: the first indication that hominids were about even when the sea was still beating near the bottom of the chalk cliff. Two tiny pieces of flint could open up a whole new story. He also found that the Slindon Sands did not represent just a single episode of marine deposition. There were three distinct beaches one on top of the other, indicating a fluctuating sea level over a relatively short period, which in turn implied an unstable climate long before any signs of the severe cold that was to follow.

And that winter the power of unstable weather was brought home in a way that everyone then in Britain would remember (not least Sharon Gerber and Simon Parfitt, whose wedding was the day after): in November 1987 a hurricane hit the south of England. Boxgrove was in the centre of one of the worst affected areas.

The winds came from the west, tearing across the downs and the plain, rattling doors, pulling at gutters and tiles, thumping against walls and whistling around chimneys. Anything loose went. Then permanent fixtures moved. Clay tiles flew off Ounces Barn in the darkness. You could *hear* trees being broken. And in the quarries, the wind plucked the plastic tunnels and screwed them into balls, so the next morning they lay beside the trenches like crumpled paper in a journalist's waste basket.

A couple of years before, heavy rain had led to the important discovery of exceptionally preserved archaeology deep within the silts. Now a storm seemed to have wiped it all out. When they cleared up the mess the following spring, however, the damage was found to be superficial. Plastic sheeting had been shredded, poles were bent and wooden planks scattered like straw. But underneath the protective backfill of the trenches, the archaeology was still there, full of promise. It had been exciting, but the ground had not moved.

Chapter 35

An Importance Difficult to Overstate

bison

We need to pause briefly, and reflect on the extraordinary quality of Boxgrove. Since antiquarians and collectors began scouring gravel pits for handaxes over a century ago, it was in those artefacts – in north west Europe almost exclusively made in flint, but elsewhere from a wide variety of fine grained rocks – that people most readily saw the oldest skilled hominids. Handaxes thrown around by ancient rivers are common – quarries in England and France have produced literally thousands, and casefulls lie gathering dust in museum basements. They are a convenient size for collecting and displaying and they communicate unmistakeably of a creative intellect.

But what do we make of these unstratified archaeological remains? Do all those handaxes have any value, or are we in reality – whatever archaeologists might claim – just hoarding old flints that can tell us nothing? It is a question that has been well exercised by anthropologists in Africa, digging up jumbles of bones and stone tools.

They were finding handaxes at Boxgrove, but here, thanks to the survival of the ancient land surfaces – unique in their size and the richness of their evidence – the stratification was almost perfect. So not only did they have the axes, they were also finding much that spoke of the world of manufacture and use of those tools. And they were finding huge quantities of bones. It was the juxtaposition of these discoveries, the blending of the evidence from artefacts and animals, of the geological clues to landscape and climate, that made Boxgrove so uncommonly special. Yet the very uniqueness of Boxgrove means that the other evidence – the collector's hauls of stained and battered flint axes – is important too. These give us the broader picture of how the Boxgrove hominids used their whole landscape, and how their descendents adapted to changing worlds down the millenia. That is why in 1991 English Heritage began a thorough survey (the English Rivers Project), checking up on all the old handaxe finds, recording the relevant geology and the state of mineral extraction and other development.

Boxgrove has its rolled and battered handaxes, too. But far more important are the remarkable land surfaces. With such exceptional preservation, they were uncovering the moments that time and geology normally blur into millennia. And by doing that they were conjuring up a real world of hominids and animals that could put flesh on the countless thousands of dry stones in museums all over Europe. It is an achievement whose importance it would be difficult to overstate.

Archaeological data can tell us where and when hominids were part of the ecology, what constituted that scene and, to a greater or lesser degree, how these creatures fitted in. But can they tell us anything more? Can we read from them clues as to how the hominids behaved, how they thought? Or are we left to use our imaginations to bridge the gap? The popular conception of neanderthals as brutish idiots is one such guess. So is Robert Ardrey's vision of bloodthirsty killers.

But we don't have to rely only on our imagination. Almost everywhere we look, if we understand that which we seek, is physical evidence. At Boxgrove Mark was slowly, but unmistakeably, beginning to penetrate a very, very rare world of 'preserved action'.

Chapter 36

Three Million Years of
Evolving Minds

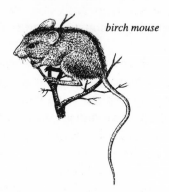

birch mouse

Suppose we placed modern chimpanzees at the start of the hominid narrative, and modern humans at the end, how might we set about filling in the story? In the absence of any further evidence, we could draw a line between the two points, separated by, say, six million years, on which to hang the slowly progressing hominids. On this basis, relative to chimpanzees, our imaginary ancestors would have been '50% human' three million years ago – good candidates for 'the missing link'. The Boxgrove creatures, at a mere half million years from the end of the tale, would have achieved '92% humanity'. The actual date of our separation from chimpanzees is not that precisely tied down, but even if we allow for an over-estimate of a million years (in fact, the current tendency is to look to before seven million years ago), we still find at least '90% humans' at Boxgrove. Most of us can probably think of people we know we might like to classify as less than 90% human relative to a chimp. The Boxgrove hominids were, it would seem, pretty much like us.

Of course, there is a major flaw in this logic. Modern chimpanzees do not lie at the root of our ancestry, but share with us a common ancestor. That ancestor was undoubtedly more like a chimp than a human, but how much more like? This is an area of evolution still poorly represented by fossils. Fortunately, we do not have to rely on such a procedure for assessing the appearance and development of a human-like intellect. Although we cannot dig up ancient IQs, there are ways of indirectly approaching the issue with real evidence. First, we can look at physical changes in the brain, as seen in preserved skulls. Then we can study lifestyle and means of getting food, as revealed by excavated artefacts and other debris. Finally we can look at a single category of artefact, the stone tool, and ask how much it can tell us about thinking skills. These are naturally controversial fields – but then, so is the meaning of a concept such as IQ in our own world. And there is, in fact, a surprising amount of agreement on some major points.

An advantage of considering a single skeletal feature (cranial capacity, an almost exact reflection of brain size) is that we can, at least for the time being, ignore the controversies that surround the distinction of one fossil species from another, and who is related in what way to whom. All we need to know is that the brains in question are in some sense part of the family.

Given that a larger brain has been shown to permit increased information processing capacity, it is little surprise to find that over the past few million years, hominid crania have indeed gradually increased in size. A chimpanzee brain (400 cubic centimetres) is about a third to a quarter of the size of a modern human's. The first measurable hominid skulls, dating from around two and a half to three million years ago, show brains little bigger. By a million years ago, the brain has reached twice the size of a chimp's, and by 500,000 years ago there are hominids with brains that fall within the lower range of modern humans'.

Over this period of change, however, it was not just brains that were growing: our ancestors were getting taller, too. There is clearly an automatic relationship between body size and brain size (an elephant is not necessarily vastly more intelligent than a gerbil), so we need to allow for these broader changes. Relative brain size is measured by a statistic known as the 'encephalization quotient', or EQ. Encephalization, the extent to which a brain is bigger than we would expect for an animal of a given body size, is an important part of our attempt to picture the emergence of modern human intellect.

Fig 30 shows how relative brain size slowly grew for a few million years, before speeding up around one and a half million years ago and taking off only a few thousand centuries ago. This is not the steady growth pattern we might have imagined. Something interesting was definitely going on.

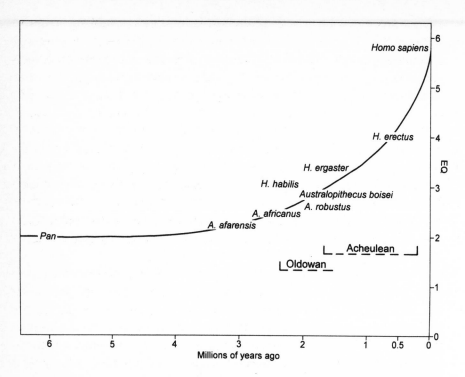

fig 30: 'Encephalization quotient' (EQ) is a measure of brain size corrected for body size. This graph shows clearly that over three million years of hominid evolution, the brain has grown by significantly more than would be expected simply as a result of the expanding body. Modern chimpanzees (*Pan*), with whom we share a common ancestor alive perhaps six million years ago, have an EQ slightly less than a typical *Australopithecus* individual. Of course, using the chimp as the ancestor is strictly cheating, for we know little about how chimpanzees have themselves changed. The actual number of hominid species is likely to have been more than those represented on this graph. Oldowan and Acheulean are the major early stone tool making industries, both found only with *Homo* species. (data from McHenry)

This trend is quite clearly reflected in the broad pattern of tool use as seen amongst surviving stone artefacts. The first simple stone implements, known as 'oldowan', date from about 2,500,000 years ago. A significant development occurred 1,750,000 years ago when the first 'acheulean' tools appear, representing as they do an advance in technological mastery. These are replaced by an altogether new and more sophisticated technology that first appears about 200,000 years ago.

We will look soon at these longterm changes in stone tool manufacture, but first we will focus on the most recent development, not least because there is an unusual degree of accord amongst archaeologists as to its importance. It was once referred to as the

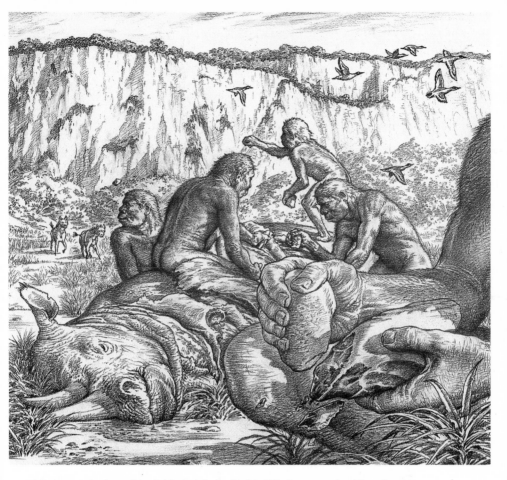

1. While hyenas look on, hominids attack the freshly killed corpse of a rhino that became extinct nearly 500,000 years ago, using flint handaxes with razor sharp edges. These tools, of which hundreds have been excavated at Boxgrove, are surprisingly sophisticated; their manufacture implies a level of intelligence for the hominids that has surprised most archaeologists. (Drawing by John Sibbick, courtesy of *National Geographic Magazine*.)

2. Mark Roberts surrounded by soil samples at his first small excavation at Boxgrove in 1983. (© Boxgrove Project)

3. The exploratory 1983 dig, Duncan Lees supervising (standing). (© Boxgrove Project)

4. Mark (above) and Tony Tynan erecting shelter over the First Trench in 1984. (© Boxgrove Project)

5. November 1984, excavation shelter in bottom of East Quarry with silt lagoons behind. (© Boxgrove Project)

6. Mark shows Louise's Trench in the West Quarry to specialists in 1987. He is standing on the preserved land surface from 500,000 years ago. (© Boxgrove Project)

7. At the back of Louise's Trench as seen in [6], this dense scatter of flint flakes was found where a hominid had sat to make a handaxe. (© Boxgrove Project)

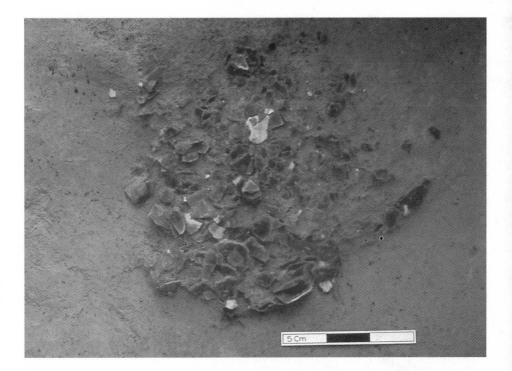

5 Cm

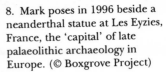

8. Mark poses in 1996 beside a neanderthal statue at Les Eyzies, France, the 'capital' of late palaeolithic archaeology in Europe. (© Boxgrove Project)

9. The skull of a small wolf from Louise's Trench. (© Boxgrove Project)

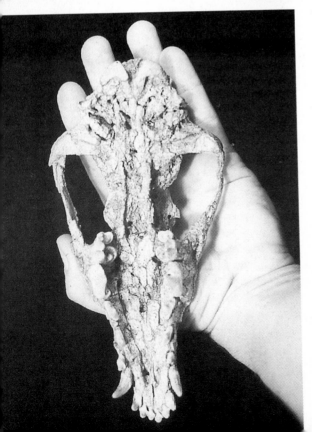

13. (*Opposite*) Laying out flints from the Horse Butchery Site for refitting at Ounces Barn, 1991. (© Boxgrove Project)

10. The Horse Butchery Site under excavation in 1989, looking west. (© Boxgrove Project)

11. Still in the ground, the controversial horse scapula at the Horse Butchery Site with the impact wound clearly visible top left as a large semicircular notch. (© Boxgrove Project)

12. Flint flakes (black flags represent smaller removed pieces) *in situ* at the Horse Butchery Site, later refitted to make a nodule from which a handaxe had been made. (© Boxgrove Project)

14. Ounces Barn 1995, looking west. (© Michael Pitts)

15. The Sand Project in the East Quarry, 1990. The best archaeology is in the Slindon Silts (being removed) and on the underlying Slindon Sands (dug out in foreground). (© Boxgrove Project)

16. Simon Parfitt at the wet sieving
post (where small bones are
washed out of excavated silts),
looking across the West Quarry to
the 1996 excavations below the
steps on the far edge.
(© Michael Pitts)

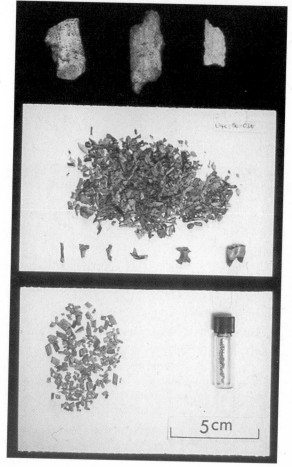

17. Animal bone fragments picked
out from the residue of wet sieving
about 100 kg of silt.
(© Boxgrove Project)

18. Mark with the hominid tibia near the end of the 1995 dig, looking north. He stands in the base of 1993 Trench 5, at the tibia find spot. (© Michael Pitts)

19. 1995 dig looking west. The two crouching figures are at the site of the first hominid tooth find. (© Boxgrove Project)

20. The surface of the marine sands where the hominid tooth was found in September 1995. (© Boxgrove Project)

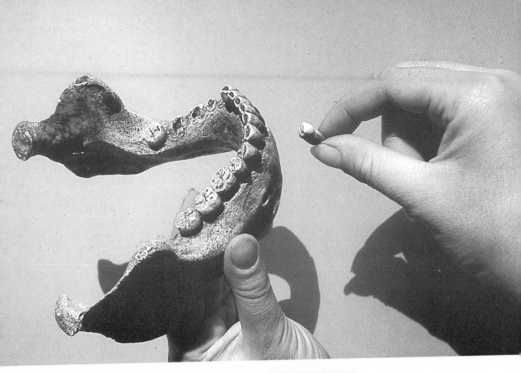

21. Cast of the jaw found at Mauer, Germany, in 1907 and the first Boxgrove tooth. Both are assigned to the species *Homo heidelbergensis.* (© Boxgrove Project)

22. Laura Basell holding the tooth she found, after the press conference at the dig. (© Boxgrove Project)

23. 1995 dig looking north. (© Michael Pitts)

24. Excavation of the surface of the marine sands 1995, with several *in situ* handaxes visible. (photo D W Webb, © Boxgrove Project)

25. Simon examining a bone hammer for knapping flint at his dig workbench in 1995. (© Michael Pitts)

26. John Mitchell with a Boxgrove handaxe in his Oxford laboratory. (© Boxgrove Project)

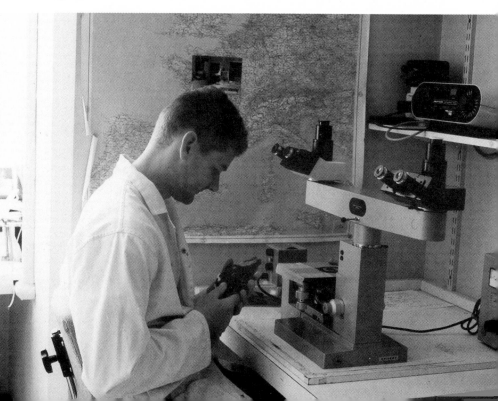

27. A large flint nodule (length c 30 cm) rebuilt from flakes found at the Horse Butchery Site. The cavity probably represents a handaxe roughout. (© Boxgrove Project)

28. Refitted handaxe thinning flakes from Louise's Trench. (© Boxgrove Project)

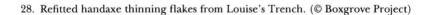

29. Bone hammer from the East Quarry. Scraping marks from removing the fresh membrane are visible at the left end; the pitting is caused by hammering flint (microscopic flint fragments are embedded in the holes). (© Boxgrove Project)

30. Part of a butchered rhino pelvis and a smaller bone fragment lying on a hand-axe on the marine sands in the 1996 dig. This may be the other half of the pelvis illustrated in fig 53. (© Boxgrove Project)

31. The large Beach Section in the east Quarry, looking north east. Main features, from bottom up (behind the figures): white beach gravels and chalk cliff collapse, lying on the marine platform in the chalk rock; dark brown bands of pure beach cobbles and sand; more light coloured cliff collapse; from the top, dark solifluction gravels have weathered down into the chalk debris. Immediately behind the far ladder is the surviving three metres of the ancient chalk cliff, originally as high as 75 to 100 metres. (© Michael Pitts)

32. Slightly further out to sea from the cliff, in Collcutt's Trench there is more marine sand than chalk. From the bottom up: chalk platform with wave-rounded blocks of chalk; beach pebbles on the chalk; marine sand; beach (behind Mark's head); more sand; a layer of chalk cliff collapse, covered by a little sand; grey Slindon Silts topped by a thin dark line of mineralised peat (the Fe Horizon); brickearths and fan gravels formed at the start of the cold climate era; dark solifluction gravels. (© Michael Pitts)

33. The winning team, 1996. Left to right, back row: Simon Parfitt (Assistant Director), John Gaskell (Supervisor), Jules Tipper (Site Manager), John Mitchell (Oxford University), Francis Wenban-Smith (Senior Site Supervisor), Wil Roebroeks (Leiden University). Front row: Tony Tynan (Site Manager 1983–91), Mike Anderton (Finds Assistant), Mark, Hans Kammermans (Leiden University), Matt Pope (Supervisor). (© Michael Pitts)

34. 1996 dig, looking west. (© Michael Pitts)

'middle-upper palaeolithic transition' but catchy phrases have since come into common use: 'the symbolic explosion'; 'the Creative Explosion'; 'the Great Leap Forward'; 'the upper palaeolithic revolution'; or simply 'the human revolution'. They may not know what to call it, but scientists certainly seem to agree that something special happened.

The change is clearest and most abrupt in Europe, where it occurred as recently as 30–40,000 years ago – which may be less than 2,000 generations from the present, barely a flicker in the evolutionary kaleidoscope of life on Earth. Before, the archaeological record is monotonously simple, consisting of little more than heaps of stones and bones – the material which has so exercised archaeologists like Binford and Isaac, and hundreds of others. After, and remember this is still in 'the ice age', long before things like farming or metallurgy, there is literally an explosion of variety, including the sudden appearance of what some people consider one of the great artistic achievements of the human species.

The Cambridge archaeologist, Paul Mellars, has documented this change over the past two decades as the details of the pattern have emerged, and he was among the first to pose the question: why did it happen? First, he notes a multiplication in the number of types of tools and other artefacts that are made. Instead of a basic handaxe and a few rough flake tools, now there are a large number of distinct implements that would seem to have their own special purposes (what the latter were remains largely guesswork, although Mellars notes wryly that the presence of different tools makes teaching undergraduates easier!). These distinct tools come and go with unprecedented speed. What's more, for the first time several are made from bone, antler or ivory, which is frequently extensively and skilfully carved. And instead of simple tools that are held in the hand, there are strong indications of complex assemblages using a range of materials – such as a wooden spear with a stone tip, launched with a sophisticated thrower made from antler.

There is more to it than this, however. For the first time, there is copious evidence that people were doing things that cannot possibly be explained as an essential adjunct to eating, drinking, breeding and maintaining body temperature. Here are the first personal ornaments: perforated animal teeth and shells, and carved beads. Here is the first decoration, ranging from stylized carvings of animals on bone and antler tools to the justifiably famous painted caves found especially in France and Spain. And, in the shape of little carved 'figurines', here may be the first intimations of magic or myth. Deliberate burial of human bodies becomes common practice. There are even suggestions of music, in the form of bones with whistle-like perforations.

The people who did all these things seem to have lived at a higher population density than had been achieved before. They made camps with recognizable hearths, holes for posts and so on. They obtained goods and materials from far afield. Sometimes they specialized in intensive hunting of single migratory herbivores, sometimes they fished. And for the first time they were able to penetrate the coldest parts of Europe and Asia, and, with the use of boats, to cross into Australia and, ultimately, the Americas (the world map then was essentially the one we know now).

'Most workers agree', says Paul Mellars, 'that these changes would be inconceivable in the absence of some form of relatively complex, highly structured language.' In fact, no one has really come up with any other explanation. We are witnessing the emergence of fully modern cognitive skills, the human capacity for communication, innovation and culture. The 'explosion' in Europe is a regional phenomenon, as Robert Foley, an anthropologist who teaches at a college but a few streets from Mellars', has pointed out. In Africa the changes can be seen appearing earlier and with less of a united rush. But all are agreed that, if archaeology is at all capable of identifying the moment when modern humans appeared, then this must be it.

The obvious question is what, then, had been happening for the previous three or four million years? Hominids had, apparently, got pretty sophisticated at making stone tools, their brains had been getting bigger, they had colonized most of Africa and Asia. And yet they had done none of those things that should signify a fellow human were we to look them in the face. Are we missing something?

One of the most interesting projects to explore this problem is that conducted by Thomas Wynn, an anthropologist at the University of Colorado, in the late 1970s and early 1980s. Is it possible, he asked, to see stages of intelligence, as recognized in the development of modern European children and adolescents by the Swiss psychologist Jean Piaget, in the evolution of the early hominids? Does every man today have millions of years of 'child-man' behind him? Was there a 'youthful era' without which the modern woman would not be modern? Wynn looked at early stone tools, and found what he was after.

The first tools are, to our eyes, pretty crude, consisting of little more than cobbles with a few pieces bashed off, or of broken flakes and chunks. The Leakeys called such artefacts oldowan, after the site of their excavations in Tanzania (see Fig 31).

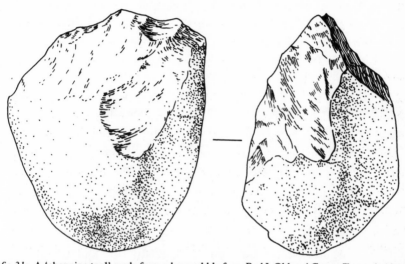

fig 31: A 'chopping tool' made from a lava pebble from Bed I, Olduvai Gorge, Tanzania (dated c 1.85–1.7 million years ago), excavated by Louis and Mary Leakey. These simple tools have a cutting edge formed by the intersection of a few flake scars, and, with rough flakes, are the earliest type of recognisable stone artefact found. They are known as 'oldowan', after an alternative spelling of Olduvai. (redrawn after M Leakey)

Wynn studied tools from the lower beds of Olduvai Gorge, dating from around two million years ago. He felt that their makers had no preconceived idea of what they were trying to do, but rather by a process of trial and error were able to come up with objects that somehow looked right. They would then go off and use them for whatever it was they used them for. In Piaget's terms, these actions would indicate 'pre-operational intelligence'. Put another way, seen through their tools the earliest hominids were no smarter than chimpanzees. Whatever else lay behind the origins of encephalization, hitting rocks together was not part of the story.

Things changed, however. Wynn also considered the acheulean

handaxe. Specifically, he chose to examine a collection of artefacts from a site in Tanzania dated to around 200–300,000 years ago. But his conclusions should apply to the whole of the acheulean era: while handaxes do vary in shape and quality, so must have the personal skills of their makers, the effects of varied raw materials and so on. The basic acheulean concept emerged over one and a half million years ago. Any development in hominid intellectual capacity inherent in this concept must be at least that old.

Placed beside the oldowan chopper, the acheulean handaxe has obvious new levels of sophistication (*see* figs 32–3). The typical oldowan tool owes most of its shape to the original cobble; the acheulean is flaked more or less all over, to a roughly symmetrical plan and profile. For over a million years in Africa, and later in Europe and parts of Asia, implements were being made to the same basic pattern. They have one more or less continuous sharp edge, often come to a rough point at one end, are a little fatter near the other end, and have a diamond-shaped cross section. Sometimes they are very finely made indeed, with sharp, regular sides and thin section.

This indicated to Wynn something beyond the capabilities of a chimpanzee. 'Acheulean hominids', he wrote, 'employed in their stone knapping the infra-logical operations of whole-part relations, qualitative displacement, spatio-temporal substitution and symmetry'. If you were ever trained to teach school children, you will probably recognize these as characteristics of what Piaget called 'operational intelligence': for the rest of us, it means grown-up thinking. The makers of the acheulean handaxe had brains wired like our own, potentially capable of dreaming up such uniquely human constructs as family trees, myths, language and art.

This flew directly in the face of the archaeologists' arguments that modern thinking is first indicated by the relatively sudden explosion of artefact styles and culture no more than 40–50,000 years ago. On top of this, at well over a million years ago, Wynn's modern humans appeared before encephalization had really taken off: small-brained but already as brainy as the best.

Nicholas Toth and Kathy Schick, at Indiana University, were archaeologists able to respond to Wynn's claims from both detailed knowledge of the east African material and modern knapping experiments. They felt he had underestimated oldowan skills. Although they look primitive, these oldest tools in fact required talents beyond the chimpanzee.

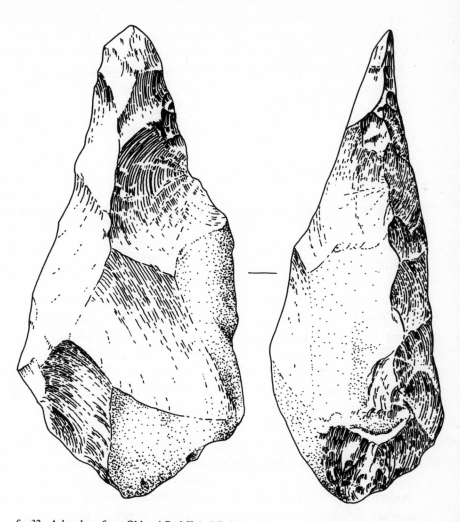

fig 32: A handaxe from Olduvai Bed II (c 1.7–1.2 million years ago) made from a large lava pebble. This 'bifacial' (worked around two faces) axe is of a type known as 'acheulean', after a town in France. (redrawn after M Leakey)

Recently they have been able to prove this with a highly intelligent captive bonobo called Kanzi. Kanzi, who can apparently understand sentences with no immediately obvious application in the west African jungle such as 'Go fetch the tomato from the microwave', was taught to make stone tools. Like Abang in Bristol Zoo, Kanzi soon learnt to knock off a stone flake, cut the string and open the box. Unlike Abang, however, Kanzi did his own experiments. To make it possible for Abang to make contact between his hammer and another stone, Richard Wright had glued the stone to a larger piece of wood. Kanzi soon worked out for himself that the easiest way to get a flake was to throw rocks onto a hard floor. Neither animal understood the most basic principle of controlled stone flaking – the importance of working from an edge, and maintaining there an adequately sharp angle.

So although they appear technologically simple, felt Toth and Schick, oldowan tools imply cognitive skills not possessed by apes. They further claimed to find evidence, in an experiment replicating simple choppers, that the makers of the ancient tools were mostly right-handed. This characteristic is particularly developed in modern humans, and is thought by some related to the ability to talk. Strong 'handedness' in these early hominids could indicate the first changes in the brain that later made language possible (we will look further at the question of language later in the book).

In fact, in their other work Toth and Schick side with the majority of archaeologists in believing that the modern human intellect is a relatively recent phenomenon. Taken by themselves, however, at face value their experiments with stone tools support Wynn's hypothesis for a much older origin – or, indeed, even older, on their assessment of oldowan technology.

For a completely different point of view, we turn to Australia, whence archaeologists Iain Davidson and William Noble argue that the acheulean handaxe is not a tool at all, but a waste product.

Conceptually, stone tools can be grouped into two classes, referred to by archaeologists as 'core' or 'flake' tools. You make a core tool by knocking bits off a lump of stone, and use what's left in your hand. You make a flake tool from one of the bits. Core tools are big; flake tools are small. When the technology is very basic, there can be real problems in telling whether an artefact is, say, a chopper (a tool) or a core (a by-product of making flakes). But Davidson and Noble are saying that even acheulean handaxes are deceptive, and that these objects are nothing more than accidents of making flakes according to a mindless formula. Again, they conclude by saying that the really big leap occurred around 40,000 years ago, and that this was powered by language.

There is clearly substantial disagreement between archaeologists as to how early hominids made stone tools, and what skills were

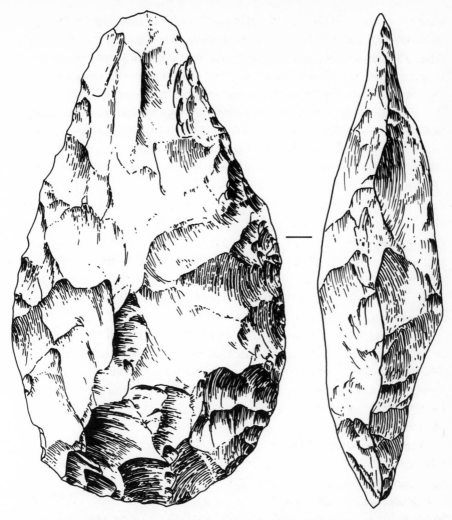

fig 33: A finer acheulean handaxe from Olduvai Bed IV (c 800–600,000 years ago). Compared to the older axe from Bed II (fig 32), this specimen, also made from lava, has a greater number of smaller flake scars and a thinner profile. The result is a straighter, sharper and more continuous cutting edge. The deep scars on the Bed II axe (fig 32) were made with a stone hammer; the finer flakes on the Bed IV axe might have been removed with a hammer of antler or bone (compare figs 42–43). (redrawn after M Leakey)

required. This may explain why tool-making plays a relatively minor part in discussion of hominid thinking, useful for anecdote and illustration but less so for enlightenment. But could it be that the very difficulty we have in understanding those stone tools is telling us something?

It is a characteristic of archaeology that significant contributions to debates that can at times be highly intellectual (not to say academic) can occur as a result of something as down-to-earth as road building or the laying of electricity cables. That is what happened at Boxgrove in 1989. Renewed extraction at the quarries brought a new threat to the preserved archaeology. This was an opportunity for more digging that Mark was not going to miss. But even he was unprepared for what they found. It was the beginning of a re-assessment of all the stone handaxes they had been finding. It was, you might say, extremely thought provoking.

Chapter 37

Battle Stations

wild horse

'Come on you lot, get up. Look at this. It's battle stations!'

It was 6.30 in the morning. Mark had been woken by a thumping great noise out in the quarries, a heavy rumbling that shook the gravels and sands and came up through the floor of his room at the end of the old milking parlour. Everyone had to see this.

They stood sleepily on the edge of the pit, a small knot of weary foot soldiers untimely dragged from their tents. It was like watching a movie. Empty lorries tumbled in from the south in a row and dropped down the sandy ramp into the East Quarry. Massed wheels threw up clouds of dust which hung chokingly in the thin May light. More lorries filed in as the first left, not bouncing with a hollow din now but sinking into the sands as they clawed their way out. They were taking the quarry away.

Everyone knew it was going to happen, but somehow they hadn't expected it would be quite like this. Early in 1989 Mark had reported to English Heritage that ARC were planning to remove sand that underlay potentially valuable but uninvestigated archaeological deposits in the western end of the East Quarry. There were, he said, two options. They could start a new project to sample the threatened area, with three years of excavations starting in 1989, and study and reporting continuing into 1994, with a total cost of around £175,000. Or they could buy the land, offering ARC an amount that would compensate them for the loss of the sand, which a back of the shovel

191

calculation showed to be worth three or four times the cost of the projected dig.

Mark was told to start digging at once.

It was like revisiting 1984. Greg Bell and Tony Tynan were to supervise the initial evaluation, and on the strength of this, full scale excavation would be conducted where thought necessary. When Greg and Tony had finished the fieldwork, Mark and Simon – who in the meantime were to continue working on the study of the earlier digs, preparing them for publication – would be able to step in and write it up.

In the course of what we will call the Sand Project, they would dig 17 test pits, open two large trenches (one beside the First Handaxe Trench, the other about 100 metres to the north), sieve 15 tons of silt, and recover hundreds of animal bones and thousands of flint flakes. It would be the largest sampling programme conducted to date at Boxgrove, and would contribute significantly to understanding the preserved ancient land surface. Among the finds would be a single wing bone from a great auk, a large penguin-like bird whose last living representative was tracked down and killed by collectors in Iceland in 1844: the Boxgrove specimen is thought to be the oldest known in the world.

All this happened as planned. Except for one thing.

As they were walking about early in the season, before any volunteers had arrived, Simon and Mark came to a scrubby, weedy patch at the back of the East Quarry. They had dug there in 1986: Geological Test Pit 17, they'd called it. They had opened a long straggling area, sieving the silt by metre square, aiming to collect large samples of animal bones. They found the scattered remains of part of a rhino, which could have been the same animal whose tooth Greg found out in the quarry to the north that very summer. They stopped when they got to the bottom of the land surface.

At the same time, in the West Quarry, Louise Austin had been digging in the lower silts, and finding exceptionally well preserved flintwork, including the unique scatter left by someone making a handaxe. Nothing like that had ever been found in the East Quarry: there were no signs of hominid activity in the deep silts there. Except that when Mark had got into GTP17 to dig down a square to investigate some puzzling geology, he'd found quantities of animal bones and flints.

'We really must do something about it, Otto,' said Mark as they

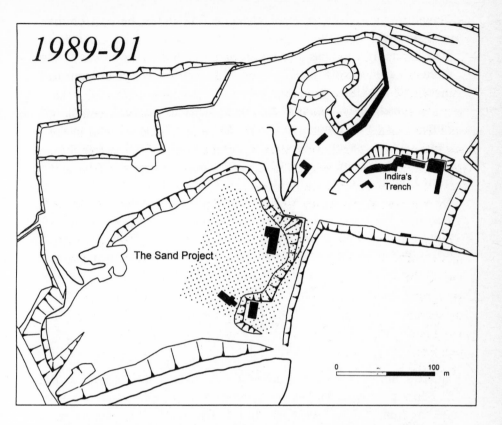

fig 34: In 1989, ARC began a new programme of sand extraction in the East Quarry. English Heritage sponsored three years of excavation to investigate the preserved land surface before it was destroyed. Many small test pits and two large trenches (one near the original First Trench) were dug within the shaded area. At the same time, Indira Mann supervised a dig in a previously opened trench, going deeper into the silts above the sand. Here large amounts of stone artefacts and broken animal bones were found in completely undisturbed condition (*see* fig 38).

looked at the torn sheet of black plastic rippling in the breeze. All they needed was a good supervisor.

Indira Mann, then an undergraduate sudent at Edinburgh University, had first dug at Boxgrove in 1986. In 1989, on her way back from holiday she thought she'd drop in to say hello to old friends. It was the end of April, and only Mark and Simon were there. Mark offered her a job. She remembered the test pit: they'd found a phenomenal amount of flint. Now it was a mess, weeds everywhere, collapsing sides and silt rain-washed in over the black plastic. The first thing was to clean back the sections. Then, leaving a baulk around the original pit so that, in time, it stood up like a square box, she cleaned the surface around.

They found a handaxe but not much else. There were only four or five of them at the start, then Jamie Mackenzie, her boyfriend, came down from Edinburgh and the students arrived. The bottom layer was sitting there, all cleaned off, ready to yield its story of what had happened there half a million years ago.

They had several discussions about what to do next, Indira and Jamie, Mark and Simon and Louise. Mark wanted something quicker than Louise's system: they couldn't afford to sit around, yet there was no point in digging if the record wasn't as good as that for the flints from Louise's Trench. The hold-up there had been the photographs. Someone would come down from the Institute in London to take the overhead shots, then they'd have to wait as much as a week to get the prints back. If they could find a darkroom, Jamie could do it; he'd learnt photography at college, studying communications and publicity.

Indira laid out three pits, and gridded them up with string into 50 centimetre squares. They did a lot of dummy runs with the camera, working out the correct height on the tripod, dropping a plumb bob from the centre of the lens, setting the focus, so that once they got going they didn't have to adjust anything except the exposure. They took a couple of shots each time, one with and one without the square's numbers on the ground, and bracketed the exposures. By mid-July they were in full flow, and flints were rising like fish in a feeding frenzy: things went very fast. In the pits they'd carefully prise out the grains of silt to expose as many flint flakes as they could, and take the photos. Then Jamie would pedal up to the Anglesey Arms with the film, process it in the lab above the bar (landlord Chris Houseman was a keen photographer), make a set of eight by ten prints (trying to bring out the edges of the flints – they weren't very good as art photos) and cycle back, often flapping the prints about in the breeze to finish the drying. By the time he was at the site, they were ready with another film. Then they'd mark up the new prints, outlining each piece of flint and writing out its number, and filling in the record sheets before starting on the silt again in readiness for the next shot. He'd get so many prints through that Jamie had to change his chemicals every two or three days.

It was like Louise's Trench, but it was different. Everything was incredibly fresh, but there weren't any obvious discrete scatters – more of a concentrated spread. This spread was heading west; there wasn't a lot to the east. So they expanded the central pit westwards into an area about six by 12 metres. And there were so many pieces of bone, all mixed in with the flakes. Some of the bones even had little bits of flint stuck in them: you could see them when they were washed in the shelter of the barns. It was difficult to escape the conclusion that something gory had occurred, right there, on the ground where they were working.

Simon had first realized that some animals had been butchered with flint tools at Boxgrove when he identified cut marks on bones in the winter after the 1986 season. He'd been given his first short contract that year as Supervisor, and he spent the time when they weren't digging examining the bone collection. He knew full well the dangers of misinterpreting a variety of scratches and fractures as artificial cut marks, but these were the real thing. They were rare: but their presence put a new perspective on everything.

Until this definitive proof that hominids had had something to do with the deposition of bones at the site, it was right to assume that all the animals were there as a result of natural processes. It's not difficult to see such agencies today, even in an industrial environment. A dead bird or garden vole rapidly becomes a dry skeleton. If you ever walk in areas where sheep or cattle roam free, you will have come across dead animals, seen the bloated corpses that so quickly turn to dry bones that are trampled on and kicked. Not all, but many of these bones can work their way into the soil. Some insects bury complete rodents as food for their larvae. A dead sheep out on the moor can sink into peat bog. Even large bones can be taken under by the everyday activities of insects, worms and other animals.

A 'natural assemblage' accumulated in this way has the potential to tell a vivid story about the ancient landscape: every animal has its niche, its particular liking for light or shade, this or that plant, degrees of dry or wet. In a striking piece of research in modern east Africa, Kay Behrensmeyer walked across the savannah for hundreds of kilometres, picking up animal bones. The varying numbers of the species whose remains she collected corresponded very closely to the living populations. But the cut marks on the Boxgrove bones told of something different, of an animal visible not by its own bones, but in the scars it left in the dismembered frames of other creatures. And of course it was this animal that everyone was seeking above all others.

Larger bones were dug out individually, measured in and recorded in detail, and every year, tons of sediment were sieved and washed to recover the minutest scraps. In 1987 Simon and his wife Sharon Gerber (who came to Boxgrove from West Virginia in 1985) together excavated a test pit to help them think about how they were recovering

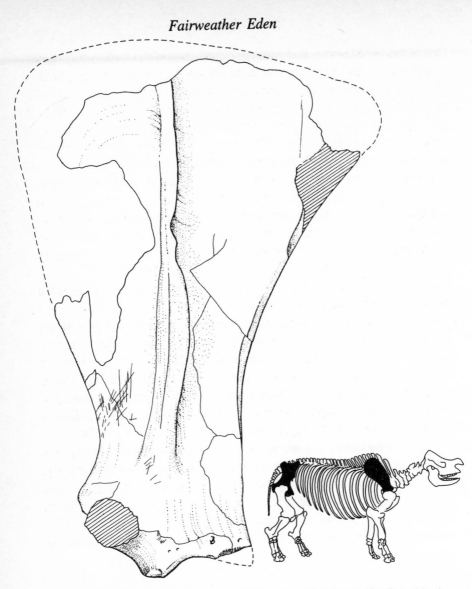

fig 35: Evidence for butchery and the range of butchered animals represented at Boxgrove are probably unique for a site of this age. In certain layers bones survive in extremely good condition. From the large sample (still under analysis) we illustrate the remains of four bones, the first to have been seen by the outside world. Thanks go to Simon Parfitt for providing the data in advance of his own academic studies.

This rhino scapula lay just beneath the old land surface at the Horse Butchery Site, and shows filleting marks that conform precisely with cuts found in modern butchery, both in their direction and their positioning. The first two sets, at the top and lower left side, are classic indications of slicing through blocks of muscle attached to the shoulder blade. At the base the flint tool has scored the bone as it was used to disarticulate the scapula from the humerus (upper leg bone), cutting through tough tendons and ligaments. Bone missing from the blade and the shaded areas was probably lost by damage after burial in the ground. Locations of this bone and the pelvis (*see* fig 53) are indicated in black on the sketch of a modern rhino skeleton. Length c. 21 cm (drawn by Phil Rye) the bones – Simon's own journey into the site's taphonomy (*see* Chapter 21). One interesting outcome of this project was the discovery of a 'warm fauna' – bones from animals that would normally live in a temperate climate – in a seam of brickearth; and a cold, arctic fauna beneath. The bones, like Simon Collcutt's sands and gravels, told of a seriously fluctuating climate. They took this pit down into the deeper silts, but there was nothing there.

Large mammals are relatively easy to identify from their bones. Some classes, such as birds, can be very tricky. In 1988 a herpetologist – a specialist in newts, toads and snakes – came to visit. He was Alan Holman from the Michigan State University Museum, and later, with the help of his own National Geographic grant, he was able to identify nine of his species, including slow worms, common spadefoots (the first specimen of this burrowing toad from Britain) and an ilium from Britain's oldest natterjack.

Another such specialist to take an interest in Boxgrove was Brian Irving, a keen fisherman turned archaeologist who was a postgraduate student at the London Institute when he first came to the quarries. At Boxgrove he found fish ranging from a large conger eel and a blue finned tuna to sticklebacks. These finds are very useful in helping to understand the marine and freshwater deposits, but there is nothing to say whether or not hominids had eaten any of them.

Simon would identify a dozen or so different large mammal species that had at one time or another been cut up and, presumably, consumed by the hominids. But never were they to find anything quite like the bones from Indira's Trench. And that first winter, up in London, Simon found cut marks on some of those bones. Not for nothing were they calling it, already by the end of the first season, the Horse Butchery Site.

Indira's Trench was immensely successful, and so was the huge Sand Project. But really the excavations were over. The butchered horse bones would not have been found if it weren't for the Sand Project, and this would not have taken place had ARC not decided to move sand extraction into the archaeologically sensitive area. By definition, when the sand was gone, the archaeology there would be finished too. What would be left was either safe under preservation agreements, or buried under deposits that one couldn't imagine ARC would ever find worth the cost of removing. There would be no more excuses to dig.

In March 1990, Mark was back at Ounces Barn to clear up the mess left by whoever had got into the barns in the winter and stripped them.

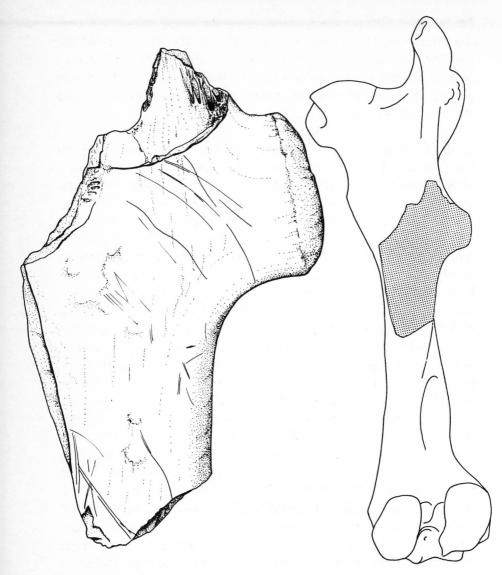

fig 36: Part of the femur (upper rear leg) of the horse from the Horse Butchery Site. Like those on the rhino scapula (fig 35), scores on the bone indicate filleting, in this case cutting away huge blocks of thigh muscle (the Boxgrove horses are the largest true horse species ever known). The progression of oblique cuts across the bone from lower left to upper right follows the course of the work, as the hominid pulled at the muscle, perhaps with the left hand, cutting repeatedly with the right as the meat came away. The slightly circular stepped edge at upper left results from crushing, probably with a flint hammer. Many bones were broken after muscle removal to reach the marrow. Length of fragment c. 11 cm. (drawn by Phil Rye)

He collected what remained of the scattered tiles and retiled the roof at the office end. They started digging again in May, Greg supervising the Northern Sand Trench, Indira and Jamie at the Horse Butchery Site. Mark went to Florida for a holiday in the summer, and he started playing rugby again. And that winter, he lived alone with his dogs in the barns. It was like old times.

In the summer of 1991 they started to refit flakes from the Horse Butchery Site. In a scene whose like had not been witnessed in Britain since Worthington G. Smith filled his house with debris from the Bedfordshire brick pits, they laid out an old carpet in the barns, gridded it in 50 centimetre squares and put the flakes on it exactly as they'd been in the ground a few hundred metres away. Walking around the transplanted site in bare feet, one of the many Institute student volunteers warmed to the task. From the area of a few squares he reconstructed a whole flint nodule. But it wasn't just a strangely shaped lump of flint: if you opened it up gently, separating halves like slicing a ripe honeydew melon, you found a cavity in the centre that was a roughed out handaxe. The student had been fitting pieces that were at least four centimetres across. Perhaps if he'd looked at the smaller flakes, tirelessly, patiently searching for clues to patch them back together, he'd have been able to reduce the cavity until the final, perfect handaxe, nested in all the tiny removals of the last finishing touches, revealed itself, the ghost in the stone.

It was when the digging finished, later that year, that the recording system came into its own. There were so many volunteers on site, so many people working, you couldn't keep a total watch on everyone. It was inevitable that the odd error would slip through – a flake recorded as lying on its back when it was the other way up, a misidentification by an inexperienced worker. The photos allowed you to check everything. There were 7,500 artefacts, and you could sit and check every single one, matching the record sheets against the photographs, against the flints in their numbered bags. Every artefact was checked for every detail, and every single one of the record sheets was rewritten.

Jamie was possessed. He'd spent three summers helping to remove and record these pieces, and he had to make sure everything was perfect.

With hindsight, they'd got it wrong at the very beginning. To help the recorders in the trench, Jamie had printed the negatives so as to make each excavation square fill an eight by ten print. The result, it

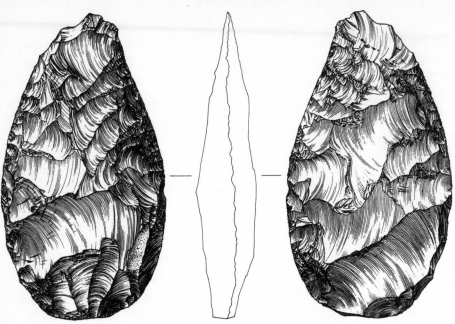

fig 37: A flint handaxe from Boxgrove, with a 'tranchet' edge at the tip formed by the intersection of large flake scars. Apart from at the base, the whole edge of this axe could have been used for cutting: the tip is razor sharp, the serrated sides are tougher but still very sharp. This is a fine example of the flint worker's art. Note the long diagonal scars in the right view, created by flakes that ran from the edge to more than half way across the axe (concentric ripples radiate from points of impact). Removing such long shallow flakes is an efficient way of thinning an axe, requiring skilful use of a soft hammer. Some European archaeologists still find it difficult to accept that these techniques could be as old as 500,000 years. Others argue that handaxes were accidental products of making flakes for use. We find this view frankly absurd: most flakes taken from this axe would have been far too small or thin to use. Length 16 cm. (drawn by Julian Cross)

seemed to Jamie, tracing the photos onto huge sheets of plastic drawing film, was a really silly scale. Then he had the idea to reduce the sheets to a better scale by photocopying them, and trace them all over again onto new sheets of drawing film.

He and Darren Norris, a local man living in a caravan behind the barns, packaged everything up and drove to London. Simon had told them about an industrial-sized machine, near the Natural History Museum, that was big enough to take the sheets. They reduced the drawings to an eighth of the originals, but you could still see even the smallest pieces of flint. Indira had contoured the site on film nearly two metres long, which was copied and reduced to the same scale. They were in the shop for six hours, and it cost nearly £400. But Jamie's scheme was working.

Back at the quarries they set to copying every flint and the contours onto a single plan. Then they added the bones. And then, like figures

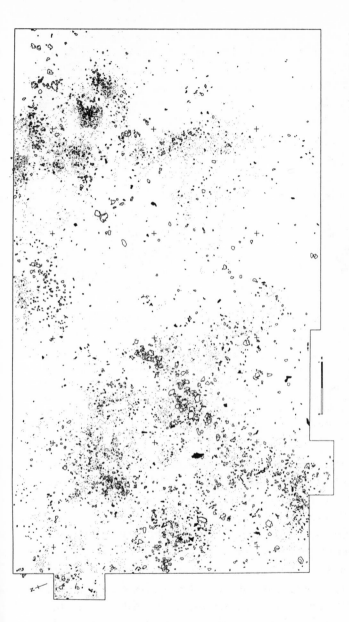

fig 38: In this plan of the central area of Indira's Trench (or the Horse Butchery Site) all flint artefacts (white or stippled) and bones (black) are plotted. The great majority of the identifiable bones are horse, which could all have come from a single large animal. The large bone lower centre left is part of a scapula with a putative spear wound. Flint flakes occur in small concentrations. Refitting suggests these each represent the action of a hominid making a handaxe with which to butcher the horse. The axes made and used in the area of this excavation were discarded elsewhere. This is typical of the activities represented at Boxgrove, where stone tools were made for immediate use and disposed of soon after (elsewhere in the quarries very sharp handaxes are found in large numbers). There was no fire or camp at the Horse Butchery Site, so there was no need to tidy up by moving the thick spread of razor sharp flint waste.

coalescing in the chemical bath in the thick red light of the darkroom, pulling the diggers into a world once gone but now recreated, the horse rose from the drawings, heavy on the ground, surrounded by squatting figures knapping flint knives; they could all but hear the clatter clack of falling flakes, the chatter of creatures crawling over the horse's warm, still form to cut and saw and chop with flint edged skill, as they found the handaxe within the nodule, the flesh and marrow within the spread-eagled corpse.

On the plan, with everything pulled together at a scale they could read, they could see as many as six or seven distinct knapping areas

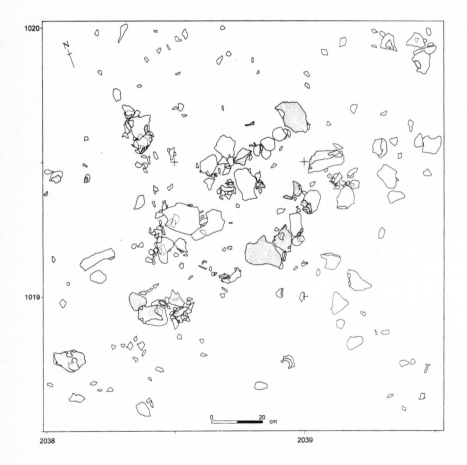

fig 39: A closer look at one of the scatters of flint flakes at the Horse Butchery Site. Cortex from the outer surface of the original nodule is stippled: in this case, an axe was made from scratch from a complete nodule brought to the spot (*contrast* fig 26).

(one of these was the refitted handaxe debris). And they could see concentrations of bone in separate places. After three years of high precision excavation and months of obsessive recording and drawing, they had painted a scene of hominids grouped around a dead horse, making their tools and cutting it up. Nowhere, never, had anyone before seen anything like this. Not for half a million years, anyway.

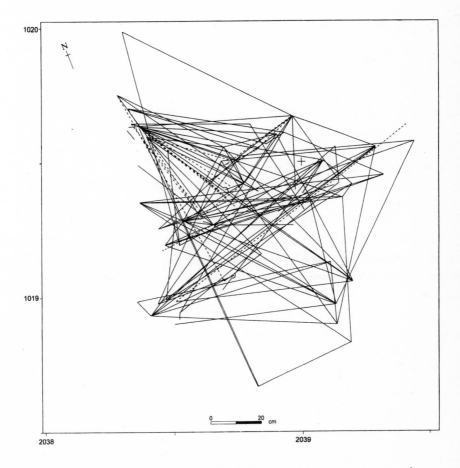

fig 40: Drawn at the same scale as fig 39, this plan shows lines that connect flint flakes that fit back together. Most of the flakes lie within a single square metre.

203

Chapter 38

'They're Tearing My Site Away'

natterjack toad

1991 was to be final season for the whole Boxgrove field programme. After that there would be several years of research and writing to look forward to, to realize the full potential of everything they had recovered. But 1991 was not the final season.

Fate intervened at Boxgrove, not for the first or the last time, and as before, it was the rapacious demands of roads, construction and investors that launched the new direction. It was an unusually anxious director that English Heritage Inspector Amanda Chadburn found on her visit to the site in May that year. The preserved areas included the west half of the West Quarry and the east end of the East Quarry. In between was a strip of ground around 500 metres across where there had been little archaeological excavation. The deposits there were not good enough for commercial extraction, so there was no threat to the archaeology – which of course still lay buried and out of reach. Now, suddenly, they were going to take it all out: *everything*, without even stopping for breath at the bottom of the gravels. All that archaeology was about to vanish, and there was nothing Mark could do about it.

In fact work had already started, for over the winter the West Quarry had been extended to the east and gravel removed so that now only a few metres were left covering the prehistoric land surface. The plan was to sell this last gravel immediately or use it for a silt dam across the centre of the quarry, then take out the sands. In the East Quarry the prospect was if anything worse.

Over 37,000 square metres of ancient land surface with everything on or in it was about to be hauled out and dumped with barely a pause for a flask of tea. Mark knew that the upper deposits were calcareous in that area, which meant the animal bones in the land surface below would be well preserved – dissolved chalk in the percolating rain water would have removed its destructive acidity. As he walked around the quarries, it seemed everywhere he trod there were rich deposits of unknown archaeology about to go. It was so big he couldn't see it all in one sweep, which of course made it bigger still: the preserved areas were puny by comparison. Mark felt powerless in face of the scale of it all. 'Look at all these machines,' he said to Chadburn. 'They're tearing my site away.'

Amanda Chadburn appreciated Mark's concern. She also knew to trust his judgement. She told the English Heritage hierarchy of the situation, and quickly came back with a brief: they wanted a full assessment of the archaeological potential of what would be lost.

Mark proposed digging 45 small test pits across the threatened area, using a relatively rapid recording technique. If the pits revealed critically important remains, the only options in the circumstances were to let them be destroyed by the new quarrying or to stop the extraction programme – which would mean buying it out. English Heritage found the money for the initial digging. On 1 August 1991 'Boxgrove C' or 'the Eartham Quarry Project' was begun. Project Director was Greg Bell, Supervisor since 1985. Mark was to continue with his studies of the earlier digs. Greg had a staff of two, digging and survey equipment, a hired van, access to specialists and consultants, and fifteen months. And only a few weeks before they'd thought it was all over.

They expected to find bones and flintwork in their test pits. Anything new was likely to be in the form of previously unencountered animal species, or in novel arrangements of debris. What they didn't expect at all was that the silts that contained the archaeology would not even be there: which was the case in the east part of the West Quarry, where the chalky gravels lay directly on top of the sands.

But all was not totally lost.

At the western edge of the test pitted area were dense concentrations of bones and artefacts. In one pit were six handaxes. But this was surprising too, because these finds were not lying at the top of the fine silt, or buried within it, where previous such discoveries had been made, but right at the bottom, lying on the surface of the sand. And there was more. The sand surface was not flat, but gullied and pitted.

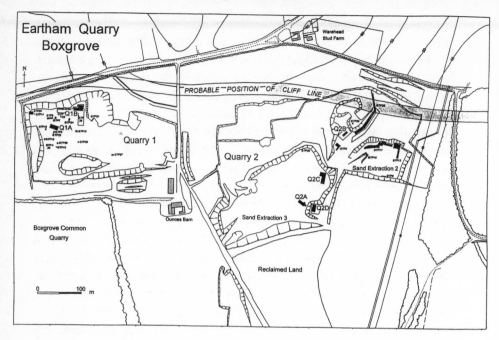

fig 41: Gravel and clay extraction in 1991 posed a new threat to the archaeology, when areas previously thought safe from quarrying were opened up. Many archaeological test pits were dug either side of the track north of Ounces Barn, revealing ancient activity beside a shallow water course. It was to further investigate this channel that Mark, Simon and Roger Pedersen dug some pits in the 'L-Shape' (here marked 'Q1B') in the West Quarry in 1993, finding the hominid tibia in the last trench.

Over in the East Quarry, things were more familiar, with good bone preservation. In the south west, however, the geology was odd. Whatever the explanation for these new phenomena, it looked as if movement of water had something to do with it. Water had channelled the surface of the sands, water had deformed the overlying silts, and further east water had taken away the silts altogether. It all seemed to fit with evidence from the L-Shape in the West Quarry, north west of the pits that Greg Bell was digging. This was the big trench opened in 1987 and 1988 to see how bone and flint occurrence varied over a continuous wide area. The size of the trench meant that in the time available they had not been able to go down very deep. It was clear, however, that they were in a former lake or pond, with artefacts and animal bones concentrated along the edge. Subsequent work in the laboratory indicated the presence of a spring, perhaps in the chalk cliff behind, that fed this pond. This, then, appeared to be the source of the erosive water revealed by Greg's Project. And in 1991 they went back to dig in the L-Shape, finding evidence that confirmed this interpretation.

This was all tantalizing in the extreme. Greg had had to dig his pits in the shadows of machinery, whipping in quick between the removal of gravels and the later extraction of sand. But as the months went by, the pressure dropped off. By October 1992, when archaeological excavation ended, as fast as it had appeared the market for unprocessed gravels had gone, and the sub-contractors with it. What still remained in place was safe. There really would now be no more digging at Boxgrove.

It was tantalizing because what had turned up so late in the whole project was evidence that might help to resolve one of the great problems of palaeolithic archaeology. Why do you find such rich concentrations of bones and artefacts beside water courses, in Africa as much as in northern Europe? Was it because hominids were making camps there, as some archaeologists thought, or was it simply that it was beside water that most of the good things in life occurred? Were there bones beside rivers because that was where animals naturally died, irrespective of the activities of hominids? And were stone tools and animal bones simply washed together from all over the place? As we shall see, the answers to such questions have profound implications for our understanding of early hominid species.

Well, they would have to work with what they had. No more digging, just a great deal of laboratory work and writing.

Except that, six or seven months after Greg had packed up, Mark took his dogs for a walk and decided he could not carry on without a last quick dig to help him understand this strange geology. He had no money to pay anyone: but that shouldn't bother Roger Pedersen. For Roger, digging was a hobby.

PART SIX
A GAME OF CHESS: 1994–1996

Chapter 39

Return to Boxgrove

hedgehog

So on 20 December 1993 the tibia found at Boxgrove almost exactly a month before was finally confirmed as hominid (Chapter 11). Twelve years' digging (for Mark) and ten years' funding (for English Heritage), and the field project was supposed to have ended, with a couple of years' research and writing up still to come, a fat monograph to produce and maybe a few articles for academic journals. An exciting decade by any standards.

English Heritage could see the bottom line. Geoffrey Wainwright knew the importance of the archaeology, and if he ever had doubts there were advisers like Clive Gamble to remind him that nowhere in the world was there anything quite like Boxgrove. The bottom line was the archaeology, and if Mark felt something needed doing, he could usually be trusted to be right.

As soon as English Heritage learnt of the tibia, they knew they would have to dig again. The find had minimal context – just that small trench – yet the results of everything else they'd done indicated that a bit more excavation would surely provide the most complete environment for any known fossil hominid of that age. There wouldn't be an archaeologist in the country who would begrudge more spending.

And no one at English Heritage complained about the publicity following the release of the news. As their chairman had reminded the media, 1994 was their tenth anniversary. Ten years' work at Boxgrove had produced no more than a handful of press stories, mostly in the local papers; even many archaeologists were unaware of what had been happening. That one bone had changed everything. There was no telling what more excavation might turn up. English Heritage was on the map.

But public knowledge created a new problem. People knew about Boxgrove: they knew there were rare and valuable things in the quarries. There was no legal protection for the site, no security guard, not even an enclosing fence. Anyone could dig there (subject only to trespass law), without consulting English Heritage or other archaeologists. The fossil find had changed a safe site, where quarrying was ended, into a potentially endangered one.

For Mark it was a moving discovery, too. After all that time digging, looking for his rubbish, his faint spoor amidst the sands and the wild animals, now they'd found the man himself (such a massive bone had to be male). It was a real gut wrencher to look at that bone and think, That was one of them – whatever 'they' were.

But there was more than a bone. In all the fuss, few had even noticed something that bothered Mark in the way that so many little things had irritated the pit of his thinking over the years. After Roger Pedersen had moved the bone out of the trench into the safety of the barns, he carried on digging, going down until he had taken out all the fine silts and reached the top of the Slindon Sands. And there, on this firm surface, were seven beautiful handaxes in mint condition, heaped up like eggs in a nest. In its way, that discovery was as special as the tibia: unprecedented. What did it mean?

That little dig that a few friends had kept quietly to themselves in the autumn of 1993, in 1995 and 1996 was to become the biggest archaeological excavation ever seen at Boxgrove and one of the largest in the country. And you don't do that in the Eartham quarries without finding anything.

Chapter 40

Autumn 1994: News for the Press

wild cat

Naturally the Boxgrove team would have loved to have found more hominid remains and, as we saw in the previous chapter, there were new questions about the archaeology that needed answering. But for Simon and Mark there was something more than this that drew them back to the quarries. There was more than the opportunity to provide a full context for the tibia, which was what the Project Design, the funding bid they made to English Heritage, emphasized: more than the chance to make new headline discoveries; more than the promise of another year's digging. Once the initial press mania was over and they were able to return to work, as they combined reporting on the entire 12 years' previous efforts with preparations for the new project, something hit them: maybe they had the real answer. Maybe with all the evidence before them, preserved as no other remains of this age were, they could tackle the questions raised by Glynn Isaac and Lewis Binford, Robert Ardrey and hundreds of other archaeologists and writers. How did these creatures behave? What went on in the minds of these early hominids?

Early in September, Simon had an unexpected chance to talk to the press. The British Association for the Advancement of Science has an annual meeting designed to bring together specialists from wide-ranging disciplines and highlight research results for the media. The 1994 conference was at Loughborough in central England, and the

Natural History Museum took up an exhibition of its work, with a few scientists and public relations people; Simon was asked to come along.

He wasn't expecting anything special: he was there to meet scientists, not journalists (having missed the May press conference, he was still a little naïve when it came to media workings). But journalists wanted to hear about Boxgrove, which of course was why the PR people had wanted Simon there. They searched out an empty room and with the help of some slides of the dig, they had their own relaxed little meeting.

The discussion was not what Simon might have expected from his reading of the press coverage of the tibia. These were mostly specialist writers, several with scientific degrees (though not one in archaeology or anthropology). He could talk about the old excavations and his work on the bones just as he might with fellow archaeologists who didn't yet know about Boxgrove.

Although it was nearly a year since the original identification of the tibia, he told them research on this one bone was still in progress: the value of the finds from the excavation lay partly in the battery of expertise that was available for their study.

Boxgrove Man was male. We still know very little about *Homo heidelbergensis*, but every other hominid species, and especially so in the distant past, shows a significant size difference between males and females. If the Boxgrove tibia had been a typical female shin, this would imply an almost impossibly enormous male. He was at least in his early 20s when he died. This was known from a thin section of a scrap of bone examined under a microscope. As longbones age, canals carrying nerves and blood vessels continually reform. The density and pattern of these canals relate to the age of the bone. In time, more detailed study should be able to pin a more precise age on the Boxgrove hominid. Mineral content of the bone might reflect the ratio of meat, fish and plants in the creature's diet. Analysis meant destroying a small but sizeable fragment of bone, so experiments were being conducted to test what was still a new technique.

X-rays, however, were not destructive, and the bone had been heavily bombarded in a sophisticated computer-linked scanner at University College Hospital in London. The scans showed a cross-section that was flat and massive compared to a modern human tibia. 'The bone is incredibly thick,' said Simon Parfitt, as reported by the *Independent*, 'with extremely developed muscle ridges.' 'This means . . . that Boxgrove man must have been an active runner,' reported *The*

214

Times. 'He belonged to a very mobile community,' said Parfitt, 'whose home range covered a large region.'

What really caught the imagination was the news that gnaw marks had been identified on the tibia. Although the actual cause of death was not known, it was clear that an animal like a wolf (and this was the commonest of the large carnivores found in the excavations) had sat and chomped away at the knobbly ends of the shin bone, leaving only the straight shaft.

Simon went on to tell the journalists about the butchery marks. To date, all flint cuts were found on the large animals – horse, bear, rhino, giant deer (a huge extinct deer we will meet again later) and red deer; even smaller deer, such as roe, appeared not to have been eaten. These bones were scattered over the excavations wherever conditions were right for the survival of this precious evidence. But in one trench an actual butchery episode of a single large horse had been identified. Simon's microscope work on the remains from the Horse Butchery Site had identified five butchered bones that had also been chewed by wolf or hyena. On three of these bones the marks intersected, and in each case, teeth had dug into grooves left by flint. It looked as if the hominids had first access to a fresh carcass, whilst animal scavengers (in the case of hyena, probably at night) had moved in to finish off the remains – and incidentally kick the flint and bone debris about a little.

Did this mean the Boxgrove hominids were hunters? Most archaeologists were agreed that this far back in time, hominids simply did not possess the skills or intellectual capacity to plan a complex hunt, but instead relied for meat on the scavenging of dead carcasses (Chapter 2). Deep down, Simon may have known the answer to this question already. But for now he was hesitant.

'One of the biggest debates in stone age archaeology', he replied, 'is whether these people were actively hunting or whether they were scavenging from carnivores. The study of the site will answer the question.'

Two months later, Mark had his own story for the press. To appreciate its significance, we need to think a bit more about how stone tools are made.

For many years some archaeologists had been arguing that early stoneworkers used what they called 'soft hammers' for finer tooling.

There were one or two reports of the use of deer antler as hammers by indigenous craftsmen in north America a century ago. In the 1930s and 1940s a few archaeologists in France and England who had become highly skilled self-taught knappers, were convinced that some of the finer late palaeolithic stone tools (dating from, say, 30,000 years ago) would have been almost impossible to make without a soft hammer. In their own experimental work, these 'hammers' were shaped like a baton, a short rod of bone or antler that fitted comfortably into the palm of the hand. The far end of the hammer would be brought down on the edge of a partly finished handaxe in expertly delivered blows from the elbow, to remove wide thin flakes from the surface. The more intuitively obvious material for such a hammer, stone, would take off a relatively thick, chunky flake: for the shaping of a thin, smooth surfaced implement, such a flake might be just too chunky. Or, worse still, it might just crush the thin edge of the axe.

The mechanics of the difference between the effect of a 'hard' and a 'soft' hammer are still not fully understood, but are thought to lie in the way in which the stone being struck sinks into the softer material a little, so that the force of the blow is dissipated away from a single impact point. What many experimenters *have* shown, however, is that there is very definitely a difference between typical soft hammer flakes and those made with a hard hammer – a difference that is best appreciated from a diagram (fig 42).

It is these characteristics that encourage modern knappers to switch from a hard to a soft hammer when finer shaping is required. Knowing only this much about making a handaxe you can perhaps begin to see that it's not quite as simple a process as you might think. Most archaeologists believe that soft hammers first came into use much later than Boxgrove, although the particularly fine appearance of many of the Boxgrove implements certainly implies that their makers did know something about this soft hammer technology.

Well, so much for the theory. What of the evidence? Ancient bone hammers are not uncommon in Europe in deposits contemporary with the neanderthals. The oldest known antler hammers belonged to modern humans, and would have been used to make highly accomplished flint implements of a variety of forms (this was long after handaxes had disappeared from the tool repertoire). But even the neanderthal hammers are very recent compared to the age of the large

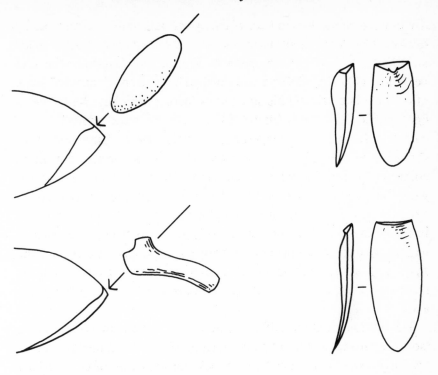

fig 42: Hard and soft hammer flaking. The stone hammer (top) removes a thick flake with a prominent swelling or 'bulb' at the butt end. A soft hammer flake (bottom) is thinner, and often has a small lip on the edge of the butt. (modified after Newcomer)

handaxes, not least those at Boxgrove. So, it seemed in 1987, the case for the use of soft hammers that far back must lie in the stone tools and debris. Then no longer digging at the site, Francis Wenban-Smith had set out to see if he could find such evidence in the flakes from Boxgrove.

He and John McNabb made piles of handaxes with flint collected at the quarries. They divided the process into two stages, which they called 'roughing-out' and 'finishing'. 'Roughing-out' is normally conducted with a hard hammer, and suitable stones for this task could be found at Boxgrove. Not only was there good fresh flint in the chalk cliff, but rolled flint pebbles ideal as preliminary working tools could be picked up from the beach at the bottom: a feature of the location which early hominids must have appreciated. With such a pebble, a raw lump of flint can be tapped for clues about internal flaws (good flint rings like a bell), opened up and gradually reduced by taking off flakes until a large rough handaxe shape is obtained.

The skilled knapper will spend some time choosing the right flint

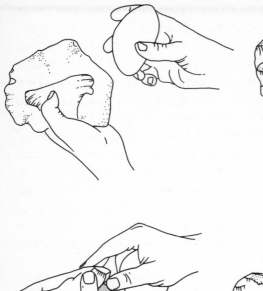

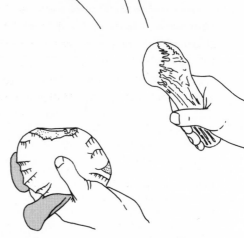

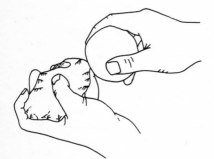

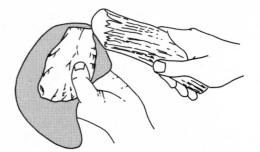

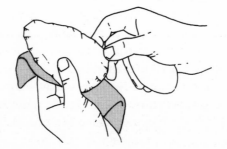

nodule, turning it, examining the shape, looking for the finished tool in the untried block which their expertise will reveal – much as a sculptor would describe the way they seek a figure buried within a block of marble resting on the floor of an Italian quarry. The Danis in Irian Jaya (the western part of New Guinea annexed by Indonesia) have an old myth about the stone axes they used to make. The axe is already in the rock when you pick it up: what you have to do is liberate it.

The *un*skilled knapper, of course, could not make a good handaxe.

Once the roughed-out axe was ready, Francis put down his hard hammer and selected a soft one. The aim now was to produce quality sharp-edged oval handaxes like those from the excavations. The Boxgrove hominids had had three likely materials to choose from for such a percussor: bone, antler and flint fresh from the chalk with a white crust or 'cortex'. Antler is most popular with modern knappers,

fig 43: Seven moments in the making of a flint handaxe. With a flint nodule and a quartzite pebble from the Boxgrove quarries, Francis Wenban-Smith begins (*top left*) by removing large flakes around the edge from both sides. He already has a clear idea of where the finished axe will be in the flint. As he works around the nodule (*top right*), the cortex (the outer crust on the flint, shown dotted) is removed and flake scars on one face serve as striking platforms to remove flakes from the other. He is protecting his hand from the sharp flint with a piece of towel. Professional gun-flint makers in nineteenth-century Norfolk, who were extraordinarily skilled at their art, wore large leather aprons and knee-pieces (they supported heavy flint cores on their legs) made from bits of old leather boots.

Once the roughing out is finished (*second row, left*), Francis examines the flint from the side as he decides how to start the thinning and fine shaping. At this stage, which might be reached after ten or 20 blows, the flint is still quite thick and the edge is irregular. For thinning (*second row, right*), he switches to a 'soft hammer' made from red deer antler. The antler hammer produces flakes that are longer and thinner than those made with the stone hammer, which allows Francis to thin the flint across the centre without taking off too much at once and potentially losing control. The Boxgrove knappers used a variety of antler and bone for hammers like this: they are the oldest found in the world.

As the axe takes shape, the risk of making a terminal mistake increases. A single misplaced blow can break the axe in half or remove too much flint, so that, if the axe is not to be abandoned, it would have to be reworked into a much smaller implement than originally envisaged. The angle of the edge to be struck is critical. In the next drawing (*third row, left*) Francis is strengthening the edge by rubbing with the stone hammer to wear back the wafer thin flint which would just crush if struck. He then takes off the intended flake with the antler hammer.

Many of the Boxgrove axes were finished with a 'tranchet flake', a large flake taken off the side or end that left an extremely sharp cutting edge. Here (*third row, right*) Francis lines up his hammer in preparation for a tranchet removal (he has changed hammers, but that was not necessary). He has previously prepared the platform, and knows exactly where he wants the flake to come away. He can only do this by examining the axe carefully before he strikes: the flake will come off from the face that is invisible as he holds the axe in readiness for the blow. The force required to get it right is considerable, but overdoing it will remove too much. In this instance, the flake came off on the third attempt.

The finished axe (*bottom*) took about 15 minutes to make. Typically between 25 and 50 flakes would be removed with the soft hammer. In a pioneering experiment at the London Institute of Archaeology in 1971, Mark Newcomer worked a 230 gram handaxe from a 3 kilogram flint nodule, in the process removing 51 larger flakes and over 4,600 small flakes and chips over a millimetre across. (drawn by Michael Pitts) who treasure the tools of their craft as an angler a favoured rod. Bone is convenient, as unlike antler which has to be carved and trimmed, a large dry tibia, for example, can be used as it is; but it is not as dense as antler, which means more force is required, and it quickly shatters and splinters. Flint is an anomaly, only recently recognized by experimenters as a potential 'soft' material. At the interface between a flint nodule and the parent chalk is a soft white layer which, if present on a hammer, can cushion the blow so that the effect is similar to that achieved with bone or antler.

As they were hoping to find out whether the Boxgrove knappers used soft or hard hammers, John and Francis also finished, as best they could, several handaxes with the hard pebble flint hammers they had used for roughing-out. When all the axes were made, Francis collected the heaps of bagged debris (each one carefully numbered and wrapped as it fell to the floor) and recorded a series of features and measurements. Could he figure from these data which type of hammer had been used? And if so, what story did the flakes from Boxgrove tell, a group of 27 selected from a scatter in the First Handaxe Trench?

One thing was immediately clear from the analyses: there was a strong distinction between soft hammer and hard hammer flake assemblages. In a sophisticated statistical plot (fig 44), all the flakes from axes made with hammers of flint or quartzite (a hard material popular with modern knappers) fell on the right side, and all the antler and bone flakes fell on the left. Three groups of flakes made with a cortical flint striker were nearer the centre, but still close to the hard hammer flakes.

This was no surprise, as knappers had been saying this was the case for many years – although it was perhaps the clearest demonstration of the fact yet presented. The most significant features were the presence or absence of a point of percussion (common on hard hammer flakes, rare on soft) and the surface area relative to flake thickness (soft flakes were wide and thin) – *see* fig 42. But what was especially interesting was that the flakes from handaxes finished with bone or antler were also distinguishable from each other. And furthermore, the flakes from the First Handaxe Trench, which were clearly struck with a soft hammer, looked as if they might have been made with bone (fig 44).

This was the first substantial demonstration that soft hammers had been regularly used as much as half a million years ago. And as Francis wrote in the publication of the project that eventually appeared

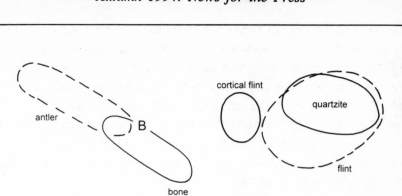

fig 44: This diagram shows how statistical analysis of flint flakes described by eight measurements enabled the type of hammer used to make the flakes (in a modern experiment) to be distinguished. Each ellipse encloses all the flakes made with a particular hammer. For example, five groups of flakes made with an antler hammer plot within the left cluster. While there is some overlap between the antler and bone hammers, and especially between the quartzite and flint, there is a clear separation between the soft and hard hammers. 'B' is where analysis of flakes dug up at Boxgrove placed this scatter: they were struck with a soft hammer. This study, conducted by Francis Wenban-Smith and John McNabb in 1987, was the first to prove the use of soft hammers as long ago as half a million years. (adapted from Wenban-Smith)

in 1989, there might be implications for the intellectual processes of early hominids. It could not be assumed that suitable bone or antler for making hammers would be just lying about at the very moment they were needed to make a handaxe, implying that a little future planning was necessary: a soft hammer would likely have been made at some time before it was needed, and then kept. 'Once this level of planning is reached in any one activity', wrote Francis, 'it is reasonable to expect planning and organisation to be occurring in all aspects of the life-style.'

And then, right at the end of November 1994, seven years after two of his former excavation supervisors sat down and made handaxes to prove that a Boxgrove creature had once used a hammer of bone or antler, Mark, with beaming face and booming voice, held out some scraps of bone to attentive audiences in London. They were, he said, by around 400,000 years the world's oldest bone hammers. They had been used to make handaxes and this implied something about the way the hominids thought.

But as yet still no one really knew why they were making the handaxes in the first place.

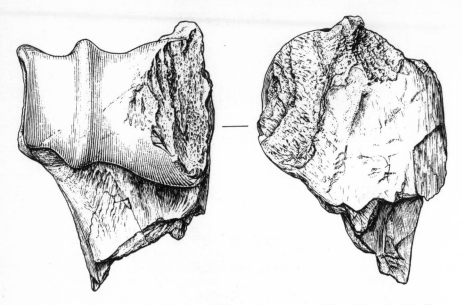

fig 45: For sophisticated flint working, a modern knapper uses a range of 'hard' (stone) and 'soft' (antler or bone) hammers (*see* fig 43). Before Boxgrove, the oldest known soft hammers in the world were made no more than 100,000 years ago; only modern humans (*Homo sapiens*) were thought to have made hammers in antler. Perhaps because of the superb preservation at the site, soft hammers at Boxgrove are as common as stone hammers, a ratio never before seen at an archaeological site. The soft hammers display heavy ware, suggesting they were intensively used, and small slivers of flint struck from tools being made are embedded in their working faces. This elbow end of an upper front leg bone (bison) has been battered away on the right side. The shaft broke off in antiquity, and may have been present when the tool was used. Found in freshwater silt in the 1996 dig. Length 8.5 cm. (drawn by Julian Cross)

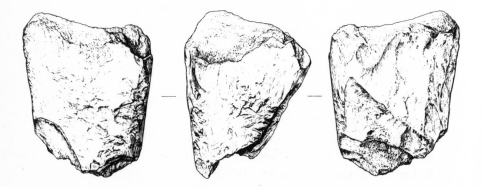

fig 46: Fragment of elephant bone found in 1996 resting on the marine sand. It has been massively scarred by hammering flint. On the left and side faces as drawn are many small depressions, and on the right some large flakes have come off the bottom. Several of the bone hammers from Boxgrove have flint scrape marks left when removing gristle and membranes, suggesting they were made from fresh bone, perhaps at butchery sites. Length 10.5 cm. (drawn by Julian Cross)

Chapter 41

February 1995: A Perfect Butchery Tool

red deer

Peter Dawson is often to be seen in the covered market in Oxford, at the counter of a traditional family butcher, a pheasant feather in his hygienic white hat. But one day a student asked if he would assist him in a butchery experiment, and he found himself out at a farm with none of his accustomed tools. He didn't know it, but he was about to advance the Boxgrove story forward another key step.

Peter Dawson stood behind the corpse on the table and smiled at the camera. An experiment that meant a great deal to Oxford research student John Mitchell (a year to organize, it had cost him nigh on £250 and Peter was the fourth man who'd agreed to help him – the others had pulled out at the last minute) was about to begin.

After studying geology and archaeology at Bristol, John Mitchell went to Oxford for a masters degree with Derek Roe. In one of his lectures, Derek described the work of his former student Larry Keeley. In the 1970s Larry had spent countless hours looking at the edges of palaeolithic stone tools under a microscope at around 200 times magnification. His idea was to try and identify how the tools had been used by distinguishing very fine polishes left on the flint by different materials such as wood or bone. This was not a new idea: for a century various archaeologists had been claiming success in this enterprise.

Yet their conclusions were so contradictory – and the work was so tedious – that 'microwear studies', as they were known, normally inspired little more than a great deal of scepticism. Larry claimed to have cracked the problems, through use of sufficiently high power microscopes and parallel study of modern replica tools whose use was known. Mark Newcomer, the London based flint knapper, was still unbelieving, so supplied Larry with tools he had made and used, challenging him to identify the tasks correctly. In nine out of ten cases, he did.

This was the sort of methodical, stringent research that appealed to John Mitchell. In the library he discovered that no one had looked at handaxes in this way since Larry – and he had studied less than a dozen axes. His second surprise came when he sought money for a big handaxe project. Everyone tried to put him off. 'Wasn't microwear trashed in the 1980s?' was a typical response. Despite Larry's success, it seemed, few archaeologists yet realized the potential of what he had done.

But three years later, after digging in England, working on ceramic petrology in Athens, and constantly rewriting grant proposals, he hit the target with the Science and Engineering Research Council. They were prepared to back a programme that featured advanced use of computer imaging – displaying a microscope view on a digital screen, whence it could be analysed statistically (a technique that had been pioneered in microwear studies at the London Institute). On the first of April 1993 he began his D Phil.

It started as a study of British handaxes, but soon acquired a heavy focus on Boxgrove. One reason so little work had been done on handaxe use was that suitable objects to study were very rare. Stone microwear is an exceedingly subtle polish on the very edge of the used tool. If the artefact has been kicked around, rolled in a river or weathered by slightly acidic water (which patinates or 'corticates' the surface) the use wear is destroyed. Already in 1993 Boxgrove could provide an exceptional group of mint condition handaxes, to say nothing of the rich context with information about the environment and hominid activities. And Mark proved to be very helpful, willing to try anything – not a universal characteristic of archaeologists digging things up.

But before he looked at anything from Boxgrove, John studied the collection that Larry Keeley had built up when he was doing his own pioneer research: all his stone tools and records were in Oxford. He spent weeks and weeks experimenting with ways to clean a freshly excavated tool, aiming to remove everything except organic residues that might still be sticking to the edges from when it was last used (perhaps an unlikely possibility, but one he could not afford to miss). Then one day he had an inspired idea for an experiment.

Archaeologists really hadn't a clue what handaxes were made for. They were all purpose tools or they had no function at all; they were for throwing like a discus at running game, or they weren't tools but waste from making other things; they were knives, scrapers, hammers or spades. A popular theory was that they were butchery tools, and a number of archaeologists had cut up animals with newly made axes to test their efficiency. Indeed, a few fresh animals had been butchered at Boxgrove, including a deer that Chris Bergman dissected for a National Geographic film. So, handaxes could cut up meat; but there were problems, such as how to avoid shredding your own hands on the axes, how to keep hold of the tool as it became covered in slippery grease and blood, why axes often had a cutting edge all round when it would have been easier with only a short straight edge, and so on.

John's idea was to find a professional butcher to do the work. As far as he knew, this had never been done before – certainly not as a controlled experiment. When you think about it, the situation is the same one that held back understanding of ancient stone tools in the nineteenth century. Burdened with an unconscious assumption that ancient hominids were incompetent and dim-witted, it never occurred to many early archaeologists that making stone tools was a sophisticated skill (*see* Chapter 30). Perhaps butchery held secrets that only a skilled artisan could unlock. And when the experiment was over, John could put the flints under his microscope to compare with those from Boxgrove.

'Can I start now, then?' asked Peter.

Sir John Lubbock in *The Natural History Review*, 1862:
Almost as well might we ask to what would they not be applied. Infinite as are our instruments, who would attempt even at present to say what was the use of a knife? But the primitive savage had no such choice of tools; we see before us, perhaps, the whole contents of his workshop; and with these weapons, rude as they seem to us, he may have cut down trees, scooped them out into canoes, grubbed up roots, killed animals and enemies, cut up his food, made holes in winter through the ice, prepared firewood, built huts, and in some cases at least, they may have served as sling-stones.

Reginald Smith (Keeper of the Department of British and Medieval Antiquities, British Museum), *Flints: an Illustrated Manual of the Stone Age for Beginners*, 1928:
It is difficult to compare it with any modern implement (except perhaps a schoolboy's pocket-knife, which has innumerable uses) . . . it is, after all, more important to recognize a 'hand-axe' or *coup-de-poing* when found than to explain precisely how it was used. The main fact is that such implements are obviously of human origin.

Richard Leakey and Roger Lewin, *People of the Lake*, 1978:
. . . carefully fashioned teardrop-shaped implements for which, embarrassingly, no one can think of a good use . . . Perhaps they were simply the way a stone-tool knapper demonstrated his skill: a kind of prehistoric trade-mark!

The butcher had 13 tools from which he could choose laid out on the table. Mark and John had gone round the quarries at Boxgrove with a wheelbarrow collecting fresh flint, and given it to Phil Harding. Phil had made 16 beautiful handaxes (John had been expecting three or four), all of types found at Boxgrove. From these John had picked out nine, and added four large flint flakes. Now they lay on the damp wood arrayed like a mini arsenal.

Peter picked the first flint.

'Stone number one', he said, holding up a small handaxe for the cameras.

Originally it was to have been a fallow deer, but this had been badly shot up in the forequarters. Instead he had a wild roe deer from the Cotswolds, killed cleanly four days ago. The carcass had been gutted, and was now missing the head and lower limbs. Peter took hold of a rear leg.

'In modern butchery, to get the best out of the hide, we use a square cut.'

With repeated short down-swipes he cut into the skin on the inside of the leg.

'We follow the seams.'

He made it sound like unpicking a shirt. Hair came loose from the hide in handfuls and gathered on the slightly jagged edge of the tool. As he cut down the leg, Peter gently pulled the skin away from the muscle.

226

John Coles and Eric Higgs, *The Archaeology of Early Man*, 1969:
A feature of certain axes of acheulean tradition is a reverse S-twisted cutting edge. A number of specialised forms of acheulean axe are known. The main type remained pear-shaped, but ovates, lanceolates (with elongated straight-sided point), ficrons (elongated but with slight concave-sided points) and cordiforms (small and heart-shaped) occur. There are a number of minor forms, as well ... Handaxes must have been multi-purpose tools.

Thomas Wynn, 'Handaxe enigmas' in *World Archaeology*, 1995:
... it would be difficult to overemphasize just how strange the handaxe is when compared to the products of modern culture. It does not fit easily into our understanding of what tools are, and its makers do not fit easily into our understanding of what humans are.

'Stone number two.'
Peter continued in short swinging cuts, opening up the hide along the belly, working swipe by swipe towards the neck. With the axe in his right hand, he grasped the skin flap firmly in his left, and pulled sideways. The edge of the axe stroked between the membranes, politely acceding to their request to part. There was no blood, no mess. He held the centre of the axe between his thumb and fingers, as a monger might hold a fish, or an experienced driver cup the wheel of his vehicle in a relaxed caress.
'This one's quite successful. It seems to have a better edge.'
No one noticed Peter having any problems with the first axe.
'Normally we'd hang it for a week. I like to have it when there's just a little bit of white spot, when the mould begins to grow on the inner membrane. Seven to ten days, depending on the weather.'
Swipe, swipe, swipe.
'This is skinning extremely easy.'

William H. Calvin in *Tools, Language & Cognition in Human Evolution*, 1993:
Surely the symmetry, the edging, and the point are indicative of some function that we have failed to comprehend. I suggest that classic handaxes may be better appreciated in the context of the waterhole ambush ... That handaxes are regularly found along watercourses and lake margins (as if lost in the mud like a golf

ball; often they are standing on edge *in situ*) supports this explanation ... Unlike Frisbees that roll along the ground for some distance, a spinning handaxe will soon impale its point in the ground and come to a sudden halt. Consider throwing a handaxe into the herd ...

Eileen M. O'Brien in *Current Anthropology*, 1981:
A thrown handaxe performs its task outside the hand, simultaneously eliminating the constraints its design imposes on manual manipulation and the necessity of a hand-hold. Intentional edge modification all around maximizes edge surface area, thereby optimising efficiency by making random edge impact effectively while minimally affecting its ability to be thrown barehanded. Its usually symmetrical form decreases air resistance and enhances balance ... These experiments were performed at the discus/ shotput practice field at the University of Massachusetts.

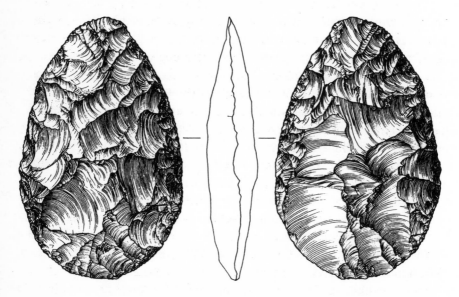

fig 47: This fine, slightly pointed oval shape might be called the classic Boxgrove handaxe. In the 1996 dig alone, over 250 axes were found, most as sharp and fresh as they day they were discarded 500,000 years ago. Length 10 cm. (drawn by Julian Cross)

'That shows you how sharp that is, I've gone through the skin.'
    Peter poked a finger through the hole, thrusting a plume of silvery brown hair onto the white membrane. Peter hadn't been expecting these flints to be so sharp. He made a mistake with stone number three.

'That is perfect for tanning.'

He rolled the loose hide, which folded heavily, like chain mail beneath a beautiful soft coat. He looked at the two membranes, one on the pelt, the other on the flesh: not a nick in either (except for the hole).

'This tool is much larger. It's easier to grip. If you take this edge', turning the axe as he spoke to show the serrations caused by the meeting of many flake scars, 'it's got more of a saw edge to it. This edge' – showing the slick straight curve where the knapper has taken a single long flake down one side of the axe, what archaeologists call a 'tranchet edge' – 'this edge is very fine, it's a better cutting edge.'

By now Peter was getting into the swing of things. With tool number four, he selected the best edge for the task before he started. He wiped the axe across the exposed flesh, gathering hairs that had fallen everywhere. John asked him if he was worried about cutting his hands.

'The art is you keep one dry.' And looking at Peter's hands, John saw that while his left was covered in drying blood and hairs, his right was as clean as fresh flint. This hand never touched the meat; the axe never touched the meat, except at the very edge.

'I started off as a butcher's boy when I was approximately nine years old. We had our own little slaughterhouse in Wantage, behind the shop. We'd go to the local farms, pick up on Monday morning in the van, dead on Tuesday, hang it, and deliver it round to the local outlets. You learnt a little bit more every time.'

He examined the fifth stone, selected an edge and began to cut around the neck, the hardest part of the carcass to skin.

Iain Davidson and William Noble in *Tools, Language & Cognition in Human Evolution*, 1993:
The regularity of handaxes can be seen, not as the result of design, but rather as the unintended by-product of a repertoire of flaking habits ... The fallacy of the finished artefact is not only about whether the forms were tools, but also about whether there was a sense in which they were finished.

Iain Davidson in *Antiquity*, 1991:
Tranchet axes, such as those from Boxgrove, would be viewed not as specialist tools with a tranchet edge, but as bifacial cores for which tranchet blows were the next appropriate source of flakes ... the 'handaxe' was a by-product of stereotyped motor

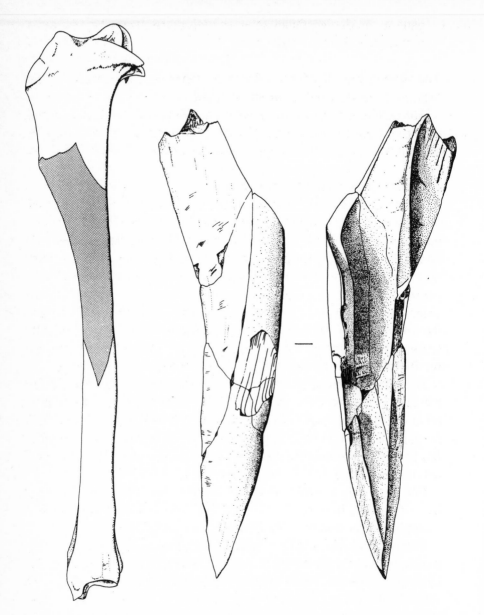

fig 48: From the marine sands in Simon Collcutt's Trench (and thus dating from very early in the Boxgrove sequence) came this piece of red deer tibia (lower rear leg). It shows small horizontal cuts from skinning along the front edge of the leg (left side of left view), and a classic fracture where the bone was broken open to expose the marrow. On the outer face (right side of left view) is a distinct percussion scar, and on the inside (right view) crushing at the point of impact; a fracture surface runs along the edge in a helical twist characteristic of breaks in fresh bone. This bone was broken with considerable force. From more complete specimens, it appears that bones were sometimes placed on a stone anvil and hit from above with a hammer. Length of fragment c. 20 cm. (drawn by Phil Rye)

patterns producing flakes for use, with no decisions beyond the removal of the next flake.

The opened hide lay flat on the table. Peter held the carcass by the legs, and the skin fell away as he lifted.

For butchering the meat, he went back to an axe he'd used before, rather than taking a new one. He chose stone number three. When he stroked its edge gently along the top of the firm meat, the flesh just fell open.

'This proves that it is very sharp.'

He cut down the neck bones: swipe, swipe, swipe. No hack, no pull or twist, just cut, cut, cut, and the first shoulder came free. It was a definite surprise to the butcher that these flints worked so well. He boned the shoulder, then moved to the chest. Pulling the handaxe edge over the ribs with a staccato crunching, he found that for this task, cutting bones, the flint was not up to it. (It is at this point, watching the video that John made of the experiment, that students sometimes leave the room.) Peter tried a number of different axes. He eventually snapped the ribs along the scoring. He got his spare ribs this way, but for the other side he decided to remove the meat in one piece.

He came up against the same problem on the back: using the handaxe like a steel chopper, he tried to cut through the vertebrae to separate the rear legs and pelvis, but it didn't work. Neither did sawing. 'We're making a slight impression on it, but nothing terrific. It's just sort of mutilating the bone.' Later he sliced gently around the pelvis rather than attempt to go through it.

For cutting meat again, he chose a former axe. 'Back to stone six,' he said, brandishing the black flint. He looked closer. 'No it's not,' swapping it for another. 'Stone three'.

Stone three was a larger, beautifully made handaxe with a fine tranchet edge. Of all the pieces on the table it was the nearest to the ideal Boxgrove axe. 'Why should I use a piece of stone,' he said, when John tried to encourage Peter to use the flint flakes (which were, after all, part of the experiment), 'when I have a perfect butchery tool?' It might have been 150,000 years or more since someone had used one of those tools with such consummate skill.

There was only one accidental cut: John bled a finger getting the flints out of their box.

Chapter 42

March 1995: Differences of Perception

rabbit

Mark was seething.

Things had generally gone well over the winter, after the successful autumn conferences and subsequent press coverage. With English Heritage's help they had put together a detailed proposal for the new dig (the largest document they had produced since the published report in 1986), and the budget of around £230,000 was on the way to being approved. To secure greater control of the site, English Heritage were negotiating with the landowners over a lease on the West Quarry, where the tibia had been found. Progress seemed slow, but eventually it would all be signed up and then for the first time there would be a sense of security, a feeling that at last no one was going to appear on the horizon without warning to drag away all the archaeology.

Public interest had continued. In the new year issue of *Discover*, the Disney science journal, Mark talked up his hominids. 'You have to remember', he told the magazine, 'that this time in sunny southern Britain we were surrounded by lions and hyenas and various other big cats ... these people had the ability to secure a carcass, whether they were hunting or scavenging ... this shows a higher level of social organization'.

But none of this had any bearing on Mark's pique. It was set off by a short article in *British Archaeology* for February. What sort of characters were Europe's earliest hominids, it asked? The answer was blunt: no co-operative behaviour, no storage pits, no ritual, no distant links between local groups. 'Moreover,' said the author, 'the absence of structured campsites, with hearths and "conversation rings" of debris, is the clearest indication that people of this date did not use spoken language. Speech has its own archaeological signature, found in evidence for the arrangement of people around hearths so they could hear one another.' The piece was headed 'Boxgrove Man didn't speak and ignored strangers'. It was written by his research supervisor and one of English Heritage's academic advisers for Boxgrove, Clive Gamble. He was concerned that Mark was getting carried away in his excitement about all the Boxgrove finds.

Over the previous decade, Clive had been working towards his own understanding of palaeolithic Europe. He had begun as a research student at Cambridge in the late 1970s. His magisterial archaeological survey was published in 1986. The European impact of Binford's *Bones: Ancient Men and Modern Myths* (published five years before: *see* Chapter 21) is already apparent in Clive's *Palaeolithic Settlement of Europe*. In fact the two men had been steering towards similar goals from different starting points. Both wanted to know what the earliest hominids were doing and both believed the route to such an understanding lay in modelling human and animal behaviour: in thinking about how early hominids organized their lives in landscapes very different from the present.

When Clive was a student, the level of argument about hominids in palaeolithic Europe – especially for the earliest period, as today represented by Boxgrove – rarely went beyond descriptions of lumbering brutes avoiding extinction by luck more than by skill (most of the research effort went into refining dating schemes based on styles of stone tools).

Against such a background, Clive argued that the controlling features of hominid life in early Europe were not the weather forecasts. Rather they were the creatures' abilities to exploit varying plant and animal resources, which abilities were themselves determined by social and communication networks that made possible particular degrees of planning, cooperation and survival skills.

This might be clearer if we summarize his analysis of palaeolithic Europe as a sequence of three different modes of organization.

One of these, which we can without doing too much violence to his description call the neanderthal life-style, lasting from around 200,000 to 40,000 years ago, he labelled 'meat storage and self-sufficiency'.

Hominids moved as individuals and in small groups to exploit the four main herd animals that roamed the open landscapes of ice age Europe. As both geology and oxygen isotope curves indicate (Chapter 28), the 'normal' climate was neither fully glacial nor warmest interglacial, but temperate or cool, with vegetation ranging from broken woodland to steppe. As they pursued bison, horse, red deer and reindeer, neanderthals repeatedly returned to caves, hunting stands and other points in the landscape in areas where they knew that at particular times of the year they could rely on certain animals. In doing so, a single group ranged over perhaps 3,000 square kilometres.

In the subsequent upper palaeolithic, 40,000 to 10,000 years ago, the era of early *Homo sapiens*, painted caves and the rest (*see* Chapter 36), a strategy of 'planned competition' permitted access to a greater variety of foods, and witnessed a larger hominid population. Temperate plant, river and sea foods require more intensive labour and craft skills than demanded of the earliest hominids in tropical Africa seeking similar resources. With more complex and robust 'alliance networks', humans were able to move in an increasing number of specialized groups: their knowledge of their environment and their ability to communicate and act on that knowledge were highly sophisticated.

By contrast, the very earliest hominids (for whom, in the early 1980s, there was really very little evidence at all), lacked the social organization necessary for complex planning. For them, the critical factor was the long winter dearth which Clive proposed they survived by eating frozen carcasses of large mammals (aided by fire for defrosting). The Clacton 'spear', he thought, might be a probe for poking about in deep snow in the quest for iced mammoth.

Their quarry occurred in huge four-legged parcels needing rapid consumption. So they would live in large groups, the better to find and defend meat from carnivores, but move over relatively small areas. They possessed only a very broad set of skills, such as those required to locate carcasses or succeed at limited summer hunting (and of course also – a significant base-line – the skills that made possible the exit from north Africa and colonization of new environments in Europe). This, said Clive, was a mode of life that could be described as 'meat management'.

It was this earliest lifestyle that he had summarized in his *British Archaeology* story. Mark sat down and banged out a reply to the editor.

'The character Clive Gamble describes in his article ... differs widely from my perception.' There is, he wrote, 'overwhelming evidence for speech at this time, as demonstrated by the research of Leslie Aiello and Robin Dunbar.' Mark was here referring to a study by these two anthropologists (described later in more detail: Chapter 50) which argued that the increasing brain size of evolving hominids implied they were living in such large groups that physical contact would have been inadequate to maintain social relationships. The only way round this would have been rudimentary spoken communication. It was a complex theoretical argument partly based on studies of monkeys and apes. But Clive Gamble's case was pretty theoretical, too.

The idea that archaeologists could dig up 'conversation rings' originated with studies by American Lewis Binford. In his work with Inuit in Alaska, and other hunters, he noted that people often sat down around a fire, and as they ate, or worked at some craft, threw rubbish over their shoulders, so that a ring of objects that a future archaeologist might dig up lay on the ground around the gossiping men and women. Clive had written that if there were none of these 'conversation rings', then there was no conversation. Unfortunately for him, he had not then seen detailed plans of the Horse Butchery Site.

'At Boxgrove', wrote Mark in his letter, 'in the horse butchery area, there are at least five discrete knapping scatters around a complete carcass.' For Mark this was enough to suggest the hominids were sitting beside the dead horse, talking as they prepared to cut it up. The Horse Butchery Site was clear evidence for cooperative behaviour. The species was not stupid and conservative, but 'supremely well adapted to cope with life in Europe during the middle pleistocene'.

This public disagreement set the agenda for the new excavations. Two men with very different backgrounds and temperaments but a shared interest. On the one hand was a powerful intellectual and a palaeolithic authority, arguing that these earliest intellects were something other than human and, at least by implication, somehow inferior. On the other, a beefy hunting and fishing man for whom the evidence for ancient hominids surviving off giant horses, rhinos and deer – a world in which every beast was a modern hunter's record-breaking prize, great herds of horses the size and build of a cart horse, deer with the biggest antler ever seen – conjured up a picture of cooperation, planning and sophistication. Was it possible they were both right?

Whatever the case, there was a feeling in the air that the right questions were being asked, that the new interest generated by Boxgrove was inspiring the right research; and that out there under the silky fine silts in the Sussex quarry, might be the right finds, just waiting to be asked to join the party.

Chapter 43

May 1995: The Dig Begins

Deninger's bear

Mark had put an ad for volunteers on the Internet, and the excavation was fully staffed for the whole season. The name 'Boxgrove' had drawn many people, but there was something else too: they offered a subsistence allowance. This used to be standard practice on excavations in Britain, and generations of highly skilled itinerant workers made a major if largely unsung contribution to understanding the ancient past. 'Circuit diggers', they called them. These days many people actually pay to work for a project. Of course, this can help the finances. But it can also make discipline tricky: if you have laid out cash to dig you might not take too kindly to being told that you are doing it wrong.

In fact after years of penny pinching there was now money for all sorts of things. The timbered roof on Ounce's Barn, bereft of its tiles, had finally fallen in, taking some of the flint walling with it. This was being made safe, the last job in tidying up the complex of stables, old bull pens and cattle sheds. Running south from the barn, just touching its south east corner, was a flint and brick milking parlour. The roof had been refelted to make it completely waterproof, and the small room at the north end, Mark's bedroom and the site office, had been covered with what was left of the tiles that had otherwise been stolen, and all the windows had been fixed. This wing was the central store and site headquarters for what was officially termed 'the Hominid Project'.

In the office there was a telephone line. There was even a fax line, and a computer, shelves for Mark's books and an old carpet on the floor.

The staff team had been preparing for a few weeks, Mark, Simon and Francis setting up equipment in April, then joined in May by the Supervisors, John Gaskell, Matt Pope and Hilary Stainer and Site Manager Jules Tipper. It was all ready by 15 May, when the first volunteers arrived. Down in the quarry, the debris that covered and protected the archaeological layers had been removed with machines, until there was just a thin layer to be taken out by hand with picks, shovels and wheelbarrows. Also to be hand dug was the dirt backfilled into the trench where Roger found the tibia. This small rectangular pit was in the centre of the cleared area. Once all the lose material was gone, the far edges of the site cleaned and straightened, they would survey in the eight new trenches. The first would be numbered 'six': Roger had already dug five.

Chapter 44

June 1995: First Reports from Atapuerca

giant deer

English Heritage held another press conference in the quarry to publicize the new dig. This was a different affair from the events of May 1994. Geoffrey Wainwright, David Harris (Director of the Institute of Archaeology) and Chris Stringer were all there to answer questions, as well as, of course, the excavation team. So despite English Heritage's press releases which still claimed the tibia was found in silts dating from 130,000 to 730,000 years ago, that Boxgrove Man was over six feet tall and that he is 'the oldest European human ever found', media stories were much better informed. In particular there was now a consensus that the tibia was contemporary with the jaw found at Mauer near Heidelberg in 1907.

What Chris Stringer most wanted was a jaw from Boxgrove.

'Any find would be marvellous,' he said, 'but I would love to get a jaw bone with teeth to compare with that found at Heidelberg.'

'I am confident we will find more remains,' said Geoff.

The Times followed up with a story by Nigel Hawkes, in which he reviewed the case for the Boxgrove fossil being the oldest in Europe. The 'short chronology', he said, as supported by Roberts, Gamble and Roebroeks, would have no hominids in Europe before five hundred thousand years ago. But other archaeologists in France, Spain and

Italy claimed to have much older evidence. We reviewed this in Chapter 30, and came down firmly in favour of the short chronology. There was one site in Hawkes' story, however, that was not in the running in May 1994: Atapuerca.

Near Burgos in northern Spain is a limestone sierra riddled with caves and fissures where archaeological investigations have been underway for two decades. It is one of the world's most extraordinary hominid sites, famed in international academic circles, and to the Spanish public through extensive media coverage, not for the preservation of activity areas like Boxgrove, but for the sheer quantities of bones. In the suitably named Sima de los Huesos – 'the bone abyss' – where the claw marks of cave bears still score clay on the wall of a side passage, in just this one site, nearly 1,500 hominid bones and fragments have been recovered – and they're still digging. These date from around 200,000 years ago. But it was the new claim that Hawkes was writing about. Unlike Boxgrove, where hominid activity is restricted to a relatively brief period of a few centuries, at Atapuerca different deposits together span hundreds of thousands of years. They had already published finds of animal bones and stone tools that looked approximately contemporary with Boxgrove. Now they'd found, in these same layers, some hominid bones.

'. . . the most recent finds', said journalist Hawkes, 'from a different cave in the same complex, are said to be considerably older': about 700,000 years old, or nearly half as old again as the Boxgrove tibia. In fact the first hint at such a claim had been reported in 1994, soon after the international Boxgrove coverage, by Paul Bahn in the *Daily Telegraph*. 'Tests are being carried out on the latest remains . . .', wrote Bahn, a free-lance archaeological writer specializing in things palaeolithic, 'to determine if they are older and, if so, by how much.' 'We need more research', said team leader Juan-Luis Arsuaga to the American magazine *Science*, 'to know if [bones from Atapuerca] are older than Boxgrove.'

No one at Boxgrove took these press stories too seriously. Atapuerca was recognized for the enormous importance of its fossils, but it was also known as a site where definitive publication of data was slow (a feature that characterizes most of the claims for very early humans in Europe). Until the evidence was available for critical scrutiny, it could not be judged. There was a distinct feeling that someone had been prompted by the huge publicity received by Boxgrove – 'the first European' – to set out to prove that Atapuerca had yet older bones, even if the place where they had been found had previously been described by the archaeologists as being the same age as Boxgrove. They could only wait and see.

What *had* excited them was news from Oxford that John Mitchell had identified his first use wear on a Boxgrove handaxe. After months of scrutinizing experimental pieces, he'd finally decided, one morning, to slip an axe from the excavations under his microscope. The polish shone from the edge almost at once.

'Come and look at this, Derek,' he cried, running across the landing of the Baden Powell Research Centre towards Director Derek Roe's office.

John knew immediately that what he saw flickering on the video screen attached to his microscope was a type of wear caused by cutting meat.

Chapter 45

July 1995: 'We're Making New Creation Myths'

hazel doormouse

Things were going very well at the dig. No one had ever seen anything like it.

The fields north of the quarries had just been harvested, and large square mounds of baled straw seemed to have dropped from a passing plane and landed on the gold stubble. A hot breeze raising fine dust smudged the air.

BBC TV's *Horizon*, by now holding several hours of unedited video tapes, had flown Wil Roebroeks and Thijs van Kolfschoten over from Holland, and after a day filming with Simon in the Natural History Museum, they were down in Sussex, walking briskly out to the excavations with Mark.

They were laughing and joking, old friends, colleagues in the hunt to understand past times. First stop was the wet sieving post (the 'vole machine'). They looked at the marine ply box, the plastic tub, the hose nozzles from the garden centre, the Holsten Pils crates stretched with stainless steel sieve mesh.

'All this cost only £150?' asked Thijs, impressed.

'We made something like that,' said Wil. 'But we used Mammoth beer crates.'

They looked at old geological test pits, and discussed the meaning of the contorted layers of coloured sands and gravels. They took photos of each other with white sun tan lotion splashed onto their noses. They talked about digging.

'You came here on a good day,' said Mark to the Dutch visitors after greeting one of his Supervisors at the excavation. 'We have nine handaxes.' Nine handaxes lying on the sand, more or less where they had been dropped, and all exposed on this one day – bringing the total so far this summer to around 70, vastly more than they'd found throughout the quarries in all those years before the tibia came up.

Thijs climbed into one pit. 'What is that bone?' he asked Simon.

'It's a terminal phalanx, but I can't see enough to tell what species.'

Thijs agreed. He stared in wonder at a tiny, perfectly preserved bird skull, a frail cage in ivory.

'You have to see this,' said Simon, motioning him towards a larger flat fragment of bone, still part buried, which they both knew at once to be part of a rhinoceros pelvis. A little bit of gristle, and it could have just come from an exotic butcher's shop window. It was covered in thin grooves, where a knife parting the attached muscles had scored the surface. Not a steel knife, of course: a flint one.

None of them had seen anything like this before.

'Forget the lager,' said Mark. 'Let's have Champagne.'

In the Anglesey Arms, all the talk was about digging.

'Yes, now we must carry on,' said Mark in answer to Wil's question.

'But the old problem is money. Where will the money come from?'

Wil was more sanguine. What about the American National Geographic Society, whose writer and photographer had visited the site yesterday? Or European Union funding?

Wil Roebroeks had begun in the 1970s as a modern history student in Neijmegen. Archaeology was a hobby then. But he started going to prehistory lectures, and the hobby took over. He dug up palaeolithic remains in the quarries at Belvédère, with grants channelled through the University of Leiden, just as Mark got his money through the London Institute. One day he took some bones from his dig to the museum in Maastricht, and met Thijs.

'We're making new creation myths,' he said to Mark. 'We need fixed points in life. What could be more important than the boundary between what is human and what is non-human? People have been arguing about this for years. There were drawings of club wielding cave men long before there was any archaeology. Clive Gamble is brilliantly provocative – one of the most creative people in palaeolithic archaeology the world over. But can there be a solution? There are a lot of questions we can't answer.'

Back in the quarries, Simon took Thijs to his hut, gave him a small polythene bag containing what looked like a crushed Weetabix biscuit – in fact the residue from wet sieving 21 kilos of the Fe Layer – and sat him down opposite his binocular microscope. Thijs emptied the bag onto a black plastic tray, and picked out specks of bone with tweezers. He found a tooth from a hazel dormouse – this animal was extremely rare in European deposits of this age, until Boxgrove.

Then Simon brought out a little jaw, about a couple of centimetres long, with tiny little pointed teeth at the tip; from an European mink, the oldest ever found. Thijs looked up. 'You really have marvellous material.'

At Pontnewydd, north Wales, the only other site in Britain beside Boxgrove and Swanscombe (Chapter 29) where early hominid remains have been dug up, they do not have the quality of preservation found at Boxgrove. But they have, at Pontnewydd, just found two further hominid teeth, perhaps two hundred thousand tears old.

'Pontnewydd 2,' reads the fax hanging from Mark's hand, 'Boxgrove 0.'

Chapter 46

Early August 1995: Another Extinct Killer

extinct panther

About once a fortnight Simon took the train to London to spend a weekend with his wife Sharon Gerber and a day or so catching up on office work at the Natural History Museum. This morning he had a tooth from the excavation, found near the bottom of the silts where it might be a century or so older than the hominid tibia. He had brought it to the Museum because he thought it was a new species for the site: it was a milk tooth, a shearing, cutting carnassial, from the jaw of a carnivore, probably a cat. But *which* cat?

The Boxgrove fossil collection was slowly taking over shelves in the Museum's store. Everything was labelled to say when it had been dug up, where it had come from. Much of it was slightly more recent than the hominid tibia (we're only talking centuries here); some, like the remains from the Horse Butchery Site, probably very slightly older. Simon pulled out a drawer, packed with card trays containing test tubes, each holding a piece of bone. In a box by itself was a wolf skull, flattened by the pressure of the overlying deposits, but otherwise complete. It was small: hardly the stuff of medieval folklore.

In another drawer was a tray containing a solid mass of tiny bone fragments, an accumulation of mink droppings found in a previous dig near the edge of the water hole where they were now working. European mink are extinct in the west today, so it wasn't until they received some fresh scats in the post from a colleague in north eastern Europe that they were sure that that was what it was ('a recent donation from Estonia', read the citation in the report, 'has been gratefully received').

Around the edge of the store were open shelves crammed with leviathans. An Indian elephant skull on a shield; the monumental head of a one horned giant rhino from Siberia; and, less modern, the dark chocolate brown bones of a mammoth from Alaska, presented by Captain Kellet and Lieutenant Wood RN in 1850. The adjacent shelf was laden with yellowing teeth, each as big as a floor scrubbing brush. Ever curious, Simon pulled out a mounted African black rhino skull, and noticed machete marks similar to the lines on the rhino skull fragments coming out of the ground at the dig. In the centre of the forehead, which was as big as a large man's chest, was a round hole two or three centimetres across. No label recorded the fate of the person who had fired that shot. The bone had healed around the wound; the rhino survived.

As he had expected, Simon did not find what he needed here. He made for the main carnivore collection. From here he took the lift (floor guide: Large Ungulates 1, Primates 7, Carnivora 8) and came out into the tightly packed collection of modern wolves and cats.

The sheer numbers were overpowering. Lions, *Panthera leo*: each tray, twelve skulls; each cupboard, six trays. There were four cupboards of lions. Four cupboards of *Panthera tigris*, tigers from the Bombay Natural History Society. Shelf after shelf after shelf of wolf skins, snow leopard skins from Kashmir, wild cats, pumas, cheetahs.

On every skull he picked up he noticed cut marks – Simon had never looked before. The best match for his fossil so far was a young lion from Ethiopia, but the cusps on the teeth weren't quite right: definitely not hyena, nor otter, nor glutton. A female cheetah from Nigeria provided a better fit. And so on, and on, searching the files. But Simon never found a match, a perfectly identical jaw with identical teeth. Eventually, after further work in the library, he decided it was – almost certainly – an extinct, jaguar-like cat, *Panthera gombaszoegensis*. He wasn't completely certain because remains of this animal are so rare that there is very little comparable material: there were no *gombaszoegensis* hunting anywhere after the Anglian glaciation.

And so another animal was put tentatively into the prehistoric zoo, set loose in the ancient forests and parklands of northern Europe:

another killer whose twitching nose would have scrutinized the smell of *Homo heidelbergensis* drifting through the grasses.

This new cat (whose identity is still awaiting final confirmation as we go to press), indicated by a single tooth, would have been no bigger than a modern jaguar. But some other creatures were huge. The Boxgrove lion – represented again by no more than one bone, but well known from other contemporary sites where only animals have been found – was the biggest lion species that lived, a quarter as big again as the lions we know today. The horse was also very big, as were the red deer – to say nothing of the aptly named giant deer, two species of which are found at Boxgrove. From other excavations around Europe it is known that there were two species of elephant around half a million years ago, although from the few scraps of bone yet identified it is not possible to say which were feeding on the plain beneath the chalk cliff. One of these was truly enormous, weighing in at nearly twice a modern African elephant, a beast fit to hold its own against some of the greatest dinosaurs. Indeed, the very hominids were amongst the largest representatives of our own genus.

One reason for all this grandeur would have been the quality of the environment. Today we associate large herbivores and carnivores with the severe world of the African savanna, where seasonal drought forces large migrations. In a temperate Europe, however, such flights from scarcity may not have been necessary. Think of the lost landscape Mark has excavated:

Fresh water is springing from the bottom of the cliff, feeding a lake that periodically overflows and washes across the plain. The rich silts of this plain, which may have been ten kilometres or more wide and stretched for long distances to east and west – though broken by the massive river valleys that come down through the chalk, themselves creating rich environments for fish, water birds and plants – support herbs and grasses and shrubs. On top of the cliff and continuing inland for hundreds of kilometres is dense forest, a mixture of deciduous and coniferous trees that we no longer see in wild woods. There is a great variety of habitats and a wealth of resources. The climate is neither very cold nor very hot, but similar to that found in Sussex today. It seems reasonable to imagine that not only were the animals big, but so were the herds – of bison, five species of deer, and horse – that swept the land trailed by giant cats, hyenas and large packs of wolves.

It was a world in which an intelligent bipedal mammal could hardly fail. As long as it lasted.

Chapter 47

Late August 1995: 'El Primer Europeo'

robin

Meanwhile in Spain, with nine pages of informed text, colour photos and diagrams, *El Pais* featured Atapuerca. But this wasn't just an update on new discoveries. There had already been plenty of those. In one Sunday supplement (a 1993 *Blanco Negro*) the story had been flagged on the front cover. Atapuerca had style. It had dramatic overland scenery, stunning cavescapes, photogenic bronzed staff, and bones: caves full of stiffs, skulls and jaws and limbs scrunched together like Toblerone – as another supplement once expressed it in a colour diagram, Atapuerca had more than 70 per cent of Middle Pleistocene post-cranial remains (that is, bits that don't come from the head) found anywhere *in the world*.

What prompted *El Pais* to leap to colour this time was age. Boxgrove had shown that what really got world headlines was being the oldest. The Atapuerca team greeted the 1994 Boxgrove coverage with a mix of bemusement and envy. All that fuss over *one fragment of bone*? They were already convinced they had stone tools much older. So they were quite understandably jealous of the interest this English fossil attracted. While the national media had done Atapuerca proud, who outside Spain had even heard of them?

Well, dating changed all that. Or rather, *re*-dating did. In 1994 in one cave, known as Gran Dolina (and code-named TD), they had found 36 hominid fossils in level six. They had previously published this level, which had produced respectable evidence for stone tool manufacture, as contemporary with Boxgrove at around half a million years old (relying on the tried and tested animal indicators, backed up by palaeomagnetism). So over 30 hominid remains (representing at least four individuals) would add vastly to our knowledge of the early European *Homo heidelbergensis*, hitherto known by little more than the Mauer jaw and the Boxgrove tibia.

But what the excitement was about was that a statistical re-analysis of the palaeomagnetic data (recording the direction of magnetic north: *see* Chapter 28) had suddenly plunged TD6 into an era of reversed magnetic polarity (an apparently valid if complex argument). The Atapuerca scientists took this to be the Matuyama reversal, which ended around 780,000 years ago (*see* fig 21). So the hominid remains found at this level would have to be older than that. As *El Pais* said on the front cover of its colour magazine, over a photo of an Atapuerca skull: 'EL PRIMER EUROPEO'.

Nature had first rights on the Boxgrove tibia story (or rather it should have done): its American rival *Science* had Atapuerca. On 11 August this journal had backed up a couple of technical articles with an editorial feature, in which two highly respected American specialists, Carl Swisher and Clark Howell, were quoted as apparently enthusiastic supporters of the new date, while Clive Gamble and Wil Roebroeks, perhaps sounding a little churlish, were seen to be sceptical.

It was part of the excavators' case that these ancient hominids were pretty hamfisted, and made only poor quality stone tools – a popular argument from people claiming evidence for very early hominids in Europe, as we have seen (Chapter 30). Clive was not impressed.

'I fail to see how tools like that could give anyone an edge over a saber-tooth,' he said to the *Science* writer JoAnn Gutin on the phone from Berkeley.

'In general,' said Wil Roebroeks, 'sites seem to get older once hominids turn up'.

If the Spanish archaeologists imagined this sounded too much like sour grapes, they needn't have worried. Atapuerca was to gallop into journalistic folklore as the site of the earliest European (just as Boxgrove had the year before), even, by the year end, appearing thus in an archaeological encyclopaedia.

Back at Boxgrove there was excitement over something else that the Atapuerca team would have found hard to comprehend. They had at last found the hoped-for hominid remain to add to the tibia. It wasn't the rest of the skeleton (in fact, as it was found at a deeper level than the tibia, it was older than this bone by as much as a century or so). It wasn't a compressed mass of ribs and toes, with lines of teeth glinting gruesomely out of the red earth, as was seen in Gran Dolina at Atapuerca.

It was a tooth.

Nearly a whole one.

Chapter 48

September 1995: Laura Finds a Tooth

thornback ray

By late August they had dug down into the base of the fine silts. The sheer unexpected quantity of artefacts and animal bones was slowing them down. They were behind schedule. They could run out of time and money while they were still removing the most productive layers at the dig.

They had eight trenches in a block, each separated from its neighbour by a metre wide baulk. The firm creamy walls looked like reinforced concrete. The volunteers were all to go at the end of September. It was looking as if they might finish the trenches but have to leave the baulks in place.

The finds had changed as the dig progressed. At first there were few artefacts: most remains were small fragments of animal bone. This was curious, as it was at this level that Roger had found the hominid tibia, which now stood out for its size compared to all the other bones.

Beneath this, in the Slindon Silts, were many flint flakes and handaxes as well as more animals. These finds, along with the silts themselves, had all been churned about a little in an unusual freak of local geology that they were now beginning to understand – which of course was one of the goals of the current project. Fresh water had been flowing from the spring at the foot of the cliff to the north, at first as an exposed stream and later, as the silt-forming lagoon developed, percolating through the silts and losing itself in the open water. Then the climate changed radically and glaciers began to spread from the

251

northern highlands. Intermittently freezing and thawing sludge – clays, broken chalk and flint gravels – guttered over the high cliff, as the cliff itself collapsed from the top in large blocks. The weight of these gravels moving over the finer sediments, saturated by the spring water, caused the two formations to mix where the one passed over the other, tongues of chalky grit and clay reaching down into the silts.

As the archaeologists dug deeper into these silts, it was clear that there had been less disturbance lower down. At the very bottom, at the contact with the old sand left by the sea that cut the cliffs, things looked pretty fresh. This had been a land surface that, with everything on it, had been buried very gently with the deposition of the first fine silts. It was on this surface they had found the remains of a butchered rhino, and also bones of butchered deer, bison and horse. And it was here that Laura Basell had found the hominid tooth.

When Mark told her she would be on the front page of all the papers, Laura thought he was joking. It was brilliant finding it, but in the bigger scheme of things it was only a tooth. Then, on 7 September, came the carefully engineered press conference. Suddenly Laura knew that Mark was not joking.

Laura Basell was a nineteen-year-old student on an Ancient Mediterranean course at Bristol University. She'd heard Mark lecture at Bristol in 1994, and she and two other students had been inspired to dig at Boxgrove. She came for four weeks in August, but enjoyed it so much she stayed on into September, resolved to change her studies to full time archaeology. This time the media had more than a bit of shapeless bone in a London conference room: they had a recognizable tooth (with all the possibilities that offered for dental puns) at the site of its discovery, and they had a vivacious girl with cascades of fair hair who performed tirelessly for the cameras like a professional model ('I can't quite believe it. It's like a dream. It's brilliant').

It had been a busy week at Boxgrove. On Monday Simon had added Samson, a former resident of Halnaker (he left a partner, Delilah) to the rotting mess in the old cattle trough where he rendered down modern animals to add to the bone collection that he used for reference when identifying fossils. Samson was his first African boa constrictor. The next day he was in London to show a puzzling bone from the old Horse Butchery Site to Sir Bernard Knight, Home Office forensic scientist then on call as a witness at the trial of Rosemary West.

And while all this was going on they made a truly remarkable find. It was a soft hammer for flaking flint. And this hammer was made from a piece of antler – carved in the stem of a huge, sprawling antler once sported by a giant deer, *Megaloceros dawkinsi*, that became extinct early in the Anglian glaciation half a million years ago. So this one find leapt straight into the record books not only as the oldest antler hammer in the world (the only other soft hammers of this age, in apparently unshaped bones, all came from the same dig) but as the only one of giant deer antler – indeed the only artefact of any kind ever found made from the remains of this long extinct animal.

It had the immediate effect of convincing Adrian Lister (a palaeontologist at University College who specialized in ancient deer), who had still been harbouring some doubts, that Boxgrove really was half a million years old. And it fuelled the growing feeling that the creatures who made those handaxes were really pretty smart. Francis Wenban-Smith had shown, through his studies of the flintwork, that soft hammers had been used. Then, years later, they had found some bone hammers. But this piece of antler was different. If the bone tools were opportunistic (they may not have been, but it was difficult to tell) it was likely that this hammer had been laboriously broken out of the hard antler and flaked into shape before it was needed. Shed antler are found only at certain times of year and in certain places. So it was likely that this hammer had been made not simply as part of the process of knapping a flint axe, but as a separately conceived act. Then it had been used so much, perhaps to make over a hundred handaxes, that the antler had worn down until the end was barely recognizable – implying that it had been carried around, 'owned' by an individual, treasured even (or, as Lewis Binford would say, 'curated'). As Clive Gamble said to the *Horizon* camera in the week after the find was made, 'It does make them look a lot more like boy scouts in terms of being prepared. This is an item of personal equipment.' (For Mark, a find that impressed Clive in this way was well worth making.)

Indeed it took little imagination to see that the huge animal whose antler had yielded the tool might, possibly, through its size and its strength, the fearsome points arrayed around the edge of its great sweeping horny trees held with impossible span high on the stag's massively muscled neck – that all this towering strength might have been perceived by the hominid who used that hammer, not just as a hunter appreciates the strength of its prey, but as a creature who used that hammer to make a tool for dismembering such animals might feel the strength in the tool and in itself. As a symbol: it was easy to imagine that.

Eric Trinkaus is a specialist in early European hominid fossils – much of his career has been devoted to studying neanderthals in particular. A week after the press conference for the tooth, almost exactly two years after Roger found the tibia, Eric spent the entire day in London at the CT scanner in University College Hospital. Typically for a bone like the Boxgrove tibia they'd need five scans, produce five digital images of the bone as if it had been sliced through. This time they did 120! 'Really it's just another bone,' said Eric, 'that will help fill in the picture.' What's so important is the site itself – the context for the bone. But media interest had galvanized specialists.

In this case – courtesy of the BBC – it had brought Eric over from the States. Tall, thin, large boned, he sat at Boxgrove on a plain chair with a foot up on his left knee, in yellow nylon jacket, clean shiny white running shoes and white socks. He was clean shaven with a moustache in the American fashion.

Chris Stringer, said Eric, wanted the tibia to be *Homo heidelbergensis*. 'I couldn't give a damn. I'm interested in problems of behavioural adaptation.' The australopithecines, the very early hominids like 'Lucy', are biologically basically apes. 'Boxgrove man would stand out a bit today, but we would recognize him as human.' In fact, going a little beyond evidence that can actually be dug up, most specialists, when pushed, would agree that the Boxgrove creatures probably had body hair not unlike a modern human's (which, if you think about it, gives considerable latitude) and perhaps skin colour and head hair of Mediterranean types. Beyond that, for example in matters of infant growth rates, sexual cycles, family or group sizes, for a very specific place and period of time such as are represented by the heidelbergs at Boxgrove, we can really do no more than guess.

But that was good enough for Eric. What really moved him was what anatomy had to say about lifestyle; how these hominids lived. Behaviour and environment shape bones – both down the generations, by natural selection, and in the individual as they grow and age. The bones in a modern tennis player's lower right arm can be up to 60 per cent stronger than their left. Vigorous walking can increase the leg bone density of an octogenarian. Those CT scans showed how *massive* the Boxgrove tibia is. These hominids were very active for a long part of the day, and the bone built itself up to resist constant use – just as you might find in marathon runners – and the stresses and strains caused by very powerful muscles.

Tall (around 1.8 metres, or nearly 6 foot) *and* strong, the picture Eric conjured up from the tibia fitted with something Francis Wenban-

Smith had once said about a large nodule from the excavation, reconstructed by refitting flint flakes: 'I don't think a modern knapper could have handled that,' Francis had said. 'It's too big. You'd need to be a Russian wrestler on steroids.'

The neanderthals, who much later descended from the heidelbergs and about whom we know a great deal more, were shorter – typically 1.7 metres (5 foot 6) for a male and 1.6 metres (5 foot 3) for a female. From Eric Trinkaus' studies we know that their skeletons (which frequently show healed injuries) had evolved to cope with heavy stress from both physical exertion and a cold climate. Like the Boxgrove tibia, neanderthal bones are very robust. Neanderthals also show a classic adaptation to a cold climate in the ratio between the length of their lower limb bones (such as the tibia) to their upper (such as the femur, or upper leg): the outer bones are shorter, fixing hands and feet closer to the warmth of the main body, giving them a squatter stature. This adaptation would be one reason for the decline in height. It was a survival strategy.

The planned end to the dig was the last Friday in September; the 29th at 4 pm. The remaining volunteers would all leave then, and there would be just the staff for a couple of weeks to finish the essential tidying up and finds processing. They'd been there before, life to the full for six months (and really, it didn't get much fuller) then finished.

The diggers – about 30 of them – scraped and brushed their spaces as if important that no one would know it was them, to leave no prints. They chorused a countdown as the second hand on John Gaskell's watch raced to four o'clock. But in one corner, shaded by the wall of the baulk, a quiet American student was too preoccupied with his last find to bother about the counting. At three minutes past the hour American Nick handed Mark, who was trowelling beside him, a tooth. Knowing instantly what it was, Mark jumped out of the trench, walked across to Simon and held out a clenched fist. When Mark opened his fingers, Simon looked at his palm and simply said 'Yes'.

'Yes!', screamed Mark.

There was instant jubilation as a wave of uncontrolled euphoria swept the team. A second hominid tooth! Simon couldn't believe his eyes, it was so like the first it might have come from the same jaw (indeed, later study showed that it did). Right at the end of the dig.

But one man was not jubilant. For 15 minutes Roger Pedersen, who'd been so calm when he found the long bone, Roger who'd let the media fuss wash over him like water spilt on a polished table, for 15 minutes Roger cried. He couldn't stop crying and laughing. He'd been very, very pleased when first told that his bone was hominid, for that meant an extension to the excavation. And then he was hoping for other finds to lead to more extensions. Mark had said that given time they'd find more. Mark had been right. Now they would dig again.

A second tooth really offered little more than a repeat of the opportunities for learning about the original owner's lifestyle provided by the first tooth, found some five weeks before. Of course, given the extreme rarity of these particular fossils, that was no mean feat at all. But for the diggers on their last day, a second tooth seemed to say only one thing: out there, in the silts, there might be more teeth, perhaps even the jaw they came from. And they all knew that if anything was likely to encourage English Heritage to come up with money for another dig, it would be the prospect of more hominid fossils.

It had been a truly remarkable season. They had expected to find quite a few handaxes, after that group in Roger's original trench in 1993. But no one could have imagined there would be so many they'd be falling over them, so many that carefully picking a route in the trenches in bare feet without kicking one out of place was a major challenge. And no one had before seen so many animal bones together in one place at Boxgrove. This sort of concentration of bones and artefacts was familiar at digs in Africa – it was an example of what Glynn Isaac had dubbed 'dense patches', whose significance archaeologists had been arguing about for years. But this wasn't like those African deposits, where rivers had jumbled everything together. Here the bones were perfectly preserved, so that butchery marks could be seen even as you stood high above the trench floor. The flint axes were as sharp as the day they were made. And the funny thing was that most of this was actually at a level about a metre deeper than the tibia that started it all, so the axes and animal bones were a century or so older. It might almost have been coincidence that the tibia was right over this extraordinary site.

It would also have to be coincidence that two teeth were found so close to the tibia, for they too were at the bottom of the trench, amongst the thick spread of bones and artefacts. For a full 15 minutes the tears rolled down Roger's cheeks. Boxgrove wasn't over yet.

Chapter 49

October 1995: An Issue Solved?

Bechstein's bat

So the digging had ended on 29 September 1995 with a second hominid tooth in the bag, and, perhaps the most remarkable thing from the season, over 150 handaxes in almost mint condition. By the following week the atmosphere had changed profoundly. All the volunteers had gone, leaving only the staff – Francis, John Gaskell, Phil Rye, Simon and Mark, and, let's be honest, a few volunteers hanging on for fun and company – to take out the baulks, tidy up, clean and pack the equipment and prepare all the finds and records for moving up to London. They all found it quiet without the students, and a release not to worry about the constant supervision. But there was another factor in the change. Mark was relaxed. He rustled a stack of fishing rods. 'I'm going to sleep. Wake me up next March.'

What we are about to describe is one of the most controversial finds made at Boxgrove. It sat on a shelf in a locked cupboard for five years after it was dug up before anyone knew what to do with it. When the horse bone was lifted from the ground in 1990, there was something about the way it was damaged that made everyone think; they were asking each other, 'Could it really be that?' On 5 September 1995, Simon received a letter from someone (who ought to know) which said 'Yes it could'. His line of work was one where scientific reserve was essential. 'I wish to be cautious in my interpretation,' he wrote, 'as I am aware of the palaeontological implications and would not wish my judgement to be coloured by over-enthusiasm and wishful thinking, which could not be later substantiated by repeated examination and more specialist techniques.

'However . . .'

We will present the evidence here, in full for the first time, and leave you to make up your own mind. Many archaeologists will say they had expected this sort of thing anyway, we knew already. Others will question the argument. But there are some basic facts which are indisputable, and we believe they add up to a unique case for something that lies at the very root of understanding of our most ancient hominid ancestors.

It was a busy day in the Medical Systems Engineering Laboratory in Cardiff. The lab had been taken over by bundles of thick electric cables, light stands, cameras, briefcases, coats and jackets, knots of people looking studiedly organized, clipboards and cups of coffee. There was a smell of dead flesh, strongest near a plastic white wine fermentation bin. Mike Jones, a researcher in the Forensic Bio-Engineering subgroup of the MSE Unit – specialities identifying the force used on stabbing victims and time of death – fiddled with some gadgets that look a bit like an interactive display at a science museum (wires, buttons, dials, swinging metal arms). The man in the dark blue tracksuit with the red green and white shoulders was Stuart Miller from the Sports Council Science Programme.

Simon took a scapula out of the wine bin. It was still fresh, the colour of raspberry ripple ice cream. It had belonged to a riding horse called Fluffy. Bending low to see closer, he noted chewing marks on the edge of the flat shovel shape of the shoulder blade. 'That's the terrier,' said Mike. 'There's a dog to keep the rats down.' A dribble of dark blood fell from the knobbled end of the bone.

The bright moveable lights with black flapping shades were all directed at a human skeleton hanging in front of a display case of specimens in bottles of preservative. Mark was in animated discussion with *Horizon* producer Chris Hale. An assistant held a clapper board: *Boxgrove Man* Roll 88, Scene 481, Take 1. Then all eyes were on the senior man in the dark navy suit, as he took up his position on the stool in front of the skeleton, blinking in the bright lights.

'I went up there with great scepticism. These bloody know it all archaeologists – I've seen so many things in the past where they've alleged skulls've been beaten in, and other fractures. Well they're obviously post mortem: at least you can't tell they're not, put it like that.'

Archaeologists who see television reports of police teams digging up murder victims are sometimes moved to protest that if *they'd* done the excavation, more information would have been recovered. Sir Bernard Knight, Professor of Forensic Pathology at the Royal Infirmary, Cardiff and Home Office Pathologist for Wales and Gloucestershire, is not impressed. 'Forensic archaeology doesn't amount to much – the body's usually stuck in the hole and that's the end of it.' He was not particularly optimistic, then, as he sat in the train to London in early September. On a previous visit to the Natural History Museum, he'd been taken by the BBC to film Piltdown Man. An assistant pulled out a drawer and Knight could see at first look that the fossils were fakes. 'It was obvious. They'd never shown them to a forensic pathologist. It's bloody ridiculous.'

But he'd long been interested in bones. In his medical training he'd taken a course in forensic anthropology, which included a trip through all the major hominid fossils known in the early 1950s. Local archaeologists soon discovered his interest and sent him their bones. He has quite a collection now.

So despite cynicism born of experience, there was still a germ of hope that maybe what they had to show him in the Natural History Museum really was something interesting. Certainly his colleagues in Cardiff, Len Noakes and Mike Jones, had been pretty keen for him to go: for they had seen photos that were almost enough to convince them that in this case the archaeologists might be right.

They were.

Bernard Knight drew the outline of a scapula with his thick black pen. The bone was incomplete, but in the middle of the broken edge there was an almost perfectly circular depression about four centimetres across, like a bite out of the side. He had been sceptical when he heard about it in Cardiff, but then he had gone London to see the actual specimen. It was half a million years old and one of many bone fragments, Mark had told him, from a large butchered horse.

'The first thing was that the edge of the defect, though it was only a third of a circle, was pretty absolutely circular. Then it had this typical terracing, which means that something had been driven through it.'

He drew a cross section through the bone to illustrate how on the underside the fracture splayed out.

'The break was so clean, which usually means high velocity – it wasn't made by something just pushing against the bone. And the other odd thing was that the edge of it had a couple of parallel diagonal marks, as if there was a rotation in it which you see in the rifling of a missile. It may be pure chance, of course, but it is a bit odd.'

So when Mark and Simon had asked if this hole could be spear damage, rather than an accidental break to the bone after butchery that just happened somehow to be circular, Knight had replied that it quite possibly could. He wrote back immediately after his visit to the museum, enclosing copies of pages from his own treatise, *Forensic Pathology*. There were photos of bullet holes in human bone, with descriptions of the process. 'As is the case when glass is penetrated, the entry side [of a bullet hole in bone] will appear sharp edged and relatively small whereas the exit side has sloping edges and is larger – in effect, a cone-shaped defect is produced which becomes larger in the direction in which the bullet has travelled.' It is also, as it happens, the principle which lies behind the knapping of flint.

'The main thing', he said, 'was the terracing, which means that something has gone through the bone with fair force from one side to t'other – from the outer side to the inner.'

'Of course,' he added, 'I can't tell you if it was ante mortem or post mortem.'

With Mark and Simon looking on anxiously, Mike Jones released the arm to which the yew point was attached, it swung down heavily and noisily and the yew point made a perfectly circular hole in the bone supported beneath. Later Stuart Miller threw a spar of wood in the park as if it were a javelin. Chris Hale's cameras recorded everything.

The scapula, like all the bones from the Horse Butchery Site, is soft, weathered and fragile. Detailed study of the circular break has yet to confirm the existence of the oblique scratches which Bernard Knight wrote 'would not be inconsistent with a spiral rotatory motion of the object which caused the defect'; this is not proof that they were never there, as the condition of the bone is poor for the preservation of such very fine marks. On the other hand, Simon has identified some butchery marks, some of which run across the 'wound' and down the edge of the break. So if it *was* post mortem, this hole would have to have been made between the death of the horse and the removal of flesh by a hominid equipped with a flint tool. This really leaves little room for anything other than a spear wound, inflicted from a distance by throwing or from close to by thrusting (but remember Knight's comment that the 'break was so clean, which usually means high velocity'). It is impossible to tell what role this spear played, if any, in the death of the animal.

We do not know of any similar bone damage of even approximately this age. But this is not the full story, for when the Boxgrove horse scapula was excavated two wooden objects that might have been spears were already known. The first and older, which we have briefly referred to before, was found in 1911 by Samuel Hazzledine Warren on the foreshore at Clacton in Essex, England, in an interglacial freshwater sediment comparable to that at Selsey (*see* Chapter 26) known for its fossils and fragments of wood. The other, a longer spar broken into ten pieces, had been preserved in ancient lake silts near Lehringen, some 35 kilometres from Bremen in north Germany. The Clacton 'spear' is thought to date from between 420,000 to 360,000 years ago (OIS 11) and that from Lehringen from around 120,000 years ago (OIS 5e) – both well before the appearance of *Homo sapiens*. It is a curious thing that these two wooden objects, one at least a pretty convincing spear, have barely featured at all in archaeologists' discussions about the likelihood or otherwise of early hominid hunting. Yet the wound in the Boxgrove horse scapula is around 100,000 years *older* than the Clacton fragment, and over *four times* the age of the German find. Let us look a little closer at these 'spears'.

In the 1970s some archaeologists got together to re-examine the Clacton object (still the oldest certain wooden artefact found anywhere in the world). They found that an earlier attempt at preservation had caused it to lose about two centimetres of its original length of a little under 40 centimetres ('It is not known', the would-be conservators had written, 'at what stage in the proceedings shrinkage and warping took place'), and that its tip drooped in a most un-spearlike manner. But the archaeologists agreed that it probably was the tip from a former spear, laboriously whittled in fresh yew wood. They looked at records of hunting spears in museums from around the world and decided that the Clacton implement was not a throwing but a thrusting spear (as the major difference between these two seems to lie in the weight and thickness relative to length – slender to throw, thick and strong to thrust – this is perhaps a debatable argument for such a short fragment). They rejected the likelihood that it was part of a game stake from a hunting pit or a stick for digging up plant roots: the shape was wrong, and anyway the care and effort given to making the long tapering point seemed appropriate only for a spear.

K. H. Jacob-Friesen, the archaeologist who found the Lehringen object (in 1948) thought that was a thrusting spear too, although here also the case against throwing is questionable: the spear is quite slender and really looks a little timid for elephanticide at close quarters. But what a find! Not only was this a complete object 2.4 metres long (albeit broken), but it actually lay amongst the ribs of an extinct elephant (or so we are told: the evidence has never been fully described). And like the Clacton fragment, the Lehringen spear is made from yew.

As a possible analogy, Jacob-Friesen referred to the hunting techniques of 'Pygmies' in the Cameroon, where, it had been reported, a lone man would stalk an elephant in the forest with a two-metre spear and thrust it into the animal's body with both hands; it would be trailed for several days before eventually it died from the deep wound.

That these objects are both of yew may be more than coincidence. Yew wood is tough (hence its use for bows in the Middle Ages) and durable (good for fence posts), features that might recommend it for spears. It is an extremely hard wood to work, and, as we found out with the piece carved for the *Horizon* experiment in Cardiff, will furnish a very sharp point. It is even possible to imagine that a poison might have been made from the fruit or leaves of the same tree. Wild browsing animals naturally avoid eating yew, but domestic stock have lost this sensitivity, which is why yew trees in Britain are often found in the enclosure of a churchyard; even dead foliage can be fatal. Whatever the wood from which the presumed Boxgrove spear was carved, it could not have been an easy thing to make. Like the antler hammers for working flint found at the dig (a second one was to be found in August 1996), a spear could hardly be the product of a creature with no ability to plan for the future.

So taken by themselves, these evidences for hunting with spears – the Boxgrove scapula and the wooden artefact from Clacton (both pre-neanderthal) and the more recent object from Lehringen – were vanishingly small. And the little interest the last two had inspired amongst most archaeologists is indicated by the fact that, as far as we know, this drawing of the Lehringen spear (fig 49) is the first to appear in an English language book. But in the new picture emerging from the Boxgrove excavation these data seemed convincing enough. Mark was by now feeling the real question was not so much *whether* the hominids were hunting, but *how*. In the meantime there was work to do: research on the earlier excavations as well as the current one had to continue (though of course it was the two hominid teeth that generated most interest), there was to be an exhibition at the Natural History Museum for the new year, and Mark had to prepare a project design for further excavation in 1996. The official line was that English Heritage was not prepared to spend more money on digging up Boxgrove – but if you've got a bit of spare time Mark, why not write a full research proposal for a second year?

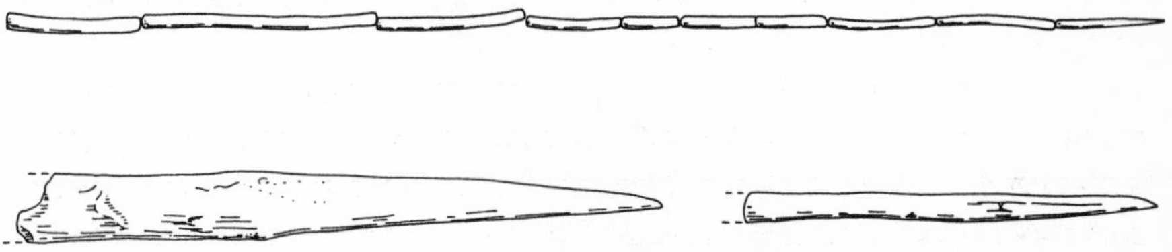

fig 49: Two probable spears, both carved from yew wood. The complete specimen (albeit fragmentary when drawn, *c*.2.4 m long), was found in 1948 at Lehringen between Hanover and Bremen in north Germany. The tip only (*lower left*, *c*.40 cm long) was found on the shore at Clacton in Essex, England, in 1911. Beside this is an enlarged view of the Lehringen tip to the same scale. The Clacton spear is dated to *c*.400,000 and the Lehringen to *c*.120,000 years ago. (redrawn after Movius, Oakley and Perlès)

Chapter 50

Winter 1995–96: Two Teeth, a Rhino and 150 Handaxes

mountain hare

17 November. From the ornate window bright light fell on the expansive clean white surface. There was a faint buzz of traffic from below and a closer hum of machinery. It was warm in the sunlight.

'What we're particularly interested in,' said Simon, 'are marks on the front of the teeth.'

Chris Jones, tall, thin, short moustache, wearing a white pinstriped shirt and dark blue trousers, handled the little boxes on the bright white surface. Inside each was a clear gelatin capsule, like a large pill, which held a tooth. There were two boxes.

In this lab at the Natural History Museum they had a rather special gadget: an electron scanning microscope that required no expensive and potentially damaging pre-treatment of specimens. The effect was like using a high power conventional light microscope, but with full depth of field – everything was in focus. It was not a particularly new technology, but had only recently become accessible, thanks to the frozen food industry searching for the perfect texture on the skin of a pea or the ideal shape for an air bubble in ice cream. The microscope stood in a dark corner of the room, where everything was draped in black. There was a black fire extinguisher on the wall with a black trumpet and hose fit to blast a bull elephant at 30 paces.

The teeth originally sat side by side in the same jaw. Simon

264

arranged the first one in its capsule, stuck onto a scrap of index card with Blu-Tack, and handed it to Chris. He placed it gently into the vacuum chamber, screwed down the door and started the little chugging pump. A fuzzy black and white image appeared on the video screen as a bright line scanned across. Chris twiddled knobs, and a quiet high pitched whine – like an operatic bee tuning its buzz – told of the metal plate that supported the tooth moving about under the control of motor driven cogs. The wall of the capsule blinked on the VDU. He slowed down the scanning rate, and the line of light moved horizontally from top to bottom with a huge improvement in picture quality. Part of the tooth filled the screen – every ripple, every speck of dirt (there was a lot of calculus) described in unreal clarity and detail.

Chris asked what parts of the tooth Simon would like photographed. Did he want more magnification?

Simon looked at segments of the scratches that ran through the enamel across the front of the tooth, and even down onto the root that must have been exposed by a receding gum. He was familiar with this type of scratch: made by a fresh flint edge. The hominid had been grasping something in its teeth – perhaps a piece of meat or the stem of a plant – and cut through it with a sharp knife, nicking its teeth occasionally when it came too close. The cuts ran in such a way that it was clear the knife had been held in the right hand. And there was no question of cannibalism or anything happening after death – the scratches were worn through by attrition from grit in the creature's diet.

Marks like this have been seen before. They are almost universal on neanderthal teeth, in one case on a child's milk tooth found at Atapuerca, an early neanderthal fossil about 200,000 years old – the oldest example known apart from those on the Mauer jaw. Until now.

Later, when Simon had the prints, he confirmed his claim that the two teeth grew side by side in the same jaw. The cuts ran straight across one enamel face to the other. The teeth sat in the front in the bottom of the mouth, right in the line of fire when the jaw was used as a vice for sawing and cutting.

And then there was all the calculus round the back of the tooth (an immediate message of these photos is that the Boxgrove hominids did not practise any dental hygiene). This is a potential mine of information on diet, trapping grit, fossil pollen grains, food debris, bacteria, perhaps even tiny fragments of charcoal and phytoliths (hard particles from green plants). The difficulty was that current techniques for analysis involve cutting up or grinding the calculus. Knowing what's in there might have to wait for new, non-destructive methods of study.

The small exhibition put on by the Natural History Museum opened on 31 December, accompanied by a few stories in the wordier newspapers. On display were the hominid teeth and the tibia, a rhino bone with cutmarks and a handaxe or two. You could also see the antler hammer found in September and a bone hammer excavated some years before but only now recognized for what it was. It was the first exhibition of finds from the quarries since the British Museum show nearly ten years before.

It was not these objects that gave the journalists their story, however, but Mark's growing conviction, fuelled by the results of the 1995 dig, that the Boxgrove hominids were intelligent and powerfully successful hunters. Analysis of cutmarks on rhino bones, he said, had revealed a complete sequence of sophisticated butchery. It began with the hunt.

'I spoke to Britain's leading expert in rhinoceroses, Nigel Leader-Williams. If you trap them at this watercourse here for example, with enough of you, I don't think hunting's a problem.' Simon's analysis of the rhino bones had shown that they were dying in the prime of life – precisely the opposite of what you would expect to find if the deaths were natural, when the bones would come predominantly from the very young or the aged.

'So they're hunting, and they're probably doing that with wooden spears.' The case for this, you will remember, lies in two probable spears, one from England and one from Germany. These are not as old as Boxgrove, but from Boxgrove itself is the horse shoulder blade with damage whose only obvious explanation is as a spear wound.

'Once the animal is down and dead, then the animal is skinned – there are certain characteristic cutmarks, especially around the head, that indicate skinning.' This would have been done as a necessary prelude to butchery, and does not in itself indicate that the skin was used for anything. The rhino was then systematically dismembered and the parts worked on separately. The limb bones of the 1995 rhino were missing, so it looked as if these parts rich in meat had been carried somewhere outside the area of the dig. After all the flesh had been cut and scraped away, the bones were smashed between a pebble and a flint anvil so the hominids could extract and eat the marrow. This, of course, would have been eaten warm and raw. But the rest of the meat was almost certainly also eaten raw. There is not yet any convincing evidence that hominids half a million years ago had mastered the use of fire anywhere in the world. In fact the first solid, undeniable hearths are much later, associated with *Homo sapiens*.

Funnily enough, against a background of giant animals, the Boxgrove rhino was quite small – similar to the modern Sumatran rhino, which, like the rhinos from Boxgrove, is a browser of bushes and trees rather than a grazer such as the larger African rhino. Nonetheless, it still packed in a lot of muscle – say half a ton of edible parts.

But Mark was puzzled.

'There's no evidence of fire at the butchery sites. I'd guess ten or 12 individuals, maybe less: how do they secure this kill? There are lions and wolves out there. How do they keep it? They sit down. Even the best butchers in the world are going to take two or three hours to complete this operation. At the Rhino Butchery Site they bring in the tools. But at the Horse Butchery Site, they've got time to bring raw material in and knap it up on the spot. And then, not just that, then they smash the bones open and they eat the marrow. Finally they take away the major muscle blocks: each man could pack out in excess of 50 kilos of meat. They're obviously organized and relaxed in what they're doing. If you think of modern lion kills, they're always being harassed by hyenas. There comes a stage when there are enough hyenas, then the lion will give up – but we don't see this.

'The view I've started to develop is that it's about recognition of species by other species in the landscape. In Africa today, in areas where there are Maasai, the lions don't bother them, they don't attack their cattle. They know that's not the thing to do. Maybe our hyenas knew not to meddle with hominids. But there's nothing wrong with saying we don't know. At the moment we don't understand how they kept things like hyenas away from these kills.'

And of course there was that hole in the shoulder blade. 'We are not saying that it was made by a spear thrown by Man,' says Mark. 'We are saying that at the moment we cannot think of any other explanation.'

All in all, wrote Robin McKie in *The Observer*, Boxgrove Man was smart and domineering. He 'had the power to plan, hunt, and make and look after tools.'

An image is slowly forming of two-legged creatures that, until modern humans walked the Earth, not only looked unlike anything else, but thought differently too: and that difference was contained in an imaginative, intelligent mind.

At Southampton University, Clive Gamble sat at his desk surrounded by books – not decorative or symbolic of learning, but for use. These books are friends whose every intimate page is known; journals bristle with paper marks; dust jackets are thumbed and torn. As he worked on his latest article the library re-arranged itself around him: a manifestation of thought in practice.

'This is Boxgrove.'

His long fingers wielded a flint axe taken from the desk in front of him. He spoke with care. 'When you hold an axe, it *is* you. Making an axe is a sequence of gestures and actions that says something about you.'

Clive was striving for a concept of intelligent behaviour that embodied something neither chimp nor human, yet was visible in the things archaeologists dig up. It is not easy. An important entry to the problem, he thought, lay in the size of the hominids' territories, the areas of landscape within which individuals worked on their relationships with other members of the species.

A few years previously, Leslie Aiello and Robin Dunbar, lecturers at the Department of Anthropology, University College, London, had studied the anatomy and behaviour of primates as reported by fellow specialists around the world. Dunbar had found that the more a particular species hung together in groups, the bigger the brain and the more time the animals spent on 'social grooming' (a form of physical contact by which relationships between individuals are defined). Then Aiello and Dunbar turned the equation round by saying that fossil brain size could be used to estimate the size of early hominid groups. They argued that encephalization (the increase in brain size beyond that expected for a given body size: *see* Chapter 36) implied that hominids were living in ever larger groups. But as they got brainier and the groups got bigger, the simple limitations of daylight hours and the need to do other things meant that physical grooming was an increasingly inadequate way for an individual to relate to the whole community. Fossil skulls suggest this problem began with the appearance of the first *Homo* species around one and a half to two million years ago, and reached a crisis with the 'archaic *Homo sapiens*', which in Europe means Mauer, Atapuerca and Boxgrove. Yet encephalization continued into relatively recent times (*see* fig 29). So hominids must have found a solution to coping with yet bigger groups and relating to yet more people. It was a solution that Mark had referred to in his letter to *British Archaeology* in March 1995 (Chapter 42). The mechanism devised to cope with large groups, said Aiello and Dunbar, was language.

Clive had for some time been tackling a comparable problem in the evolution of hominids, but from a completely different angle: that of archaeological data. For him the big question was what lay behind the relatively sudden appearance of sophisticated art and ritual, and the expansion of hominids from the core areas of Europe, Asia and Africa into the Americas and across the Pacific. This seemed to be an intellectual phenomenon – a new power of culture and society – and not a physical one that could be charted with things like brain size. Language, he felt, while not necessarily the prime cause, was essential. Yet if language had appeared much before these events – 40,000 years ago in Europe – then it would be necessary to explain why this unique conveyor of rich information, this tool for editing and storing imagination, had had so little impact on hominid behaviour that it left no trace in the ground – following Aiello and Dunbar's argument – for a million years.

Just as animal studies have thrown up a pattern relating primate group size to brain size, so archaeologists have noticed a consistent way in which early hominids appeared to have used raw materials. Common sense would lead you to expect that at any one place, most stone tools made by a hominid would be in the best available (or at least best known) local rock. Archaeological research has shown that 'local' meant between 40 and 100 kilometres in any direction. This seems to hold for a wide variety of hominid species and in all sorts of landscapes.

Clive proposed that this 60-odd kilometre radius was mapping a space within which *all* hominid activities were local: movement of an individual within an area brought them into contact with rock outcrops which they used when appropriate, carrying tools and blocks of material about with them. He called this area the 'local hominid network'. This is, in effect, the environment in which a hominid knew and understood its resources and fellow creatures by more or less direct contact. If we think of Boxgrove, there is nothing there at all that is not *very* local – all the animals are apparently butchered where they died and the tools to cut them up made from flint collected in the immediate vicinity.

From around 50,000 years ago (in Europe this coincides with the arrival of *Homo sapiens*) some objects were moved over much larger distances – the foreign items are always rare, but consistently crop up. A classic (even extreme) modern parallel is the all but contemporary scene in parts of Australia, where stone axes regularly changed hands over thousands of kilometres. In ancient Europe it is not just a few stone tools that are found far from their sources but also other things, such as shells or fossils. At the same time many of the made objects look to us as if they have been carved and decorated beyond any practical function. Antler and bone tools, for example, are very frequently covered in designs showing animals like horses or deer (this is also the time of the great cave paintings). You might have all sorts of reasons for carving the head of a horse on an antler tool, but in no way is that head going to have a material effect on the tool's use (of course you might *believe* this is the case, but that's another matter).

What was happening, said Clive, was that hominids had evolved a way of transcending their local networks: of sending and receiving information in the broadest sense far beyond the limitations of touch and see. The key to this development was the ability to think symbolically. Something complex (imagine, for example, a long walk following paths amongst trees, down one hill, up another, across open grassland, through more trees and down to a wet place where horses drink) can be replaced by a symbol (The River – an entity that contains not just the water, but everything else to do with location, use, danger and specific incidents, and so on). Although the concept is more complicated, thinking actually becomes easier.

Words are symbols (although they are much more than that). So is the horse's head on the antler tool. In fact, as soon as you are open to symbolic messages, everything anyone does or makes speaks to you symbolically. Artefacts – 'material culture' – become an important stream of information. Words do too, but language in that literal sense is not the only – or perhaps even the most significant – method of communication. By using symbols hominids extended their environments indefinitely. These were no longer just physical worlds: they were, in Clive's phrase, 'social landscapes'.

The Boxgrove hominids, leaving profuse evidence for eating, but little else, were constrained within their local networks. They didn't converse in a hut round a hearth – such a large area has now been excavated at Boxgrove, if there were any such things there we would by now almost certainly have found *something*; they didn't use materials that came from somewhere they'd never seen; they didn't carve mammoth ivory into female figurines; they didn't frame their thoughts in an imagination seeped in fantasy, ambition and symbol.

Yet at Boxgrove they littered the ground with perfectly serviceable and skilfully made flint handaxes.

'I can see a situation,' said Clive, returning the axe to his desk, 'where people make artefacts because that's what they are – how they are recognized. For a modern human, a discarded handaxe has all sorts of social value and information. For these hominids that is not the case. The axe only has meaning as part of an individual: the making of that axe and its use in butchery defines them. On the ground the axe has no meaning, so it is not seen.

'Boxgrove society was based on intense physical inspection. Perhaps making handaxes was like grooming is to a chimpanzee. Human social evolution is the process of extending the individual across space and time, of extending society beyond the physical links between individuals. The only way to do this was through material culture.'

Aiello and Dunbar had suggested that brain size and language had grown in parallel as hominids lived in larger groups. But this idea was developed without mention of a fundamental hominid trait, the further parallel of making sophisticated artefacts. Clive is now saying that perhaps artefacts were the adjunct to conventional primate social grooming that Aiello and Dunbar described as early language. It was only around 50,000 years ago that the artefacts and the mental abilities their manufacture required, were put to other uses – were taken over in completely new forms of symbolic communication.

'It was the 150 handaxes,' said Clive, thinking of a visit to the Boxgrove dig that summer, 'that changed my way of thinking.'

As we said earlier, this is not easy. There are several reasons. First, we are trying to understand something that happened in the past that would not be simple even if we could still see it happening today. You only have to think of how the way we see *ourselves* has changed in recent decades to appreciate how intangible these things are. Seen in that light, you can perhaps imagine that there may not be a single, correct way of describing how the Boxgrove hominids thought and behaved – like investigative television films, the view can change according to where we stand.

Then, of course, is the problem that Boxgrove is so very old. Not a lot survives after all that time, even at Boxgrove with its exceptional preservation. And that very preservation can make us forget that we have only one part of that ancient world. There may well be no huts or hearths down on the open plain, but is that the place where we might expect to find such things anyway? Would not the plain be an open, dangerous area entered only to do those very things we see in the Boxgrove excavation? What happened in the forest above the cliff, or along the river valleys? We cannot just make things up to fill those gaps in our knowledge, but we must remember that what we *do* know can only be a minimum.

Many academics today are interested in the question of when and why spoken language evolved. But there is here, as we have seen so many times, the danger of looking only for us in the past. We need writers like Desmond Morris to remind us how important body language is for us. Furthermore, archaeologists, by dint of trying to read stories from old artefacts, have realized how much the things we make are also a key part of our communications with each other. There is more to intelligent thought than the declension of verbs. And there, surely, lies the best hope we have of breaking this impasse. All over Boxgrove, and especially in the dig that began in the spring of 1995, are the artefacts that were central to these hominids: and in them lies fossilized body language, thoughts and intentions. The 150 handaxes, if we really understand them, can change *our* way of thinking, simply because, half a million years ago, they *were* thought.

Chapter 51

Spring 1996: Preparing for the Last Time

bison

Mark had been assessing the 1995 results. For the first time at Boxgrove, all the field records had been entered daily into a computer data base. This of course greatly speeded up the archiving and analysis, but then again there had never been quite so many finds (apart from the handaxes, for example, there were over 4,000 flint flakes that had been individually recorded). The artefacts and the animals bones had gone to stores at the British Museum and the Natural History Museum respectively; drawings and photos had been catalogued and copied; there had been meetings with specialists working on material from the dig, and meetings with English Heritage to discuss progress.

Although English Heritage had seemed decidedly ambivalent about the likelihood of further excavation in 1996, when finally in January Mark and Simon were asked to produce a project design for just that, continuation seemed the only logical option. They appeared to have dug out part of a water hole in which exceptionally informative material had accumulated. Still in the ground was the rest of this limited deposit, with the information that would relate it to known geology to the south. And amongst the thousands of items recovered, the most extraordinary were all on the southern margin of the dig: these were the two hominid teeth, a heap of chalk blocks (cricket ball sized, as a story in the press had it) with apparent scratches made by flint tools, and what looked like the sand cast of a long thin wooden object. The latter finds were still preserved in blocks of silt while conservationists decided how best to clean them.

As well as providing an immediate context for these particular finds, and of course the chance to pick up more hominid remains (not least the jaw from which the two teeth came), total excavation of the spring deposits would greatly assist interpretation. They would know, for example, if the missing rhino leg bones were there – or not, as the case may be; they would be able to state confidently, if the present pattern was confirmed, that while hundreds of handaxes were discarded at the spring, few if any were made there (contrasting with the Horse Butchery Site, for example, where axes were made but none was abandoned). They would be able to explore a poorly understood feature that looked like a large water gulley on top of the sand at the base of the silts.

On 1 of April they started preparations for fieldwork. On the 15th they were down at the quarries. Mark was setting up the site hut and directing machinery to remove the burden from where they wanted to dig. They cut into the steep slope at the back, in a series of large red brickearth steps immediately christened 'the ziggurat'. The staff and a few early students then cleaned up the wet muddy mess, Francis and Matt Pope driving dumper trucks, while Mark and Simon decided where they would put the spoil heaps from the proper excavation. The previous year's dig had been huge: this year's – the last year's – was nearly twice as big again.

One of the first tasks was to complete the wet sieving of some 30 sacks of silt saved from the previous November's baulk removal. It took about an hour to sieve a bag, up at the quarry edge. Water ran down a channel onto the quarry floor into a pool the colour of caramel pudding. At the distant side of the pit the seven brickearth steps rose red against the green cliff.

Later, sieving the dry residue through ever finer meshes in the shelter of the barns, Simon found a small fragment of tooth – part of a root. He took it to London and confirmed his suspicion: it fitted onto the tooth Laura Basell found the previous summer, the reunion of parts separated by a half-million-year-old fracture. In a few days they would have 25 volunteers, rising to 45 in the summer. Yet they'd found a hominid fossil, even before the beginning.

Chapter 52

Summer 1996: A Trip to Spain

beaver

There were 169 volunteers altogether, starting variously between 29 April and 15 September. There were eight large trenches in a row (all gridded with string) so that if you walked past steadily the effect was like watching a slow train as you waited at the railway crossing. But if you looked closer, there were differences. One trench might still have been at the level of the Fe Layer, mostly trowelled away so that it was a chocolate biscuit coloured stain caressing the small hollows and bumps of the surface. Another would be a bit deeper, so you could see the thin undulating dark line in section, like a long thread winding and snapping in the wind. The section face above the line would be lumpy and chalky; below, a very fine cream silt. A third trench would be deeper still, where half a dozen students knelt and sat on the fine smooth cool marbled silt, trowelling with a satisfactory 'scheep scheep' of chalk on a school blackboard.

And these were just the main eight trenches. The edges of the old excavated area had all been extended, there were more trenches to the west, near the spoil heap, and far across the green shrubs and weeds were a few Dutch students digging with Wil Roebroeks.

In June one topic of conversation was the charcoal from a limited area in the north west corner of the main site, in Trench 17. They'd had a little in 1995 – to be precise, 18 tiny crumbs. Now you could see the little black smudges in the trowelled silt, and quantities floated out when the loose material was dropped into tubs of water. On one occasion, Mike Anderton, the Finds Assistant from Sheffield University, processing finds from a nearby baulk taken out the previous autumn, came on a distinctive angular lump of flint; it was two or three centimetres across, its surface crazed like glaze in an old teapot, blotchy pink and purple: the signs of fire. But as the level of this trench went down, the charcoal became less common and the forest of blue flags thinned out until there were only a few and then none. Something had burnt nearby, but whether it was a hearth or a natural fire would remain unknown. It is still unclear if hominids at this date were regularly, systematically using fire anywhere in the world. Whenever evidence for fire exists, it is always in the form of scattered charcoal or burnt earth, really signifying very little. If you wanted proof that hominids controlled fire in hearths half a million years ago, then Boxgrove was not going to settle the issue. If you felt there was no such control then, the absence of hearths in all the excavations might bolster your belief.

Meanwhile, debate about the age of the first hominids in Europe had continued – and in June took on a new and dramatic twist. In January, a lead feature on 'The First Europeans' in the American magazine *Archaeology* had included a story on Atapuerca by Paul Bahn ('the human bones from the Gran Dolina must be between 800,000 and one million years old'). French archaeologist Jean-Jacques Hublin declared that the 'new evidence [from Atapuerca] can hardly be rejected by even the most vigorous supporters of the short chronology'. The editorial quoted Lawrence Straus, an American specialist, who reported that Atapuerca had 'revolutionized our understanding of the European origin of the neanderthals and of the antiquity of the hominid occupation of Europe'. Another American magazine, *Discover*, included the Atapuerca bones in its top 100 science stories of the year. Boxgrove barely existed.

The Spanish archaeologists, of course, were justifiably enjoying their new found glory. In 1995 Eudald Carbonell, Xosé Rodríguez and colleagues had presented a review of the first Europeans in the academic *Journal of Anthropological Research*. They contrasted the old 'short chronology' whose 'supporting arguments have been completely superseded' with what they termed a 'mature' theory of earlier colonization. The latter was 'now solidly in the domain of empirical facts' and 'no longer a hypothesis': 'the first settlement of Europe' occurred close to a million years ago. All the problems associated with 'the long chronology' for the arrival of hominids in Europe (Chapter 30) were, it seemed, raising their heads again.

We need to think back to the discussion of ice age time, and how analysis of marine fossils changed the ancient world landscape

276

(Chapter 28). At first Nick Shackleton had found little support among colleagues in Cambridge, who were wedded to a picture of the ice age founded on ancient pollen (Chapter 26). But there was one scientist who consistently backed him up from the start, whom Shackleton, not surprisingly, found 'always open-minded'. He was a Welshman called David Bowen.

Bowen was impressed with the oxygen isotope sequence from the oceans, and felt the only reliable way to relate it to land geology was to devise a technique of absolute dating that did for the ice age what radiocarbon had done for more recent centuries. He targeted shells from freshwater and dry land molluscs, measuring amino acid change. In a living mollusc, all amino acids are of one particular form. After death, they convert to a mirror image form until there is a balance between the two. This equilibrium takes about a million years to achieve, so by measuring the ratio between the two forms it is possible, other things being equal, to estimate the age of a shell. The technique is known as 'amino acid racemization', or specifically as applied by Bowen, 'isoleucine epimerization'.

In 1989 Bowen and his colleagues published the results of analysing shells from a series of British sites that spanned the last 600,000 years or so. If some of the jargon was a bit of a mouthful, the implications were stark. They found that the sites fell clearly into groups which perfectly matched the Oxygen Isotope Stages indicating six warm intervals between Stages 15 and 5. This was a dramatic early confirmation of the marine data and a pointer to future correlation with land geology: 'existing models of glacial and environmental history, including palaeolithic archaeology, are oversimplified, and require re-evaluation'. Shackleton was naturally impressed. And in time, as we have seen, majority scientific opinion would side with him and Bowen (Chapter 30).

This first report by David Bowen and his team did not include any samples from the higher raised beaches on the coast of southern England. In 1994, however, Bowen and his old colleague Gerald Sykes wrote to *Nature* to report on work they were doing for the Boxgrove project. It had no implications for other more recent sites in Britain, like Pontnewydd for example, where the early neanderthal teeth were found, or for anything outside Britain. But Boxgrove, they said, belonged in Oxygen Isotope Stage 11, not 13, and was 'only' 400,000 years old. While Atapuerca was getting older, it seemed, Boxgrove was moving in the opposite direction.

Then, in June, a weighty academic article by Günter Bräuer of the

Institute for Human Biology in Hamburg and Michael Schultz of the University of Göttingen's Centre for Anatomy, appeared in the *Journal of Human Evolution*. It was about a fossil jaw, and it cut right to the heart of the origins controversy.

The one rock that propped up claims for very early hominids in Europe, and conversely the one problem that needed explaining away by proponents of a late arrival, was the famous Dmanisi mandible. It was dug up in 1991 in southern Georgia, beneath a building in a mediaeval city some 80 kilometres south of Tbilisi. The shock was the date of this fossil, which came from deposits whose age had already been determined: potassium/argon analysis of the basalt below the find suggested an age of around two million years, confirmed by palaeomagnetic studies which indicated normal polarity, presumed to be the Olduvai 'subchron' of around 1.9 million years ago. Suddenly Georgia had become the gateway to ancient Europe. Did these early hominids just wait at the door for a million and a half years (to arrive at Boxgrove, for example, 500,000 years ago), or did they open it and march straight through (perhaps into southern Europe)? The replies to that question can be imagined, depending on which archaeologists you asked. Meanwhile everyone awaited full publication of the evidence.

In June 1996 Bräuer and Schultz provided the first half (leaving the stratigraphy of the site still to come). But preceding their detailed analysis of the jawbone, they pointed out that the dating was hardly as sound as some archaeologists seemed to believe. The potassium/argon analysis related to the rock *below* the jaw, not to the layer in which it was found, and normal magnetic polarity could as equally indicate other more recent periods (*see* fig 21). 'It is still not known', they wrote, '. . . how much time it took for the sediments to be deposited, and how old the bone pocket is which contained the human mandible.' So the evolutionary identity of the jaw became an important part of fixing a date: did it look like a two-million-year-old hominid?

Bräuer and Schultz's reply to this was a resounding 'No'. After exhaustive comparisons of the shape of the jaw and teeth with other fossils, they concluded that 'primitive' characteristics specific to early *Homo* species that might have been expected at two million years ago were absent at Dmanisi. Instead they found many similarities with later *Homo erectus* jaws. The differences were subtle, including such things as the size of dimples in the bone and the shape of the teeth, but they were many and they all pointed to the same thing. 'On the basis of morphology and of the affinities of the hominid', they concluded in the cautious style typical of their work, 'a more recent age [than 1.6 million years] would appear more likely.'

The later *H erectus* jaws in their analyses, excavated in Africa and China, dated from around 900,000 to 250,000 years ago. Chronologically, then (if no more), the way was open for this mandible to be the same hominid represented by the Mauer jaw (whose statistics were not included in their study) and the Boxgrove remains. On the other hand, some anthropologists believe that *Homo erectus* has nothing to do with hominids in Europe at all, but is an Asian variant that evolved from a common ancestor with *Homo heidelbergensis* (*see* fig 1). Certainly it could no longer be used as the cornerstone of theories propounding a hominid colonization for Europe as far back as two million years ago. As we have seen happening before in the search for the first Europeans, the landscape had suddenly changed shape.

In July the Atapuerca research team organized an international conference in Burgos, Spain, to celebrate the first Europeans. There was a clear hope that, perhaps, the invited archaeologists would confirm the Gran Dolina fossils as the oldest hominids in Europe.

Straight from the dig in Sussex, Mark arrived in Burgos on the Madrid train early Friday evening, travelling with Thijs van Kolfschoten. When they climbed out onto the platform they were met by José Bermúdez de Castro, a co-director of the Atapuerca project. Soon they would join archaeologists from all over Europe, including Robin Dennell and Paul Mellars from England, and Juan-Luis Arsuaga, Eudald Carbonell and the rest of the Atapuerca team, as well as Erich Mick, the mayor of Mauer in Germany. Mark had met Erich before. Like Burgos, Mauer had held a conference in honour of the first Europeans: Mark had been welcomed as a fêted guest, bringing a fossil to match their own jaw. If these people could be said to represent the ancient Europeans in their particular patches, it was a convocation the likes of which had never been seen before.

It had all the appeal of a half-term holiday away from school. Far from the doorless portable toilet and the black hosepipe at Boxgrove, Mark sank into the opulence of the hotel Puerto de Burgos. Later the archaeologists met in a restaurant by the cathedral, and over suckling pig and Spanish wine they let the dirty ache of modern travel ease from their bodies, affirming friendships, chewing the fat. Back in his room Mark fell asleep watching the Tour de France.

Saturday morning the tour buses were ready outside the hotel. Only 20 minutes later they were at the Sierra de Atapuerca, a high limestone plateau gleaming under a bright blue sky. They could see the top of the old railway cutting, a deep ravine that had sliced through the caves

279

and fissures left hanging in the rock like an ant nest in a glass box. Out of the coaches they were walked around the various excavations (first meeting Antonio Rosas directing his own dig). All the relevant specialists stood up and did their bits, four or five lectures in English at each stop. They took photos of the sections, they took photos of each other against the sections, they peered at the limestone rubble and the red clays, they photographed the trenches through the taut wire grids and forests of vertical weighted wires. At the sieving area by the river, where students were working with pumps and wet suits, everything looked very accomplished. It was a lovely river, with little pools, stretches of fast water . . . and a huge orange plume of sediment, ruining, thought Mark, some fine trout fishing.

Of course what Mark most wanted to see was the Gran Dolina, where the archaeologists were claiming hominid activity dating from a million years ago. He'd first read of their excavations in the lower levels of this sectioned cave in a 1994 issue of the *Journal of Human Evolution*. There were over 16 metres of sediment, mostly deposited by water flowing in the underground cave system. Eudald Carbonell and Xosé Pedro Rodríguez recognized 11 different levels, starting at the bottom with TD1 ('TD' for 'Trinchera Dolina' or the Dolina trench). The first level in which stone artefacts were common was TD6; higher up, TD10 and TD11 also contained many artefacts and animal bones. They proposed an age for the TD6/7 boundary of about 500,000 years (in Oxygen Isotope Stage 13): TD6 was the last level at which the chronologically diagnostic vole *Mimomys savini* was found. Supporting this was a magnetic reversal at the bottom of TD3, interpreted as the Matuyama/Brunhes boundary at around 780,000 years ago (*see* Chapter 28). The stone artefacts included some acheulean handaxes, so all in all TD6 looked to be approximately contemporary with Boxgrove: which was precisely how Carbonell and Rodríguez described it.

In the 1995 *Science* paper that reported the revised palaeomagnetic dating – pushing TD6 back beyond 800,000 years ago – the assemblage of animals formerly used to argue for a 500,000 year date was now held out to support the new date, the authors, apparently, feeling no need to explain the contradiction. The stone industry was described as primitive and pre-acheulean (in line with the 'longtimers' case). Mark heard through the grapevine that the previously reported handaxes were in fact not well contexted. But what about the fauna? The chronology of changes in small rodents in Ice Age Europe is well documented. Something didn't add up.

In *Science* Josep Parés and Alfredo Pérez-González, describing their palaeomagnetic work, estimated a sedimentation rate in the cave of about 50 centimetres every 1,000 years, or less than a finger's depth in a century. But it seemed obvious to both Mark and Thijs, standing in front of the Gran Dolina section, that the cave had in fact filled up pretty quickly. What Thijs had seen and heard of the animal bones supported this. The bones were in reasonably good condition (you'd expect very small pieces in such slowly accumulating material) and there was no dramatic change in the species between TD3 and the base of TD8.

The site geologist said they'd dug a small pit at the bottom and found that the magnetism seemed to be returning to normal polarity. If the cave had filled rapidly, as seemed the case to Mark and Thijs, this looked like a very short period of reversed polarity. But even the filling rate of 50 centimetres a millennium estimated by Parés and Pérez-González would imply a period of reversed polarity of around 10,000 years (unless a large slice of the deposits was missing, but the geologists could not see any change of this type). In magnetic history terms, this is still a brief episode.

The Brunhes is the most recent and still current major magnetic period, or 'chron'. Seven hundred and eighty thousand years of 'normal' polarity during the Brunhes (when magnetic direction is approximately north) was preceded by another chron, the Matuyama, when magnetic direction was reversed, pointing south. But there are also several minor variations within these chrons, known as 'sub-chrons'. To date, for example, eight of these have been identified within the Brunhes. Any of these subchrons could be of approximately the right duration for the laying down of the Atapuerca TD deposit. In particular, there are three that roughly match the previous dates ascribed to the site: the Biwa3 event (350,000 years ago), the Emperor (about 480,000 years ago) and the Big Lost event (around 550,000 years ago) (these events, incidentally, are all named after important geological sites) (fig 21).

Mark asked the geologists about such a possibility, but they appeared to avoid his question. Yet this explanation would fit perfectly the other evidence which Carbonell and Rodríguez had only two years before described as supporting a date contemporary with Boxgrove. This is the same type of evidence that we have used to date Boxgrove to half a million years ago, and is agreed on by mammal specialists all over Europe. The Mediterranean is, of course, further south from the ice sheets that had such dramatic effect on landscapes and ecologies in northern Europe, so some species survived longer in southern Europe than their equivalents in the north. But this is all well catalogued and understood. Asked for his opinion, Thijs van Kolfschoten laughed. 'For us mammal palaeontologists', he said, 'Atapuerca is really not a problem. It *is* contemporary with Boxgrove.'

Mark and Thijs returned to Sussex with renewed excitement about what was happening in the field of the first Europeans. For them both it was a first visit to Atapuerca, and if anything their expectations had been exceeded. The conference and the tours had been well organized, and if they still had reservations about the early date, it was a lovely site with wonderful material and the fieldwork looked first rate. And back at Boxgrove they were being shown some of the new finds laid out on the trestle table in the old milking parlour: two pieces of rare elephant bone and the first scrap of wild boar to come from the quarries. Yet again, the ghost-like map of ancient Europe was on the move.

But what of Boxgrove itself, and David Bowen's claim that it was 100,000 years *younger* than they thought?

As Mark indicated in a reply to Bowen and Sykes' *Nature* critique, things are not simple. Some of their own analyses (omitted from Bowen and Sykes' short letter) allow for Boxgrove to date from Oxygen Isotope Stage 13 as much as OIS 11. Indeed, a decade before, in *The Times* of 17 September 1984, the research team were quoted as having discovered that the high raised beach was 'approximately half a million years old. If the [acheulean] hand axes ... found in these deposits are the same age it shows that early man was in Britain a long time before his presence is commonly accepted.' But more significantly, placing Boxgrove into OIS 11 would make it contemporary with other sites sporting a very different suite of animals. It is impossible to imagine such distinctive faunas living so close together in the same environment for thousands of years.

Adrian Lister, palaeontologist at University College, London, put it well in the *Horizon* film. Imagine, he said, you had a machine that transported you to a foreign country and told you where you were with a number. 'If you looked out of the window and saw kangaroos and wallabies jumping around, but the machine told you you were in Africa, you wouldn't believe it ... you'd believe the faunal evidence and think there's something wrong with the machine.'

One could in theory select a scientific procedure (ignoring others) to argue that Boxgrove dates from any of four interglacials, should one so wish to do. However, many of these techniques are still experimental, and have produced conflicting dates elsewhere, especially for material that is older than 200,000 years. In short, we feel the mammal fauna (*see* Chapter 29), combined with substantial stratigraphic evidence from across Europe, especially from the Thames valley, argue convincingly for placing Boxgrove in Oxygen Isotope Stage 13. That is a firm base from which to assess other dating techniques, rather than the reverse.

By now you will appreciate that dating early hominids in Europe is far from simple! Much of what we have just described occurred not only as the most recent dig at Boxgrove was taking place, but also as we were writing this book. It goes without saying that the controversies will continue, that new sites with new dates will be announced and that old sites will be redated (possibly not for the first time). But we believe firmly that at any one time, it is important in such a controversial field to be highly critical. It is too easy to build complex arguments on slim or imperfectly published data and lose sight of the poorly laid foundations. To repeat what we have said earlier, at present there is still no convincing evidence that hominids arrived in Europe much before half a million years ago. At Atapuerca, the only large, quality excavation with undeniable artefacts and hominid remains where evidence has been claimed for a much greater antiquity for this event, the new dates need to be assessed fully with detailed publication of the geology, the animal remains and the artefacts. Until this can be done, we cannot accept that a rewriting of early European prehistory is justified. Undoubtedly what we need is a reliable method for obtaining absolute dates. As yet, however, as the inconsistencies in the results of studies such as amino acid racemization at various early sites in Britain show, we do not have that.

Atapuerca, Boxgrove, Mauer and a few other sites and finds (and no doubt more to come), perhaps even Dmanisi, all belong to an as yet ill-defined era in ancient Europe. It is the time of the first human-like intelligence in Europe, of the first hominids. We want to know who these creatures were, and what they were doing. No one place can answer all our questions – unless we define that place as Europe. And, in that Europe, although we are only at the beginning of an understanding, we are nonetheless already closer than ever to our earliest predecessors.

Chapter 53

Autumn 1996: Handaxe Thoughts

Mosbach wolf

John Mitchell set up camp at Boxgrove on 8 July. Planning the work in Oxford, he thought of it as his laboratory. When he arrived it was more like a squat.

Simon found space for him in his portacabin, where a trestle table leant against an end wall. On this John stood his Leitz microscope with camera attachment, a transformer for the light, a videocamera attached directly to a computer for exchanging with the still camera, a video screen showing the microscope image, a stand with another camera for photographing the flints, electronic scales, mobile phone.

John's plan was to complete his main Boxgrove handaxe sample at the excavation, going down to the site every day, talking to the supervisors, seeing the objects come out of the ground and having them in his hut before anyone else had a chance to damage them (his research had shown that a very small amount of friction can alter the surface of flint: just kicking around in a cardboard box, a handaxe could acquire edge polish that might obscure ancient use wear). Like his experiment with a real butcher, taking the microwear lab to the dig had never been done before.

On the floor beside the door was his washing kit, a key part of the process that he had spent so long experimenting with in Oxford (Chapter 41). First he would soak an axe in water, to loosen the dirt, ending with a few seconds' dip in a sonic cleaner, which vibrates the water molecules. Then he'd spray it with a weak ammonia solution, wash it again, spray with white spirit to remove any finger prints, and end with a wash in distilled water. It would be dried with a hair dryer mounted on a frame (or a 'hot air fan' as he writes in his thesis).

John had taken a job as assistant to the Dean at his Oxford college, Somerville. This gave him a little money and a free flat, in return for overseeing undergraduate discipline. The grant had run out in April, and with it went the heating, fuelled by metered electricity. It transpired that the job involved coping with the everyday problems of educated youth. Boxgrove, surely, would be better than that.

His first handaxe seemed fresh as a daisy. Yet under the microscope there was no use wear visible: the object was covered all over in a very fine polish. He hadn't seen anything like this before, but it looked natural – perhaps from a very gentle water flow? What if all the axes were like this?

Larry Keeley examined only four or five axes that were fresh enough to preserve microwear, all found in England: two from Hoxne, one from South Woodford (Essex) and one or two from Hitchin (Herts). All these had edge polish consistent with their use in butchery. Only two other handaxes had been successfully studied in this way from anywhere else in the world. These had been excavated by Peter Beaumont in a South African cave called Wonderwerk, and dated from before 350,000 years ago. On both axes Johan Binneman found wear that pointed clearly to heavy use, cutting plant material, perhaps wood and sedge. All these seven axes belong to the same acheulean tradition that is represented at Boxgrove, but none quite matches the half million years of the hundreds of handaxes from the digs there.

Coming down to Boxgrove, John hoped to study another 50 or so axes. At anything from four to seven days per axe, this was an ambitious goal. He would increase the world sample by ten times.

Larry Keeley had shown that of the materials likely to have been worked by early hominids, such as fresh or dry hide, wood, meat or bone, each left characteristic types of polish and striations on flint that were invisible to the naked eye, but clearly distinguishable at high magnification. How these polishes form is largely a mystery: sometimes they look as if material has actually built up on the surface, taking in loose grains, implying that the flint has bonded with substances, perhaps various forms of silica contained in the worked materials; other researchers believe the polish is caused purely by erosion of the stone surface, especially by small particles worn from the tool itself. Whatever the cause of the polishes, John's work had confirmed Larry's claims that they were distinctive (although it was six months of microscope work before he was first able to see what Larry described) and, with more sophisticated equipment, he was refining the technique. With the aid of new Data Cell image analysis software he had hopes of achieving quantified descriptions that would ease the task of comparing hundreds of subtly different patches of wear.

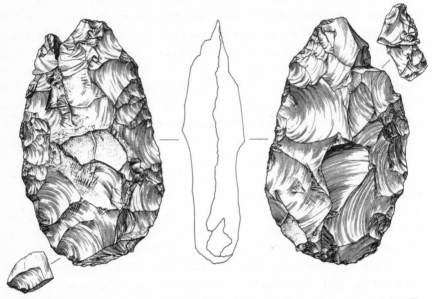

fig 50: A slightly chunky handaxe, stained a brown honey colour, with three refitting flakes. The unfinished look is probably the result of flaws in the flint (top left in left view) which caused the two refitting pieces to break off uncontrollably, at which point the knapper gave up. It would have been abandoned or used as it is. Length 150.5 cm. (drawn by Julian Cross)

After scanning two more axes that had the same fine sediment polish as the first, he explained to Mark that he had to have the freshest found on the dig. He was given a dozen handaxes that came from the base of the silt, resting on the surface of the sand. These were so fresh – he'd never seen anything like them before – he quietly checked with Simon that Frank hadn't just made them. The first one had meat polish, and a little bone wear that might have been butchery contact or from a bone hammer used in making the axe. Now he was away.

John examined about 70 (including those already looked at in Oxford). Slightly less than half of these had the fine sediment polish or were patinated. But around 40 had identifiable use wear, and all except for one which also displayed dry hide polish, had nothing except meat and bone polish from butchery. For several years they had been digging up bones which they knew told of animal butchery with flint tools. Now they had proof of what they had suspected at Boxgrove. They also had the first really substantial explanation from anywhere in the world, that came not just from the microwear but from all the other studies at the dig, for at least one thing these handaxes were used for. As the Oxford butcher said, they were the perfect tools: half a million years ago, the hominids that made the axes knew that already.

There is a little experiment John and Mark did that is worth reporting, if only for its curiosity value. It certainly has never been done before, and may never be done again. As we saw, many of the axes that looked at first sight to be in pristine condition, under the microscope displayed a continuous sheen of very fine polish. By hanging new fresh flint in the little stream that flowed from the wet sieving post, John found that a small amount of gently flowing water could do this – which would fit with other evidence from the dig for such slow water at certain levels. This gave them an idea.

The axes all looked as if they could still be used, begging the question: Why had they apparently been thrown away? Using one of the water-polished axes from the dig, Mark butchered a deer in the quarry. John then cleaned the axe and looked at it under his microscope. Not only did this half-million-year-old handaxe work as efficiently as it must have done the day it was made, but afterwards it was seen to have developed precisely the same type of meat polish that John was seeing on other axes. So the answer to the question was that whatever the reason for discarding the axes, it had nothing to do with them being worn out. It looked as if they might have been used only once, to butcher a single animal, and then forgotten.

Why? Some archaeologists will argue that this shows how little they planned ahead. Think of the effort they could have saved if they'd kept those axes for another day. But really, what actually would they have achieved? A new handaxe is like a pocket full of razor blades, and if you have no pockets (which is not unlikely at Boxgrove – although there is no direct evidence either way for the making or wearing of clothes) that is a dangerous thing. Making the axe may be intellectually demanding, but is not so physically, especially when the raw materials are so close at hand in the cliff. It is a process that need take no more than 10 or 15 minutes and, as Clive Gamble has suggested (Chapter 50) this very act might have had social significance. Perhaps, like a modern knapper, they actually *enjoyed* making axes.

Were there any other flint implements? Perhaps smaller tools were used for different purposes? Well, instantly recognizable tools – flakes that had been shaped for holding or to create a particular type of working edge, by dressing after they were struck from the core – were still extremely rare at Boxgrove. This in itself was not a surprise. There is a tendency for flake tools – scrapers, borers, knives and so on – to become commoner over time as handaxes fall out of use. Archaeologists have distinguished over 60 different 'tools' made by neanderthals around 100,000 years ago, when handaxes are much scarcer and generally smaller. But if few of these small tools were found at Boxgrove, the hominids there might still have been using undressed flakes.

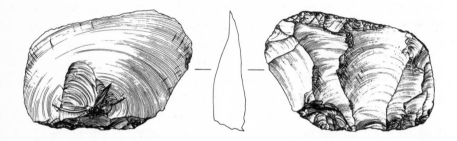

fig 51: Flint 'scrapers', of which this is the best from the digs, are rare at Boxgrove. This piece is too weathered to preserved microwear, so its purpose will remain unknown. Like the fine handaxes, tools of this type were conventionally thought to be much younger than 500,000 years. Width 10 cm. (drawn by Julian Cross)

Whenever a flint flake came out of the ground that looked as if it had been used – usually because of a patch of fine regular damage on an otherwise sharp edge – Mark passed it on to John. Over the three months he was at the excavation, he scanned hundreds of flakes. Most of these, however, once put under the microscope, showed no evidence of use. Just 40 – a small fraction of the number of handaxes – did have microwear: and this was just more of the same, meat and bone polish.

It would be silly to extrapolate from this one project and say that all handaxes all over the world were butchery tools – even if we didn't have the evidence for plant cutting from South Africa. But there is a way we can move to a broader view. The microwear studies point to the significance of one key element in the handaxe concept: the sharp strong cutting edge.

If we think of these objects as mechanisms for supporting that edge, the shape of a handaxe becomes the outcome of reconciling the demands of achieving the longest, sharpest and toughest edge with three restraints: the need to manipulate the axe, and the limitations of available raw material and of stone knapping technology. Any aerodynamic properties (Chapter 41) are simply incidental. Suggestions that handaxes are in fact waste left over from flake manufacture are also just plain nonsense. The last thing you need for efficient flake production is a long, thin edge (*see also* next Chapter). Again, plan symmetry, so far from implying a complex of specific intellectual talents (Chapter 36) need relate to no more than the drive for a long cutting edge. The ultimate handaxe, if we could remove every other imperative, would be circular. But what about the different shapes that have long fascinated some archaeologists? How do you explain that while the Boxgrove handaxes are predominantly oval, with rounded sides (of the type that some archaeologists would die for, almost), at other places they can be triangular, with straight sides coming to a point, or anything in between, with great variation in the degree of regularity? Nick Ashton and John McNabb have the answer to that.

They guessed that knapping skills, 'cultural sophistication', 'mental templates' or design sense (the sorts of explanations popular with archaeologists) had little to do with it. All the early hominids were interested in, said Nick and John, was a good cutting edge. The 'classic ovate' and what they called the 'non-classic handaxe' (typically dismissed as an ugly piece of incompetent work) were ends of a continuum. The variation was simply a matter of flint quality.

Mark White, a research student of Paul Mellars in Cambridge, set out to test this idea. Mark studied for his first degree at the Institute of Archaeology in London. Like every first year student, he was taken to visit Boxgrove; later he went there to dig. For his undergraduate dissertation in 1993 he wrote about palaeolithic flint technology. Now he is considering handaxes.

He began by taking two major shape groups of handaxes that Derek Roe had defined in Britain 30 years before, 'pointed' and 'ovate'. He then took Nick and John's proposal that the ovate, with a continuous working edge, was the ideal, while the shorter and interrupted edges of the pointed axes were the knappers' attempts to get the most out of far from ideal stone. When he looked at around twenty handaxe sites in Britain, he found this theory perfectly confirmed. All the sites where pointed axes dominated were ones where hominids had access only to derived sources of flint, in river or glacial gravels. Ovate axes, by contrast, were made in fresh high quality flint that either came direct from the chalk, or from the flinty clay deposits from dissolved chalk that cap the soft parent rock.

This immediately solved the old typological conundrum of reconciling geological stratigraphy that conflicted with a theory that coarse handaxes were older than fine ones (Chapter 26). The variety apparently had nothing to do with time, but everything to do with the quality of local flint. At any one site, the great majority of handaxes were ovates when fresh flint was close by; but if the nearest flint was gravel, most were pointed. The effect was a clear benefit in usable edge to the hominids blessed with good flint: 70 to 80 per cent of handaxes at ovate sites had a continuous cutting edge, while less than half achieved this with gravel flint. The explanation for this is simple. A good ovate needs a better quality blank than does a partially flaked pointed axe.

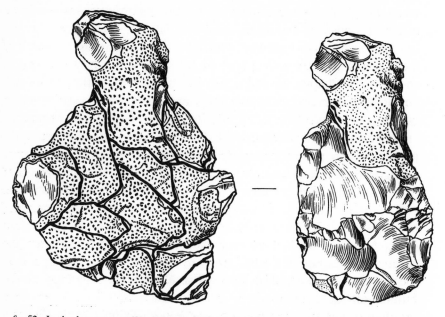

fig 52: In the last century Worthington G Smith found some remarkably well preserved flint working debris at Caddington, Bedfordshire. He was able to refit many flakes together, several onto the handaxes from which they had been struck. The flint was of poor quality, consisting of small irregular nodules. Many of the axes, including this one which he found in 1892, are uneven in shape, and clearly owe their form partly to the limitations of the original nodule. Flakes refitted to the axe are shown on the left, outlined in thick black. The axe is 16 cm long. (drawn by W G Smith)

At Boxgrove, John Mitchell could now support this interpretation with his microscope studies. The meat and bone polish on the handaxes – virtually all of which were ovates – extended all the way round. This had puzzled him at first, because in butchery experiments, many archaeologists used only part of an edge, with straight hacking movements, and actually seemed to prefer pointed axes. Then he saw Peter Dawson using a fine ovate axe (stone number three) to dissect a deer. Without commenting on what he was doing, so that it seemed almost instinctive, the experienced family butcher continuously turned the axe as he worked, using a swaying cut that spread the wear right around the tool and allowed him to use the best edge for the appropriate task.

This is beginning to add up to something big. The years of patient excavation at Boxgrove, topped by the current project, have produced the best database for early hominid activities from anywhere in the world. No one would claim that what we are seeing – efficient and unmitigated butchery of large animals – is the whole story. The apparent absence of almost anything else argues that the hominids were doing other things, sleeping, rearing young, perhaps obtaining different foodstuffs and so on – and no doubt as at Boxgrove, dying – in other places (there is now, of course, an imperative to find some of those places that are well preserved and excavate them – if they still survive; *see* Chapter 35 and fig 6). But equally the meat had to be a key to their survival. And two skills gave them access to that meat: hunting (or almost incredibly efficient scavenging), and knapping.

Archaeologists have argued that handaxes were multipurpose tools, or perhaps *no* purpose tools (Chapter 41). Faced with no apparent change in artefact styles over a huge area and span of time, they have then gone on to berate early hominids for their want of imagination, writing of a 'fixation', of 'cultural ruts' and 'more than a million years of boredom', of 'staggering conservatism' and 'tools than can charitably be described as very crude'. But if we accept that the compelling purpose of the handaxe was to provide a cutting edge, then the long and widespread survival of this tool type is not a reflection of failure: on the contrary, it is a tale of success, of a solution to a problem of survival that could not be bettered. Such a point of view requires, for many of us, a radically changed opinion of our earlier ancestors.

We come back to the question of hunting. When archaeologists, in particular Lewis Binford, first argued that hunting was a recent skill, preceded by millions of years of scavenging, there was a sense that hominid intelligence was being downgraded. Binford himself, as we have seen (Chapter 2), contrasted the old 'mighty hunter of beasts', with the new 'most marginal of scavengers'.

So now, when we propose that Boxgrove indicates highly competent hunting skills at half a million years ago, we are faced with the criticism that hominids were not then smart enough to do it. But such judgements may be missing the point entirely.

Let us suppose, for the sake of argument, that the Boxgrove hominids have nothing to do with us – modern humans – but were just another animal in that landscape half a million years ago, like the bears and the rhinos and the voles. They were there, feeding, breeding, over-wintering and dying, because, like other successful animals, they

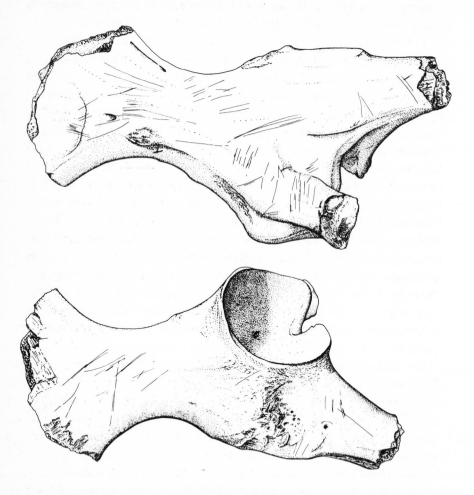

fig 53: Piece of rhino pelvis excavated in 1996 from the surface of the marine sand under the silt, where a dense concentration of bones and artefacts lay in almost totally undisturbed conditions. All marks relate to muscle removal. *See* fig 35 for location of bone in the animal. Length c. 28 cm (drawn by Phil Rye)

had found a niche that enabled them to maintain their population. Let us also suppose, as animals, that they would not do anything that didn't in some way assist their continued existence. If they did – for example, if a family had a penchant for lying out in the sun all summer and doing little else – they would soon be replaced by more survival orientated individuals (this, in essence, is how evolution works: as the environment changes around an animal, inborn differences between one individual and another, however subtle, variously increase or decrease that animal's chances of living and passing on its genes). In this world where efficiency is all, nobody is going to make beautiful handaxes if they don't promote life.

The two uses so far identified for these axes are meat butchery and plant cutting. Binneman and Beaumont suggested that the handaxes they studied from the Wonderwerk Cave were used to cut sedges, and preserved in the cave deposits were spreads of grass stem and branch tip fragments they interpreted as bedding areas. Dark layers containing plant opal (microscopic silica bodies found in grasses) and beetle remains in another cave in South Africa, Montagu Cave, have also been interpreted as indications of bedding. At Stoke Newington in the last century, Worthington Smith found so many fronds of *Osmunda regalis* (a large fern) that he thought they 'represented litter, or the beds on which the savages of old had rested themselves'. It is easy to imagine how these two activities – meat processing and gathering bedding – could be highly significant to survival. In fact, by the definition we are working to – if it ain't essential, it won't happen – there has to be something like this that is *necessary* for survival that only a stone tool can do. So necessary, in fact, that the benefits outweigh the high cost of maintaining a brain capable of creating a handaxe.

We will return to knapping and intelligence: there is more to say. The point we are making now is that we need to dissociate assessments of intellect from judgements of success. Like any other animal, early hominids will have resolved lifestyles that worked (if none had done this, of course we would not now be here). Handaxes were not made on a whim but as part of a viable survival strategy. If the Boxgrove hominids were hunting, it would have been because that was the best way to meet part of their dietary requirements. If they were not, there were better ways.

Clearly it will take, and rightly, more than one excavation and the research of people like Francis Wenban-Smith, John Mitchell and Mark White to resolve what was happening at this time all over the hominid world. As John was preparing to return to Oxford in mid-September, Mark Roberts was thinking about some new finds from Germany that hint at what is yet to come. The man who rescued them from brown coal mines at Schöningen, where he has been excavating for several years, is Hartmut Thieme. Mark had met Hartmut in the spring on a trip to Germany to see the objects, and again at the Burgos conference. Now he was translating his paper for publication in an English science journal.

Hartmut's unique find consisted of three spears that at 300,000 or 400,000 years old are by far the most ancient in the world: three spruce wood spears, one of which was two and a third metres long, shaped in every respect like modern javelins. If archaeologists thought the Clacton wood fragment might have been a stick for poking about in deep snow, or if they forgot about the more recent spear found at Lehringen, there would be no avoiding these new finds from Schöningen once they were published. At least 100,000 years younger than Boxgrove, these spears could be very different from whatever made the hole in the horse shoulder blade from the dig. But there has never been anything remotely comparable from this broad era. Early hominids in Europe were making throwing spears.

Chapter 54

September 1996: Like Playing Chess

badger

'We would then be on top a 75-metre high cliff', said Mark, setting the scene as he stood on the track above the quarries, addressing a group of English Heritage archaeologists and advisers. 'You'd be able to see the chalk sweeping across over there', he gestured to the east, to the left of the track, 'round to what is now northern France. The English Channel had not broken through.' In the other direction, across the seemingly wooded plain and beyond the spire of Chichester cathedral, the undulating grey plateau of the Isle of Wight rose like a monster from the sea. That too would have been part of the mainland, beyond the wide estuary of the now gone River Solent, debouching its rich silty waters into the sea south of Boxgrove.

It was easy to imagine. Suddenly the entire coastal plain, the hamlets and hedges, the trees and electricity pylons, the fields, the roads, the quarries, Chichester with its Roman walls and its out of town shopping and, ten kilometres to the south, Bognor Regis by the sea, where the sun now fired a thin horizontal sliver of crumpled gold foil – suddenly all of this seemed nothing but a huge expanse of open landfill that hid the real world: the sweet dense smell of earthy chalk crumbling from the top of the cliff, the wet scrubby plain below, where dimly perceived forms moved warily amongst the grasses and the pools and further out the wide still lagoon protected from the sea by a thin arm of hazy blue land.

After touring the quarries, the visitors crammed into the cow parlour to see the largest display of finds ever mounted at the dig. They listened engrossed as Mark showed them some newly dug up knapping hammers (four in flint, one antler, one red deer bone and one bear bone), cutmarked bones and more than 50 handaxes (a small selection from the summer's bag: from an area like that, explained Mark, under normal conditions they might expect to get six or seven).

There was one man and one find that had to be brought together. The artefact, the second and better preserved antler hammer (after the giant deer one found in 1995), was dug up in August, but because of its fragility and its very special nature – for some it is actually the single most exciting find of the entire project – it was not out on display but tucked away inside a small card box. The man was Phil Harding. Phil is passionate about flint, and a superb flint craftsman.

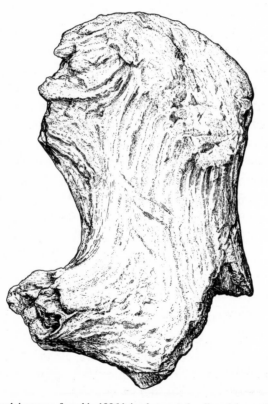

fig 54: This superb hammer, found in 1996 lying between the silt and the marine sand, was made from a huge red deer antler. The original antler would have had a projecting burr at the top, now completely worn away. A small tine projected to the left, and the main beam ran down from the bottom right. These were almost certainly deliberately removed by the maker of the hammer. The degree of wear suggests this tool was used to make a large number of handaxes. Length 15.5 cm. (drawn by Julian Cross)

'What have we 'ere then?'

He dipped his hand gently into the small card box and lifted out the piece of chalky antler. They had now found so many soft hammers that no one at this particular moment could say exactly *how* many – 20 perhaps? – or what animals were represented by all the bones used for these unique tools. But there was no mistaking this one: a huge and perfect flaking hammer cut or hacked from the base of a massive red deer antler. As big as Phil's hand and as thick as his wrist, the tough antler had been pounded out of existence at the working end. A few small splinters of flint had been seen under the microscope, embedded in the antler.

Phil was almost incoherent.

'Brilliant innit, eh? Amazing. This is to me . . . this's gotta be the most . . . it's more important than the handaxes.'

Anything more important than handaxes to Phil had to be pretty big. Palaeolithic archaeologist John Wymer came to have a look, and they started to talk about the flint at Boxgrove. They'd seen quite a few axes from the site over the years, and Phil had made tools for John Mitchell's butchery experiment with stone from the quarries.

'The thing that struck me, making these implements for John, was that anyone making a Boxgrove handaxe 'as got to have some sort of sense in their head – they ain't stupid. That flint, it's the most – well, I won't say it's the *most* awkward, but you've got to think about it. It goes in and out, you've got a little tiny bit in between all these nodules to get what you want. I ain't never knapped flint like it'.

'How long to make one handaxe?' asked John Wymer.

'It took me a fair old while – mainly because I had to think about it. You 'ave to pick the right nodule. Every one's different. Right from the start, you 'ave to see the finished axe, and think about getting acute angles for future blows. You 'ave to take decisions that are unique to each nodule, just to make the same handaxes. Unless you've got the most elementary piece of raw material, you've got to think about it'.

He paused, placing the antler hammer back into its box.

'No, even the best flint, you've got to think'.

Francis Wenban-Smith had been listening.

'The ability to make a handaxe says everything you need to know about *Homo heidelbergensis*. People say it's just banging rocks together. But ask anyone who has to make a handaxe and you'll get a different story. It's all planning: from the moment you pick up a

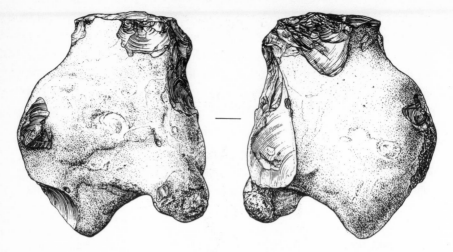

fig 55: A creamy white flint nodule used as a hammer, heavily crushed around the top. This was found in the soil horizon that formed when the sea had left a wide grassy plain at the foot of the chalk cliffs. In earlier layers, when the original beach at the cliff was still exposed, pebbles were preferred over fresh flint for hard hammers. Length 9.5 cm. (drawn by Julian Cross)

nodule, you have to have an idea of where the handaxe is. If you follow the path of least resistance, you will remove parts of your axe. The tranchet tip requires immense foresight – the edge must be left unworked till the end, to leave a platform for removal of the flake. And all the time you're weighing benefits in one area against advantages in another – thinness, straightness of edge, symmetry'.

'It's like chess', he said. 'Sometimes you have to think five or six moves ahead. And you don't think about shaping first, then thinning and then sharpening: your head is full of such abstract concepts every time you remove a flake. It's like playing chess'.

Well, two of the country's best flint knappers were agreed on one thing: making a flint handaxe is not easy, and it's certainly not – as so many academics claim – just a matter of practised repetitive movements. It's an intellectual exercise, where problems are being solved in the mind at every turn. 'Only a cabinet-maker', Jacques Pelegrin, an experienced French knapper, has written, 'can understand what another cabinet-maker is doing'.

Indeed, independently of the conversation in the old cow parlour at Boxgrove, Jacques told *National Geographic* for a 1996 article on neanderthals that you need brains to knap flint.

'It takes months, if not years, to learn to do it well', he said.

'It would be like playing chess for us'.

Chapter 55

Fairweather Eden

Hundsheim rhino

White. Pure, white. Bright soft white. Then night: dark rhythmic sounds in the damp cold black. Then bright. Then night – night brightening, blue light on shadows that work up and work down in silent muscular rhythm, moving through the smothering damp white, on through the brightening night and on again. They talk as they hang in the white, exchanging hoots and honks across the huge measureless distance of shapeless form, working on and on, more drifting now on still straight wings until they know it is time and with excited kwornks and hoots the whole long line slowly turns in a sensuous curve and starts to fall.

The forest roof is breaking up as trees lose their green, a patchwork of broken lines and surfaces, part dark and solid, part open, inviting wind and rain. The trail of swans undulates as one breaks its hold and flexes in deliberate short thrust and the movement passes down, bird after bird quickly lifting and plunging its huge straight white wings. They fly on above the trees, keeping height with rhythmic beat until they see the end of the forest and begin the final descent to the wet pool spattered plain. Gliding low towards the cliff edge they see a movement under the bare oaks and elms, a brown flow of danger, creatures swarming on the land. They hear the hoarse cries, the blundering feet in the dead leaves and sticks and mud. And with a honking and klanking they are past, falling down to the open flats.

The forest is damp and thin. Smooth trunks reach high and straight into the grey sky. Some trees still have leaves or needles, and under these there is little light or growth. There is an occasional hole where an old giant has pulled in its branches and stands dead in the vacant space, or has fallen messily into the arms of neighbours. The floor is a maze of paths across the beds of rotting leaves, through bare shrubs and brambles, past shredded bark and crushed saplings, from small leafy tunnels to wide ways torn through foliage and timber. Every creature knows its own trail. Some creatures know the trails of others. One knows them all.

Hungry. I'm hungry.

The infant looks up at its mother.

Are you hungry? I'm hungry too.

Hungry? Hungry!

Yes, I'm hungry. Are you hungry too?

The troop has been walking since before sunrise, padding through the fallen leaves, chattering and shouting, pulling at small branches, running up trees for the viewpoint, rummaging in heaps of dead wood, always on the lookout for food. With so many of them they have to keep moving. In a day or so they've stripped every grub and fungus, eaten every nut and root, and every creature knows their smell and sound. So they keep walking, knowing that soon they will find big food. Now it is time for big food.

A male with one ear bends down to the child, dark hair falling across his face, and they wrestle and punch and fall into the leaves with laughing screeches. The female looks anxious, then joins in the tumble, rolling in the mud. Others echo their cries. A wave of chatter and laughter crosses the forest floor as the dirty brown crowd flows through the trees with renewed purpose.

It doesn't take long for the news to spread. One of several small groups that ran off by themselves has come back to the troop. There is a change in the way everyone moves, in the sounds they make, in expressions. First silence, then a gentle murmur, then silence again, like tide reaching at cobbles. They come closer together, sucking in the ragged edges half lost amongst the trunks and the brambles, chattering quietly and steadily, then open out but this time in a long trail towards the low sun they cannot see, like a snake uncoiling. They're all ready for this. They know what to do.

A large male breaks free and hauls himself up the trunk of a tree. Two more follow. There is a burst of screaming and shouting from

300

high above, a cacophony of arr arr arr as startled rooks flap noisily from dark untidy nests. Small twigs and acorns patter on the ground. Ahead on the trail there are more distant cries, then these too cease. Only the scuffing of feet on the damp leafy ground remains, and the swish of bodies brushing through the forest.

They stop before they reach the cliff, hiding back in the trees. They know this place like they know every place: where to eat and drink, where to sleep, where to hide and where to break out and reach the plain below. Where to hunt. Where to find wood for spears, flint for knives; leaves for staunching wounds, roots for aches. They will be here some time. One by one, in groups of three, four and more, they break off and start to rediscover their latest home.

When they are ready and the wind is right, they move down onto the plain. This is a different sort of movement: not a mass ramble in the forest, splitting and regrouping, retracing paths and resting in trees. This is organized and efficient, every step deliberate. Most of them stay up on the cliff where they cannot disturb the prey. The whole lot of them could go down, every one brandishing a spear, but if the prey smelt them and ran, nothing could catch it or stop it. Yet one individual with true spear and crafty pace could kill it before it even knew the danger.

Not that they ever hunt like that. This time there are about a dozen of them. Most know the prey better than their mates. They know how it eats and sleeps, how it drinks and gives birth, how it talks through its nostrils and scents with its urine. They know the soft fleshy skin of the lips, the sweet glutinous swallow of the eyes and the warmth of the wet blood. They know every twist and bulge of the hard white frame inside the flesh.

They move silently down the crumbling cliff, each on a different path, finding their own routes to different places, fanning out amongst the grasses on the plain. For one of them this is the first hunt. Another has seen this more times than it has bones in its body; it lost one ear in a fight with another animal, but it still hears better than the rest of them.

And now, downwind of the quarry but too distant to make out any more than a dark shape rising slightly above the tussocks of sedge and grass, some of them know it's a female and that it's pregnant.

It's not so much that they've sat down and worked out a plan: they just know what to do. The scatter of tall scurrying figures resolves into a wide arc sweeping towards the recumbent form of the prey half hidden by grasses. Each figure carries several long thin spears, held horizontally. Each has only one in the right hand.

They are still some distance away when the rhino suddenly moves.

There is a loud snort, a concentrated rushing of air like a wave unexpectedly rising and falling from a flat tide. With a slow heave she straightens her front legs. Her ears work back and forth, scanning the plain, catching every event. Huge flocks of wigeon, teal and mallard whistle and chatter in shrill chorus, brushing the wind in rhythmic swoops. Plovers cry and trill, gulls throw high echoing laughs across the white sheets of sibilant sea whose salty spray tickles the dilating nostrils of the alerted beast. She reads the furtive rustles in the grass, the rasping stems, the flickering ripples in the shallow pools. Shaking her head, she pumps up her rear legs, quivering pipes of pure meat. She breathes noisily, reaching for the air with her lip, exposing wet pink gums. She leans on her stiff back legs, dragging her front legs until they are almost flat on the ground and her bulging stomach smears the grasses with mud, then stands erect and slowly, with a lazy whoosh of escaping air, awkwardly lets herself down until her chin is in the dirt and her mouth is closed and her dark brown eyelashes hide her sight.

Only the hunters are completely still, their strong tall bodies crossed by bundles of thin lines, like hard dead trees neither moving nor attracting motion. All she had to do was turn around and they would have lost her. Now they wait like dead trees, invisible in a silent game of chess.

By the time they start to move again the sun has fallen enough to find a thin horizontal split in the cloud, and casts a harsh light across the plain whose scrubby details dissolve into dazzling patches of water and dark silhouettes. The hunters stalk in the cold wind with sun in their eyes.

They are arrayed a sprint and a spear throw from the prey. The rhino is lying slightly askew to the wind, so on the seaward side they can pass her and face the route she will take if she runs. On the cliff side they can only reach her tail.

They hold steady, facing in, fingers on right hands loosely cradling smooth wood as they feel the balance and the weight of their spears. Heads turn from side to side as they eye each other. There is no noise other than the wind and the birds and the distant sea.

Then two hunters, one each side of the prey, break rank and move inward. They carry their right arms bent, hands at shoulder level with horizontal spears. Their left arms are out straight and stiff, gripping more spears in their strong hands. They lift their legs high over the grasses in slow deliberate movements, placing feet in the smooth mud like startled deer testing the silence.

Their goal is not to kill but to wound severely. The efficiency of their thrusts will determine how fast the rhino can stand, how much time the others have in her confusion to come in and throw and to judge whom she will charge. Although concealment is impossible, perhaps out of instinct they crouch as they walk closer, never straightening their legs or their backs. They both pause; then start again; then pause.

Unknown to either of them, while they advance a jay is picking about in the ground close to the rhino on the seaward side, concealed from that direction by a thick clump of sedge. Now it shows itself by hopping up onto the rhino's back. It sees the spear-wielding figure lit brightly against the cliff, and instantly takes flight with a piercing squark. The noise disturbs the rhino. She jumps to her feet in a flurry of mud and water, shaking her head in a determined shiver and snorting loudly. The first thing she sees is the stunned figure between her and the cliff. Without even pausing to balance, her front feet hit the ground with a loud wet thump and she swings her head down and round into a charge.

The pace slows as the light begins to fade in the woods. They settle down in small groups, in the trees, on the ground, clustered around a trunk where it rises out of the soft bed of rotting leaves, lying, standing, leaning back into the well of a high, massive fork. Children run from tree to tree, laughing and screaming. An early owl shrieks.

At the edge of the cliff a small knot of figures gazes out through serried trunks and bare shrubs across the plain. Hands caress, arms envelop. They can see the arc of hunters close in, pause, move on again. They see the still prey. They see two of their kin move slowly nearer, holding spears straight and steady.

Then something goes wrong. No lance is thrown, no back is stretched and sprung by extended arm thrusting forward to loose the stave that pierces hide like a white-tailed bird enters the sea. The prey is on its feet and they still hold their spears.

It's not the snorting beast that gives him fear. From the horn like a gnarled thumb on the end of its nose, the brown stained teeth at the back of the slobbering mouth, the rilled skin around the eyes, the thick, heavy folds where legs meet hairy belly to the short stiff tail with mangy tufts, he knows this creature as he knows himself. He knows the smells and sounds. He knows where to hurt, where to cut.

It's the bird.

The sudden noise, the brilliant flash of pink and white and blue, put him off balance. They raise within him memories of his own blood. Of pain. Of fear.

At the heat of his shock he throws his spear. It glances off the back of the rhino with a hiss as she lurches to face him with lowered head. But even before her heavy pads push at the dirt he has found his strength back again. Nothing breaks his thoughts but the needs to avoid the charge and place his next thrust true. Feet slightly apart, both arms high, his hands gripping close to the point of his spear, he stares at the rushing beast until he can see down the pink flaring nostrils, leaps forward and sideways, plunges the sharp wood into her shoulder as he rolls away from the throbbing, speeding bulk.

He is aware of other forms moving in, of the sound of wood on bone as a spear hits the rhino's opposite flank. Shouts and cries envelop him. He falls on his side into the rough wet tussocks. He feels the pounding feet in the earth, first steady, then hesitant, steady again, slowing, thumping and shaking the ground.

He lies there on his chest, listening to the voice of the earth joined with that of his own heart until his lungs slow, then raises his head, elbows into the mud. He faces the empty space cleared by the sleeping rhino. And then he sees another prone form. He knows the lips, the tousled hair, the purple ripple where the ear should be. And of all the spears there's one he knows best.

The others just lie around like scattered pine needles.

Chapter 56

Only the Beginning

giant shrew

Across the shiny steel microscope, she extends a long white arm, an arm with neither elbow nor wrist that flexes and reaches with long white fingers for a small white card box. From the open box she lifts a small buff coloured fragment of bone and places it gently between the tips of the fibre optic cables that arc towards the binocular lenses like feelers of a giant insect. She leans over the eyepieces and the heavy fabric of her long black skirt hangs unruffled over the toes of her dark blue trainers with thick white cord laces.

Lucy Gibbons is examining another shrew.

It's a narrow room in the Natural History Museum, looking out over grass through plane trees and traffic to high white buildings. So narrow that the packed shelves of books and files along the back and the cluttered worktop under the window along the front turn it into a passage, a short walk without issue. The small white card box came from a tight array in a wooden drawer that sits on the worktop. It's about two-thirds full and contains 120 boxes; there are four other drawers like this that are full. In each tray is a plastic stoppered clear glass tube a centimetre in diameter and five centimetres long (too long, so that each tube rests with its base in the box on the left and its top resting on the lip on the right, making it easy to pick up). There is a slip of white paper in each tube, whose printed words describe the origin of the bone the tube also contains, in most cases pinned down to the nearest millimetre somewhere within gravel quarries at Boxgrove.

These five trays contain all the shrew mandibles and incisors from the excavations (except for those dug up in 1996, which still await processing). For many specialists, if the entire Boxgrove project had produced nothing but these five trays of teeth it would still have been exceptionally cost effective.

Lucy Gibbons, a final-year undergraduate at the Institute of Archaeology, is looking at the teeth for her dissertation.

Beyond the piled wooden drawers are boxes of more bones, heaps of photographs and box files and, against the end wall, a bank of new metal filing trays. These contain Simon's growing collection of small modern animal bones which he uses for comparison with the ancient material. There is the immaculately cleaned skeleton of a female red fox peeled from the road by the Boxgrove quarries, a domestic cat, a mountain hare shot in Scotland, plaice and cod.

On the small table where Simon works, a blue folder lies open. It contains scanning electron microscope photos of the tooth that Laura Basell found. It looks like a dental nightmare, with the deep scratches in the dentine, very heavy wear on the chewing surface, scarring from disease and bubbly lumps of calculus. There is a rich tale lying in the two hominid teeth, just waiting for someone to work out a way of reading it. On the back wall hangs a large colour picture taken at Boxgrove in 1985. It shows a plastic horticultural tunnel standing in snow.

Lucy is comparing the Boxgrove shrews with those from Westbury-sub-Mendip, the quarry in Somerset which for a time could claim the oldest artefacts in Britain, and which is now famous for the size and quality of its animal bone collection, for the first time bringing together these two illustrious sites. Simon and Andy Currant have an idea that there is a very subtle evolutionary change in shrew tooth morphology that points to Westbury being slightly older than Boxgrove. Lucy is hoping to test this theory.

'I found some *Apodemus sylvaticus* stuff when I was picking over sieving residues at Boxgrove. I got all the books out, and then I showed Mark and he agreed that's what they were.' For Lucy, it's important that she gets things right.

For Lucy, and for everyone else, whether they've worked on the site yet or not, the Boxgrove story is only just beginning. Even as we write, many of the finds from the excavation have still not been processed. But this is just the first stage, cleaning, sorting, cataloguing.

Afterwards comes the research, the questions about this lost world that we want to answer and before never even knew how to frame.

For half a million years ago, these were not trays of glass tubes in white boxes: they were shrews. The gnawed bone in the safe was not a TV star fossil but a hominid, a being. The broken scapula in the conservation laboratory cupboard was a horse, the thousands of bones in packed racks in the store outside Simon's room were creatures that nuzzled and crawled and swam their lives in a landscape that we would recognize. Almost every animal we know today in Britain is there. The rabbits and robins and squirrels from our story books, the bears and wolves of fairy tales, wild ancestors of our domestic beasts, the rats and mice of our warehouses, the fish that we eat. Only there is more than this. To this concentration of natural history we need to add the elephants, rhinos, lions, hyenas and other extinct variants of animals we no longer think of as part of the north European scene. Yet, strangely, it was this mixture of the European and – as we now see it – the African that characterized many Renaissance and earlier depictions of Eden.

And Eden it was, really. A land too unsullied and perfect for us, fit only for an innocent ancestor, where the sun shone and the rain fell until the great ice came. And if we try to communicate with the people of that world, there is no risk that we will spoil them: the only risk is they might touch us.

Lucy stands and runs her hands through her short dark hair. It is coloured with blonde highlights. In a couple of weeks, when she comes again to see the shrews, the hair will be scarlet, and she will wear a scarlet cardigan tied around her waist.

We know what it is to make choices like that. That's what makes us human.

Epilogue

extinct lion

It all began with a determined student out to prove himself. At first Mark was concerned more with geology than archaeology. He wanted to understand the stratigraphy of the high raised beach in Sussex, and see if there really was a preserved ancient land surface as earlier finds had suggested. There was: and his geological achievements impressed English Heritage, who funded over a decade of digging to salvage information from the active quarries. When it was realized, quite early in the project in 1986, that Boxgrove was not 200,000–300,000 years old, but 500,000, and thus belonged to the era of the first European hominids, the already unique finds became yet more special. And by the end of 1996, with the hominid shin bone and teeth, and the extraordinary quantity and quality of data that came from the major excavation in the final two years, Boxgrove's significance had extended beyond northern Europe to touch the very stuff of human origins.

We have come a long way from the savage and brutal ape-humans envisaged in the past. There is a book by the American science writer and anthropologist John Pfeiffer, called *The Emergence of Man*, which particularly well caught the flavour of late 1960s thinking. In arguments that blended the then new ideas of archaeologists like Lewis Binford and Glyn Isaac with the killer ancestors envisaged by Robert Ardrey (it became a standard university text in the early 1970s), Pfeiffer considered the significance of hunting large animals.

'Big game hunting,' he wrote, 'represented ... a major challenge which perhaps more than any other single factor accounts for man's uniqueness.' There is an excitement about hunting, felt Pfeiffer, that enriched the early human brain, which was required to store ever more complex information about the landscape. 'Meat eating led step by imperceptible step to more and more elaborate hunting techniques and gradually transformed man.' And he meant 'man': as males went off to hunt, amongst all primates, women became 'the first females to be left behind.'

Pfeiffer was impressed by the evidence from three excavations in southern Europe (at Terra Amata in France and Ambrona and Torralba in Spain). Here were found quantities of stone tools with bones of large animals like elephants, horses and deer. Before long, however, other archaeologists showed that the deposits containing these finds were not as perfectly preserved as their excavators had believed. Water had jumbled things up, so that there was no reason for assuming the animals were contemporary with the tools, still less that they had been killed by hominids.

The realization that these three sites did not in fact present dramatic evidence for hunting came as a shock to many archaeologists. In Europe, as much as in Africa, they then began to think of earlier hominids as meat scavengers rather than hunters, restricted by poorly developed skills of organization and planning.

Now Boxgrove has produced the most complete case from anywhere in the world that early hominids were after all, at least in northern Europe, hunting large animals. Perhaps not all archaeologists will be ready to accept the argument, but when you think of the putative spear wound in the horse scapula, the evidence for skilled, unhurried butchery of fit and mature animals (from Boxgrove) and the three wooden spears newly found at Schöningen, you start to wonder how much better evidence you could ever find. Nonetheless, whether meat was obtained by killing or by scavenging, or a combination of the two, there is no doubt that these hominids understood their environment well and exercised a not inconsiderable degree of planning and foresight. There is also clear evidence that they were able to adapt to severe changes in climate, as flint artefacts have been found at Boxgrove in just about every geological stratum from the warmest to the coldest eras.

Are we then back to square one? Were our ancestors bloodthirsty hunters who got smart on meat? Can we feel the aggressive carnivore rising anew within us?

In one sense, it seems, John Pfeiffer was right: meat eating and the evolution of a large brain in our genus were connected. However, it was not the mental stimulus of the hunt that fired up the brain cells. If this alone was the cause, then we would have to explain why carnivores such as lions or ferrets, undeniably better natural hunters than us, are not also more intelligent. And then consider the chimpanzee (when Pfeiffer wrote, Jane Goodall had only recently reported the very first modern sighting of chimps hunting). Although meat is a small part of their diet, they do hunt, occasionally killing monkeys or baboons. The chase brings together several chimps in apparent cooperation and scheming, and causes considerable excitement within the whole troop. Yet no one has argued that this relatively rare behaviour determines the chimpanzee's intelligence. Indeed, other forms of acquiring food – think of the skills required for locating and cracking nuts – seem no less intellectually challenging than baboon hunting. No, it was meat in the diet, not the act of running around after it on the savanna, argue Leslie Aiello and Peter Wheeler, that allowed the large human brain to evolve.

If you think of it as just another part of the body, the key question is how can we afford such a big brain? The human brain eats up energy at nine times the speed of the body as a whole, yet our metabolic rate is typical of mature mammals whose relative brain size is little more than a fifth that of ours. So where, asked Aiello and Wheeler, does the extra energy come from to fuel such an expensive organ?

Their answer is that during the course of evolution, as hominid brains grew (or, to put it more precisely, as hominids became more encephalized: *see* Chapter 36), they proportionately sacrificed another very energy-demanding organ. This was the only such organ they could afford to cut down in size: the gut. They could do this because the gut is strongly determined by diet. An animal eating large quantities of food of low digestibility needs a large gut; small amounts of more digestible food allow a smaller gut. So as our ancestors' brains increased in size (all this, of course, over many generations), so they compensated by shrinking their guts, which they were able to do by improving the quality of their diet. They ate more meat.

Around two million years ago, early *Homo* species on the African savanna, increasingly reliant, according to Cambridge anthropologist Robert Foley, on the meat of large herbivores as an adaptation to the seasonal availability of other foods, were walking on two legs and making stone tools, and growing larger brains and a smaller gut. But what caused what? Meat in the diet may have made encephalization possible, but this is not the same thing as saying that eating meat made it happen.

Rob Foley has consistently argued that our hopes of understanding early hominids are greatly increased if we see them not as early versions of us that haven't yet quite made it, but as intelligent animals whose behaviour is as much subject to evolutionary pressure as was their physical appearance. From this perspective, our history is much like that of any other intelligent mammal – the significant difference is that our special interest in ourselves means that, despite obvious gaps, our story is particularly well understood. There is no sense of purpose or direction. Today there is only us, one species of *Homo*. But in the past there have been many, and several species of the australopithecines that came before and, for a period, lived alongside. Each variant evolved in response to particular local pressures, and as environments changed and competing or prey animals with them, so some were better able to adapt than others.

Anthropologists now think that not all australopithecines were vegetarian, but some were omnivorous: meat was then, two or three million years ago, already a significant part of the diet. If we approach the question of meat eating neutrally – they had to eat something, so whatever that was reflected a natural selection of the most successful strategy – then there are just two skills hominids needed to survive.

The first of these was the ability to learn about and understand their environment, in particular their prey animals, so that they could hunt or scavenge efficiently. There is no reason to see this as anything different from the type of skills possessed by chimpanzees, who procure a wide variety of foods which vary seasonally and in their ease of access.

The second requirement is the ability to make tools that allow them to get at the flesh of the large, thick-skinned herbivores that early *Homo* species seem to have favoured. If they had had to rely on teeth and nails, they could not have eaten these animals. A stone tool with a sharp edge gave them that option.

Again, tool-making and -using is not uniquely hominid, but amongst primates seems to have appeared by at least the time of our common ancestor with chimpanzees. What is unique is the type of tools we find with the first species of *Homo*, the habilines. However 'primitive' they might look, the simplest knapped stone implement is beyond the mental capacity of a chimp. Kate Robson Brown, a student of Rob Foley's at the Department of Biological Anthropology in Cambridge, has recently argued this in an extremely interesting study of stone tools from the famous 'Pekin Man' fossil producing caves at Zhoukoudian in China.

Instead of looking for a form of human intelligence (by, for example, using a Piagetian scheme of analysis), Robson Brown started with the rough tools and asked what specific mental abilities their manufacture would have required. Some skills she could see – certain spatial and visual intelligences – are possessed by all higher primates. But others, including the abilities to hold an image in the mind irrespective of the appearance and position of the object being looked at, to correctly discriminate oblique angles, and to understand the relationship between a moving object and a still one, have never been seen in studies of animals like chimpanzees. She concluded that even these very basic implements, which Thomas Wynn would say were indicative of 'pre-operational intelligence' (Chapter 36), reflected something altogether more sophisticated than the brain of a chimp. But on the evidence of the stone tools alone, this brain was not a human one. Indeed, in Kate Robson Brown's words, it 'possessed a cognitive capacity for which no current analogue exists': a form of intelligence no longer to be found on Earth.

The Zhoukoudian tools do not include anything showing the complex bifacial working found on handaxes. We saw earlier how flint knappers like Francis Wenban-Smith and Phil Harding were adamant in their defence of handaxe technology as something grossly underestimated by most archaeologists. On top of all the skills that Robson Brown saw in the simple flakes and choppers from Zhoukou-dian, is the need to hold several sets of spatial intelligences in the mind at once – what Francis compared to playing chess. And yet, as Clive Gamble has surely rightly argued, there are still many things about the Boxgrove hominids, who were among the best handaxe makers ever seen, that distinguish them from us. Their worlds were geographically limited, they did not build complex shelters or permanent hearths, they left no art or evidence of ritual. But just as making a flint handaxe is a genuine intellectual challenge for a modern knapper, so their intelligence is still within us and of us, a complex of strands that makes up but part of the wonderful, inexplicable phenomena we bundle together and call our mind.

As hominids evolved, so stone technology became more sophisti-cated (Foley pointed out some years ago that certain basic technologi-cal concepts seem to be linked to particular hominid species). All the time it was the efficiency of the stone cutting edge that was being increased: everything else was simply a by-product of this effect. It makes sense, then, that for a partly carnivorous species, there would be a natural process of selection for better knapping skills, as these facilitated the acquisition of meat. Becoming a better chess player favoured survival.

With the evolution of *Homo sapiens*, however (and that's another story), the stakes changed. The heidelbergs and their neanderthal descendants in Europe put everything into the hunt. Combining their stone working skills with sheer brute force, they could outsmart both the toughest animals and the harshest climates. But that was not enough to compete with *Homo sapiens*. Our predecessors had built yet further on the evolving brain and, with new social skills of learning and communicating, were able to take advantage of resources that were not accessible to the neanderthals. They might have chosen to eat meat: but new processes, such as cooking, for the first time enabled them to change the quality of natural foods. A gut evolved on a diet of flesh could be satisfied with anything their ingenuity could devise. In the long run, it was the sapient strategy that won.

It seems to make little sense to think of an ancestral hominid deep in our psyches. Which hominid? What part of our psyche? The human mind is such an extraordinarily complex thing, it should not surprise if we say there can be no one point in our evolution when it appeared. But if we still hanker after this antediluvian spirit, we need to search high and low for the aggressive carnivore delighting in gore. Look at Boxgrove. Every animal for which there is any evidence of interference by the hominids has been carefully, almost delicately butchered for the express purpose of consuming the meat. What distinguished these creatures was their ability to make the handaxes, perhaps in their eyes the axes themselves. When confronted with such rich resources as the plain at Boxgrove had to offer, they did not go into a hunting frenzy like a fox in a chicken coop. Instead, they sat down and made hundreds and hundreds of handaxes, discarding them when still as sharp and fresh as new as soon as they'd finished at one carcass, so that they had to keep making more.

So, yes, perhaps we can sense an ancient mind working away. It is the mind of the planner, juggling ideas, evaluating options, finding joy and satisfaction in effective solutions. We are all of us players of chess in a game that took shape hundreds of thousands of years ago. How long it will last, like everything else, is now up to us.

Glossary

Abbevillean An old term (after Abbeville, France) for roughly made handaxes.

Acheulean Bifacial handaxes (after St Acheul, France), sometimes exhibiting very fine form and technical skill.

Australopithecine Common name for members of the early hominid group that includes species of *Australopithecus* and *Paranthropus*. They are found in sub-Saharan Africa from about five million years ago, the oldest being recent discoveries in Ethiopia.

Biface Alternative term for handaxe.

Chellean An archaic alternative to Abbevillean.

Cortex The white crust on a flint nodule. Flint artefacts in the ground for a long time can start to weather, or corticate, in acidic water. This makes them unsuitable for microwear studies.

Encephalization The increase in brain size beyond that expected for a given body size.

Eolith Literally means 'dawn stone'. They were believed, by proponents in the later nineteenth century and early this century, to be very early stone tools that were so crude they had no regular shapes. Now known to be natural stones.

Erectus Common name for *Homo erectus* (coined when this hominid was thought to be the first to walk upright on two legs, though now it is believed earlier forms also had this ability.) The first fossils, from Africa, are slightly younger than habilines (q.v.), and recent finds from Nganddong, Java suggest they may have survived as a local variant in Asia until as a little as 27,000 years ago, alongside sapiens (q.v.)

Habiline Common name for *Homo habilis*, a species of hominid that appears in Africa about two million years ago, and is probably responsible for the first stone tools.

Handaxe A conventional term for a stone implement with a more or less continuous cutting edge that is typically hand-sized, and was probably used in the hand (but not as an axe). The edge is formed by flaking the stone on both sides. In America they are usually referred to as 'bifaces'.

Heidelberg Common name for *Homo heidelbergensis* (after the Mauer jaw, found near Heidelberg, Germany in 1907), in Europe from about 500,000 years ago (or longer). Ancestral to neanderthals.

Hominid Member of the family Hominidae, which comprises all species from us to our ancestors after the split with the apes (i.e. species of *Australopithecus, Paranthropus* and *Homo*).

Loess Deep deposits of wind blown dust, which in Europe are typically derived from the sparsely vegetated areas near ice sheets.

Long chronology A mnemonic for the theory that hominids have been in Europe for as much as a million years or more (opposed to the 'short chronology').

Magdalenean An upper palaeolithic stone working tradition in Europe (after La Madeleine, France), about 18,000–12,000 years ago.

Marl A mixture of clay and chalk.

Microwear A very fine polish on the edge of flint tools that, when examined under a high power microscope, can sometimes lead to the identification of materials that the tool was used to work.

Mousterian The stone working tradition (after Le Moustier, France) typically associated with neanderthal fossils. It includes small handaxes and a series of flake tools.

Neanderthal Member of the species *Homo neanderthalensis* (after the Neander Valley or Thal, Germany), found throughout Europe and west Asia about 115,000–35,000 years ago.

Neolithic The era of the first farmers, who had no metals, in Europe about 10,000–4,000 years ago.

Oldowan The oldest and simplest stone tools recognized, named after Olduvai Gorge (formerly spelt Oldoway), Tanzania. They have a rough cutting edge formed by the removal of a few flakes from a pebble or cobble. The oldest currently known, at c. 2,500,000 years, come from Gona, Ethiopia.

Palaeolithic The greatest stone age era that begins with the first stone tools in Africa about 2.5 million years ago and continues to the end of the last glaciation about 12,000 years ago.

Permafrost Permantly frozen ground, often covered by a seasonally thawing layer.

Pleistocene The geological epoch that follows the Pliocene, from 1.64 million years ago to the end of the last glaciation around 12,000 years ago.

Post-cranial All bones in the body except the skull and mandible (lower jaw).

Raised beach The old shore-line (which may consist of a cliff with sands and gravels) preserved as a geological feature when land rises relative to the sea.

Sapient Common name for *Homo sapiens*, modern humans, who first appeared in Africa around 130,000 years ago (50,000 in Europe).

Short chronology A mnemonic for the theory that hominids did not arrive in Europe much before 500,000 year ago.

Solifluction The downslope movement of loose rock and soil debris over deep frozen ground (permafrost).

Taphonomy Study of the way bones survive in the ground and can be related to the events that deposited them.

Animals at Boxgrove

This is a complete list of animals whose bones have been identified from the excavations at Boxgrove. There will almost certainly be additions as work continues on the most recent finds. Their presence in warm (marine Slindon Sands, lagoonal Slindon Silts and the soil above) and cold periods (the later brickearths and gravels) is indicated.

		Warm	Cold
Fish			
Raja clavata	thornback ray	+	
Anguilla anguilla	eel	+	
Conger conger	conger eel	+	
Clupidae	herring family	+	
Salmonidae	salmon or trout	+	
Gadidae	cod family	+	
Gadus morhua	cod	+	
Gasterosteus aculeatus	three-spined stickle-back	+	
Triglidae	gurnard family	+	
Labridae	wrasse family	+	
Thunnus thynnus	blue fin tuna	+	
Platichthys flesus	flounder	+	
Pleuronectidae	flat fish	+	
Amphibians			
Triturus vulgaris	palmate newt	+	
Pelobates fuscus	common spadefoot	+	
Bufo bufo	common toad	+	

Bufo calamita	natterjack toad	+	
Rana arvalis	moor frog	+	
Rana temporaria	common frog	+	

Reptiles

Anguis fragilis	slow worm	+	
Lacerta cf *vivipara*	viviparous lizard	+	
Natrix natrix	grass snake	+	

Birds

Cygnus cf *cygnus*	whooper swan	+	
Anser anser	greylag goose	+	
Anser sp	goose	+	
Anas platyrhynchos	mallard	+	+
Anas penelope	wigeon	+	
Anas cf *querquedula*	gargeny	+	
Anas crecca	teal	+	
Anas sp	dabbling duck		+
Aythya fuligula	tufted duck	+	
Bucephala clangula	goldeneye	+	
Perdix perdix	partridge	+	
Gallinula chloropus	moorhen		+
Scolopacidae or Charadriidae	snipe or plover	+	
Larus ridibundus	black-headed gull	+	
Rissa cf *tridactyla*	kittiwake	+	
Pinguinus impennis	great awk	+	
Bubo	European eagle owl	+	
Strix aluco	tawny owl		+
Apus apus	swift	+	
Erithacus rubella	robin	+	
Prunella cf *modularis*	dunnock	+	
Sturnus vulgaris	starling	+	

Mammals

Insectivora

Erinaceus sp	hedgehog	+	
Neomys sp	water shrew	+	+
Sorex minutus	pygmy shrew	+	
Sorex runtonensis	extinct shrew	+	+

Sorex (Drepanosorex) savini	extinct shrew	+	+
Talpa europaea	common mole	+	+
Talpa minor	extinct mole	+	+

Chiroptera

Plecotus auritus	common long-eared bat	+	
Myotis mystacinus	whiskered bat	+	
Myotis bechsteini	Bechstein's bat	+	

Primates

Homo cf *heidelbergensis*	hominid	+	

Carnivora

Canis lupus mosbachensis	wolf	+	+
Ursus deningeri	extinct bear	+	+
Mustela erminea	stoat	+	
Mustela luterola	European mink	+	
Mustela nivalis	weasel	+	
Meles sp	badger	+	
Crocuta crocuta	spotted hyena	+	
Felis cf *silvestris*	wild cat	+	
Panthera leo	lion	+	
cf *Panthera gombaszoegensis*	extinct large cat	+	

Proboscidea

Elephantidae	elephant	+	

Perissodactyla

Equus ferus	horse	+	+
Stephanorhinus hundsheimensis	extinct rhinoceros	+	+

Artiodactyla

Cervus elaphus	red deer	+	+
Dama dama	fallow deer	+	
Capreolus capreolus	roe deer	+	
Megaloceros dawkinsi	giant deer	+	
Megaloceros cf *verticornis*	giant deer	+	

Bison sp	bison	+	+
Caprinae	sheep or goat family		+
Sus scrofa	wild boar	+	

Rodentia

Sciurus sp	squirrel	+	
Myopus schisticolor	wood lemming	+	
Lemmus lemmus	Norway lemming		+
Clethrionomys glareolus	bank vole	+	+
Clethrionomys rufocanus	grey-sided vole		+
Pliomys episcopalis	extinct vole	+	+
Arvicola terrestris cantiana	water vole	+	+
Microtus (Terricola) cf *sub-terraneus*	pine vole	+	+
Microtus agrestis	field vole	+	+
Microtus arvalis	common vole	+	+
Microtus gregalis	narrow-skulled vole		+
Microtus oeconomus	northern vole	+	+
Castor fiber	beaver	+	+
Muscardinus avellanarius	hazel dormouse	+	
Eliomys quercinus	garden dormouse	+	
Sicista cf *betulina*	birch mouse	+	
Apodemus maastrichtiensis	extinct mouse	+	+
Apodemus sylvaticus	wood mouse	+	+

Lagomorpha

Lepus timidus	mountain hare	+	
Oryctolagus cf *cuniculus*	rabbit	+	

Bibliography and Further Reading

Introduction
We have avoided footnotes and references in the text to keep it clear. Through this section, the assiduous reader can check up on research and opinions we quote. It is principally designed, however, for those who wish to know more about topics that interest them, and is thus arranged thematically, rather than by chapter. If you are looking for a particular reference, first decide which theme it is likely to appear under, checking the chapter numbers given with the theme headings. For example, if you intend to pursue Wynn's work on stone tools described in Chapter 36, you would choose 'Making and Thinking About Stone Tools', which lists this chapter number. We have chosen many recent titles for their own comprehensive bibliographies: we gather some key ones together here.

Evolution
Jones, S, Martin, R & Pilbeam, D (eds) 1992. *The Cambridge Encyclopaedia of Human Evolution*. Cambridge: Cambridge University Press.
Stringer, C & McKie, R 1996. *African Exodus*. London: Jonathan Cape.
Tattersall, I 1993. *The Human Odyssey: Four Million Years of Human Evolution*. New York: Prentice Hall. A well illustrated guide to primate and hominid evolution by the Anthropology chairman of the American Museum of Natural History in New York.

Archaeology
Gamble, C S 1986. *The Palaeolithic Settlement of Europe*. Cambridge University Press.
Gamble, C S 1993. *Timewalkers. The Prehistory of Global Colonisation*. Stroud: Alan Sutton. A gold mine for the well-informed!
Roebroeks, W & Kolfschoten, T van (eds) 1995. *The Earliest Occupation of Europe*. Leiden: University of Leiden.

Geology
Bowen, D Q 1978. *Quaternary Geology*. Oxford: Pergamon Press. An influential text now showing its age a little, but still worth dipping

into.

Imbrie, J and Imbrie, K P 1979. *Ice Ages. Solving the Mystery.* London: Macmillan.

Jones, R L & Keen, D H 1993. *Pleistocene Environments in the British Isles.* London: Chapman & Hall. An up to date text that should be read with still more recent work that is less equivocal about the ages of Boxgrove, Slindon and Selsey.

Preece, R C (ed) 1995. *Island Britain: a Quaternary Perspective.* London: Geological Society Special Publication 96.

Stories of Ancient Finds
Grayson, D K 1983. *The Establishment of Human Antiquity.* London: Academic Press.

Lewin, R 1989. *Bones of Contention: Controversies in the Search for Human Origins.* New York: Simon & Schuster.

Reader, J 1988. *Missing Links: the Hunt for the Earliest Man* (2nd ed). London: Penguin Books.

Interpreting Archaeological Sites
Binford, L R 1983. *In Pursuit of the Past: Decoding the Archaeological Record.* London: Thames & Hudson. A highly readable review of the author's career.

Schick, K D & Toth, N 1993. *Making Silent Stones Speak.* New York: Simon & Schuster.

How Early Hominid Sites Came To Be (Chs 2, 28)

Many books have been devoted to this huge subject (taphonomy, experimental archaeology and understanding the meaning of early archaeological assemblages) to say nothing of countless articles. Isaac (1989) is a collection of major papers by Glynn Isaac edited by his widow. Binford (1983: reference in introduction) reviews his earlier work. Schick & Toth (1993: reference in introduction) is a well illustrated review of archaeological experimenting by two players in the game. Turn to Lewin (1987) and Reader (1988: both references in introduction), and more particularly Brain (1981, 1989) for discussions of Dart's contributions. Information on the Leakeys' work at Olduvai will be found in Leakey (1971), and again in Lewin and Reader, as well as in *National Geographic* Sep. 1960 and subsequent issues. The interview with Mary Leakey from which we quote (Chapter 2) is in Holloway (1994).

Andrews, P 1990. *Owls, Caves & Fossils*. Chicago: University of Chicago Press.

Andrews, P & Cook, J 1985. Natural modifications to bones in a temperate setting. *Man* 20, 675–91.

Binford, L R 1981. *Bones. Ancient Men & Modern Myths*. London: Academic Press.

Binford, L R 1988. Fact and fiction about the *Zinjanthropus* floor: data, arguments and interpretations. *Current Anthropology* 29, 123–35. (and see comments by H T Bunn & E M Kroll that follow)

Blumenschine, R J 1995. Percussion marks, tooth marks, and experimental determinations of the timing of hominid and carnivore access to long bones at FLK *Zinjanthropus*, Olduvai Gorge, Tanzania. *Journal of Human Evolution* 29, 21–51.

Brain, C K 1981. *The Hunters or the Hunted? An Introduction to African Cave Taphonomy*. Chicago: University of Chicago Press.

Brain, C K 1989. The evidence for bone modification by early hominids in southern Africa. In Bonnichsen, R & Sorg, M H (eds) *Bone Modification* (Orono, Maine: Center for the Study of the First Americans), 291–7.

Holloway, M 1994. Unearthing history. *Scientific American* 271, 37.

Isaac, G 1989. *The Archaeology of Human Origins*. Cambridge: Cambridge University Press.

Leakey, M D 1971. *Olduvai Gorge Volume III*. Cambridge: Cambridge University Press.

Shipman, P 1986. Scavenging or hunting in early hominids: theoretical framework and test. *American Anthropologist 88*, 27–43.

Shipman, P & Rose, J 1983. Early hominid hunting, butchering, and carcass-processing behaviours: approaches to the fossil record. *Journal of Anthropological Archaeology 2*, 57–98.

Sutcliffe, A J 1970. Spotted hyena: crusher, gnawer, digester and collector of bones. *Nature* 227, 1110–3.

Turner, A 1989. Sample selection, schlepp effects and scavenging: the implications of partial recovery for interpretations of the terrestrial mammal assemblage from Klasies River Mouth. *Journal of Archaeological Science 16*, 1–11 (with comments by L R Binford).

Discovering the Antiquity of Human Ancestry (Chs 4, 6, 8, 10, 13)
There is a very large literature dealing with the antiquarian ideas, techniques and people of the nineteenth century and earlier. Anyone new to this field should note that historical interpretations change, that writers frequently quote (or misquote) each other, rather than the

original sources, and that much still remains to be resolved and reported (not least, with regard to McEnery's life and career): which all adds to the fascination. We have included here some of the key modern and historical texts which helped us with this section. Grayson (1983: reference in introduction) is an excellent general survey. The papers by Evans (1860), Lyell (1860) and Prestwich (1860) all report on the visits to Abbeville in 1859. Pengelly published in some detail the literature of Kent's Cavern in volumes of *Transactions of the Devonshire Association for the Advancement of Science* for 1868, 1869, 1871, 1878 and 1884. His manuscript transliterations are reliable. The Torquay Natural History Society has rich manuscript holdings on the work of McEnery and Pengelly.

Buckland, W 1823. *Reliquiae Diluvianae; or, Observations on the Organic Remains Contained in Caves, Fissures, and Diluvial Gravel, and on Other Geological Phenomena, Attesting the Action of an Universal Deluge.* London: John Murray.

Clark, L K 1961. *Pioneers of Prehistory in England.* London: Sheed & Ward.

Corbey, R & Theunissen, B (eds) 1995. *Ape, Man, Apeman: Changing Views since 1600.* Leiden: Department of Prehistory, Leiden University.

Daniel, G 1967. *The Origins & Growth of Archaeology.* Harmondsworth: Penguin Books.

de Perthes, B de C 1847–9. *Antiquités Celtiques & Antédiluviennes.* Paris.

Desmond, A & Moore, J 1991. *Darwin.* Harmondsworth: Penguin Books.

Evans, Joan 1949. Ninety years ago. *Antiquity* 23, 115–25.

Evans, John 1860. On the occurrence of flint implements in undisturbed beds of gravel, sand and clay. *Archaeologia* 38, 280–307.

Frere, J 1800. Account of flint weapons discovered at Hoxne in Suffolk. *Archaeologia* 13, 204–5.

Gillispie, C C 1951. *Genesis & Geology: a Study in the Relations of Scientific Thought, Natural Theology, & Social Opinion in Great Britain, 1790–1850.* New York: Harper Torchbook.

Gordon, Mrs 1894. *Life of William Buckland.* London.

Gruber, J W 1965. Brixham Cave and the antiquity of man. In Spiro, M E (ed) *Context and Meaning in Cultural Anthropology* (London: Collier-Macmillan), 373–402.

Heizer, F (ed) 1962. *Man's Discovery of his Past: Literary Landmarks in Archaeology*. Englewood Cliffs: Prentice-Hall.

Kennard, A S 1945. The early digs in Kent's Hole. *Proceedings of the Geologists Association* 56, 156–213.

Lyell, C 1860. On the occurrence of works of human art in post-pliocene deposits. *Report of the 29th Meeting of the British Association of Advanced Science Notices & Abstracts*, 93–5.

Lyell, C 1863. *The Geological Evidences of the Antiquity of Man*. London: Murray.

Lyell, K M 1881. *Life, Letters, and Journals of Sir Charles Lyell, Bart*. London: Murray.

North, F J 1942. Paviland Cave, the 'red lady', the deluge, and William Buckland. *Annals of Science* 5, 91–128.

Pengelly, H 1897. *A Memoir of William Pengelly of Torquay, geologist, with a Selection from his Correspondence*. London.

Pengelly, W 1874. The cavern discovered in 1858 in Windmill Hill, Brixham, South Devon. *Transactions of the Devonshire Association for the Advancement of Science* 6, 775–856.

Pengelly, W (ed) 1869. J MacEnery's Cavern Researches. *Transactions of the Devonshire Association for the Advancement of Science* 3, 191–482.

Piggott, S 1976. *Ruins in a Landscape: Essays in Antiquarianism*. Edinburgh: Edinburgh University Press.

Prestwich, G A 1899. *Life & Letters of Sir Joseph Prestwich, Written & Edited by his Wife*. Edinburgh.

Prestwich, G A 1901. Recollections of M Boucher de Perthes. In *Essays, Descriptive & Biographical*. London.

Prestwich, J 1860. On the occurrence of flint implements, associated with the remains of extinct mammalia, in undisturbed beds of a late geological period, in France at Amiens and Abbeville, and in England at Hoxne. *Philosophical Transactions of the Royal Society of London* 150, 277–317.

Prestwich, J 1873. Report on the exploration of Brixham Cave, conducted by a committee of the Geological Society. *Philosophical Transactions of the Royal Society of London* 163, 471–572.

Schmerling, P C 1833–4. *Recherches sur les Ossemens Fossiles Découverts dans les Cavernes de la Province de Liège*. Liège: Collardin.

Sollas, W J 1913. Paviland Cave: an Aurignacian station in Wales. *Journal of the Royal Anthropological Institute* 43, 325–74.

Trinkaus, E & Shipman, P 1993. *The Neandertals: Changing the Image of Mankind*. London: Pimlico.
Warren, C N & Rose, S 1994. *William Pengelly's Spits, Yards & Prisms: the Forerunners of Modern Excavation Methods and Techniques in Archaeology*. Torquay: Torquay Natural History Society.

Hominid Fossils, Evolution and Early Hominid Behaviour (Chs 11, 36, 42, 50, 52)

Recommended well illustrated guides to hominid evolution are Caird & Foley (1994), which focuses on changes in behaviour, and Tattersall (1993). More detail will be found in Lewin (1993) and especially *The Cambridge Encyclopaedia of Human Evolution,* both of which have excellent text figures and diagrams. Stringer & McKie (1996) is a good recent review of hominid evolution from the 'second African exodus' perspective (all references except Caird & Foley and Lewin in introduction).

Discussion of 'Boxgrove Man's character' (Chapter 42) occurs in Gamble (1995) and Roberts' reply in *British Archaeology* 3 (1995), 10 and, in more detail, in Roberts (1996a & b).

For fossils from Atapuerca see Bahn (1996), Carbonell & Rodriguez (1994), Carbonell et al (1995) and Parés & Pérez-González (1995); the Dmanisi jaw Bräuer & Schultz (1996); the Mauer jaw Kraatz (1985); British fossils Stringer (1986).

Aiello, L C & Dunbar, R I M 1993. Neocortex size, group size, and the evolution of language. *Current Anthropology* 34, 184–92.
Aiello, L C & Wheeler, P 1995. The brain and the digestive system in human and primate evolution. *Current Anthropology* 36, 199–221.
Ascenzi, A, Biddittu, I, Cassoli, P F, Segre, A G & Segre-Naldini, E 1996. A calvarium of late *Homo erectus* from Ceprano, Italy. *Journal of Human Evolution* 31, 409–23.
Bahn, P G 1996. Treasure of the Sierra Atapuerca. *Archaeology* 49, 45–8.
Bräuer, G & Schultz, M 1996. The morphological affinities of the plio-pleistocene mandible from Dmanisi, Georgia. *Journal of Human Evolution* 30, 445–81.
Caird, R & Foley, R A 1994. *Ape Man: The Story of Human Evolution*. London: Boxtree/New York: Macmillan.
Carbonell, E & eight others 1995. Lower pleistocene hominids and artefacts from Atapuerca-TD6 (Spain). *Science* 269, 826–30.
Carbonell, E & Rodríguez, X P 1994. Early middle pleistocene

deposits and artefacts in the Gran Dolina site (TD4) of the 'Sierra de Atapuerca' (Burgos, Spain). *Journal of Human Evolution* 26, 291–311.

Diamond, J 1991. *The Rise & Fall of the Third Chimpanzee*. London: Random House.

Dunbar, R 1996. *Grooming, Gossip and the Evolution of Language*. London: Faber & Faber.

Foley, R A 1987a. *Another Unique Species: Patterns in Human Evolutionary Perspective*. London: Longman.

Foley, R A 1987b. Hominid species and stone-tool assemblages: how are they related? *Antiquity* 61, 380–92.

Foley, R A (ed) 1991. *The Origins of Human Behaviour*. London: Unwin Hyman.

Foley, R A 1995. Causes and consequences in human evolution. *Journal of the Royal Anthropological Institute* 1, 67–86.

Gamble, C S 1995. Personality most ancient. *British Archaeology* 1, 6.

Gamble, C S 1996. Making tracks: hominid networks and the evolution of the social landscape. In Steele, J & Shennan, S (eds) *The Archaeology of Human Ancestry* (London: Routledge), 253–77.

Hill, K 1982. Hunting and human evolution. *Journal of Human Evolution* 11, 521–44.

Klein, R G 1995. Anatomy, behaviour, and modern human origins. *Journal of World Prehistory* 9, 167–98.

Kraatz, R 1985. A review of recent research on Heidelberg Man, *Homo erectus heidelbergensis*. In Delson, E (ed) *Ancestors: the Hard Evidence* (New York: Alan R Liss), 268–71.

Lewin, R 1993. *Human Evolution: An Illustrated Introduction* (3rd ed). Oxford: Blackwell.

McHenry, H M 1994. Tempo and mode in human evolution. *Proceedings of the National Academy of Sciences* 91, 6780–6.

Monahan, C M 1996. New zooarchaeological data from Bed II, Olduvai Gorge, Tanzania: implications for hominid behaviour in the early pleistocene. *Journal of Human Evolution* 31, 93–128.

Parés, J M & Pérez-González, A 1995. Paleomagnetic age for hominid fossils at Atapuerca archaeological site, Spain. *Science* 269, 830–2.

Roberts, M B 1996a. 'Man the Hunter' returns at Boxgrove. *British Archaeology* 18, 8–9.

Roberts, M B 1996b. And then came clothing and speech. *British Archaeology* 19, 8–9.

Roebroeks, W, Kolen J & Rensink, E 1988. Planning depth,

anticipation and the organization of middle palaeolithic technology: the 'archaic natives' meet Eve's descendants. *Helinium* 28, 17–34.

Rose, L & Marshall, F 1996. Meat eating, hominid sociality, and home bases revisited. *Current Anthropology* 37, 307.

Stringer, C B 1986. The British fossil hominid record. In Colcutt, S (ed) *The Palaeolithic of Britain and its Nearest Neighbours* (Sheffield: University of Sheffield), 59–61.

Wood, B 1992. Origin and evolution of the genus *Homo. Nature* 355, 783–90.

Discovering the Ice Ages (Chs 23, 24, 27, 28, 29, 52)

Our history of the realization that Europe had in the past been partially covered in ice draws heavily on accounts by Hallam (1983, Ch 3), Imbrie and Imbrie (1979: see reference in introduction) and North (1943). Dawkins (1874), Evans (1872; his 2nd edition of this work is still an important text for students of stone artefacts) and de Mortillet (1897) are early archaeological attempts to define time in this era. Chapter 23 was inspired by Cornwall (1970), which though dated, is a very readable description of the ice ages as seen by a younger colleague of Zeuner. The ice age in Britain viewed from the 1970s is well described in Mitchell et al (1973) and West (1977). For current assessments of ice age chronology see Gibbard et al (1991), Hays et al (1976), Imbrie et al (1984), and Roberts (1984) and, for Britain, Bowen (1978: reference in introduction) and Bridgland (1994). For fauna see Currant (1989), Lister (1992) and Sutcliffe (1985).

Agassiz, L 1840a. On glaciers, and the evidence of their having once existed in Scotland, Ireland and England. *Proceedings of the Geological Society of London* 54, 1–28.

Agassiz, L 1840b. *Études sur les Glaciers.* Neuchâtel: Jent and Gassman.

Bowen, D Q, Hughes, S, Sykes, G A & Miller, G H 1989. Land-sea correlations in the pleistocene based on isoleucine epimerization in non-marine molluscs. *Nature* 340, 49–51.

Bridgland, D R 1994. *Quaternary of the Thames.* London: Chapman & Hall.

Cornwall, I W 1970. *Ice Ages. Their Nature and Effects.* London: John Baker.

Currant, A 1989. The quaternary origins of the modern British mammal fauna. *Biological Journal of the Linnean Society* 38, 23–30.

Croll, J 1875. *Climate and Time in their Geological Relations: a Theory of Secular Changes of the Earth's Climate.* Edinburgh: Black.

Dawkins, W B 1874. *Cave Hunting: Researches on the Evidence of Caves Respecting the Early Inhabitants of Europe.* London: Macmillan.

Evans, J 1872. *The Ancient Stone Implements, Weapons and Ornaments, of Great Britain.* London: Longmans, Green. (2nd ed 1897)

Geikie, J 1874. *The Great Ice Age and its Relation to the Antiquity of Man.* London. (2nd ed 1877)

Gibbard, P L et al 1991. Early and middle pleistocene correlations in the southern North Sea basin. *Quaternary Science Reviews* 10, 23–52.

Hallam, A 1983. *Great Geological Controversies.* Oxford: Oxford University Press.

Hays, J D, Imbrie, J & Shackleton, N J 1976. Variations in the earth's orbit: pacemaker of the ice ages. *Science* 194, 1121–31.

Imbrie, J et al 1984. The orbital theory of pleistocene climate: support from a revised chronology of the marine $\delta^{18}O$ record. In Berger, A L et al (eds) *Milankovitch and Climate* (Hingham, Mass: D Reidel), 269–305.

Lister, A M 1992. Mammalian fossils and quaternary biostratigraphy. *Quaternary Science Reviews* 11, 329–44.

Milankovitch, M M 1941. *Canon of Insolation and the Ice Age Problem.* Beograd: Koniglich Servische Akademie.

Mitchell, G F, Penny, L F, Shotton, F W & West, R G 1973. *A Correlation of Quaternary Deposits in the British Isles.* London: Geological Society Special Report 4.

Mortillet, G de 1897. *Formation de la Nation Française.* Paris: Alcan.

North, F J 1943. Centenary of the glacial theory. *Proceedings of the Geologists' Association of London* 54, 1–28.

Penck, A and Brückner, E 1909. *Die Alpen im Eiszeitalter.* Leipzig.

Roberts, N 1984. Pleistocene environments in time and space. In Foley, R A (ed) *Hominid Evolution & Community Ecology* (London: Academic Press), 25–53.

Sutcliffe, A J 1985. *On the Track of Ice Age Mammals.* London: British Museum (Natural History).

West, R G 1977. *Pleistocene Geology and Biology with Especial Reference to the British Isles* (2nd ed). London: Longman.

Zeuner, F E 1944. *Dating the Past. An Introduction to Geochronology.* London: Methuen. (4th ed 1958)

Zeuner, F E 1959. *The Pleistocene Period. Its Climate, Chronology and Faunal Successions.* London: Hutchinson.

Fairweather Eden

Geology and Archaeology of the Coastal Plain of Hampshire and Sussex (Chs 14, 15, 26)

There is no comprehensive review of the earlier archaeological and geological work on the coastal plain. This list includes a selection of references which will provide a good entry into the literature. The Sussex Archaeological Society in Lewes has typed copies of most of Gideon Mantell's diaries, on which Curwen (1940) is based. Also see Zeuner (1958, *Dating the Past* 4th ed; 1959) in 'Discovering the Ice Ages'.

ApSimon, A M, Gamble, C S & Shackley, M L 1977. Pleistocene raised beaches on Portsdown, Hampshire. *Proceedings of the Hampshire Field Club* 33, 17–32.

Bell, A 1871. Contributions to the fauna of the Upper Tertiaries. No. I. The 'mud-deposit' at Selsey, Sussex. *Annals and Magazine of Natural History* 8, 45–51.

Calkin, J B 1934. Implements from the higher raised beaches of Sussex. *Proceedings of the Prehistoric Society of East Anglia* 7, 333–47.

Curwen, E 1925. Palaeolith from raised beach in Sussex. *Antiquaries Journal* 5, 72–3.

Curwen, E C 1940. *The Journal of Gideon Mantell. Surgeon and Geologist.* Oxford: Oxford University Press.

Codrington, T 1870. On the superficial deposits of the south of Hampshire and the Isle of Wight. *Quarterly Journal of the Geological Society of London* 26, 528–50.

Dixon, F 1850. *The Geology and Fossils of the Tertiary and Cretaceous Formations of Sussex.* London: R and J E Taylor. (2nd ed. 1876)

Fowler, J 1932. The 'One Hundred Foot' raised beach between Arundel and Chichester, Sussex. *Quarterly Journal of the Geological Society of London* 88, 84–99.

Gibbard, P L 1995. The formation of the Strait of Dover. In Preece, R C (ed) *Island Britain: a Quaternary Perspective* (London: The Geological Society), 15–26.

Godwin-Austen, R 1857. On the newer Tertiary deposits of the Sussex coast. *Quarterly Journal of the Geological Society, London* 13, 40–72.

Heron-Allen, E 1911. *Selsey Bill: Historic and Prehistoric.* London: Duckworth.

Hodgson, J M 1967. *Soils of the West Sussex Coastal Plain.* London: HMSO.

330

Keen, D H 1995. Raised beach and sea-levels in the English Channel in the middle and late pleistocene: problems of interpretation and implications for the isolation of the British Isles. In Preece, R C (ed) *Island Britain: a Quaternary Perspective* (London: The Geological Society), 63–74.

Mantell, G 1833. *The Geology of the South-east of England.* London: Longman.

Martin, E C 1938. The Littlehampton and Portsdown chalk inliers and their relation to the raised beaches of West Sussex. *Proceedings of the Geologists' Association* 49, 198–212.

Murchison, R I 1851. On the distribution of the flint drift of the south-east of England, on the flanks of the Weald, and over the surface of the South and North Downs. *Quarterly Journal of the Geological Society of London* 7, 349–98.

Oakley, K P & Curwen, E C 1937. The relation of the coombe rock to the 135-ft raised beach at Slindon, Sussex. *Proceedings of the Geologists' Association* 48, 317–23.

Palmer, L S & Cooke, J H 1923. The pleistocene deposits of the Portsmouth district and their relation to man. *Proceedings of the Geologists' Association* 34, 253–82.

Palmer, L S & Cooke, J H 1930. The raised beaches near Portsmouth. *South-Eastern Naturalist & Antiquary* 35, 66–75.

Prestwich, J 1859. On the westward extension of the old raised beach at Brighton, and the extent of the sea bed at the same period. *Quarterly Journal of the Geological Society of London* 15, 215–21.

Prestwich, J 1892. The raised beaches, and 'head' or rubble-drift, of the south of England *Quarterly Journal of the Geological Society of London* 48, 263–343.

Pyddoke, E 1950. An acheulean implement from Slindon. *University of London Institute of Archaeology Annual Report* 6, 30–33.

Reid, C 1887. On the origin of dry chalk valleys and coombe rock. *Quarterly Journal of the Geological Society of London* 43, 364–73.

Reid, C 1892. The pleistocene deposits of the Sussex coast and their equivalents in other districts. *Quarterly Journal of the Geological Society of London* 48, 344–61.

Reid, C 1903. *The Geology of the Country Near Chichester.* London: HMSO.

Rice, R G 1905. On some palaeolithic implements from the terrace gravels of the River Arun and the Western Rother. *Proceedings of the Society of Antiquaries* 20, 197–207.

Shephard-Thorn, E R & Kellaway, G A 1978. Quaternary deposits at

Eartham, West Sussex. *Brighton Polytechnic Geographical Society Magazine* 4, 1–8.

Shephard-Thorn, E R & Wymer, J J 1977. *South East England & the Thames Valley* (X INQUA Congress Guidebook for Excursion 5).

Smith, R A 1915. Prehistoric problems in geology. *Proceedings of the Geologists' Association* 26, 1–20.

Smith, R A 1929. Palaeolith found at West Bognor. *Sussex Archaeological Collections* 70, 196–97.

West, R G & Sparks, B W 1960. Coastal interglacial deposits of the English Channel. *Philosophical Transactions of the Royal Society of London* B 243, 95–133.

White, H J O 1913. *The Geology of the Country Near Fareham and Havant*. London: HMSO.

White, H J O 1921. *A Short Account of the Geology of the Isle of Wight*. London: HMSO.

White, H J O 1924. *The Geology of the Country Near Brighton and Worthing*. London: HMSO.

Woodcock, A G 1981. *The Lower and Middle Palaeolithic Periods in Sussex* (British Archaeological Reports British Series 94, Oxford).

Young, B & Lake, RD 1988. *Geology of the Country Around Brighton and Worthing*. London: HMSO.

The Archaeology of Early Europe (Chs 27, 29, 30, 32, 36, 37, 49, 52)

Roebroeks & Kolfschoten (1995 *see* introduction), the proceedings of the 1993 Tautavel workshop (Chapter 30) is an up to date review of the earlier palaeolithic in Europe (Roberts, Gamble & Bridgland [1995] specifically concerns the British evidence). Bonifay & Vandermeersch (1991) is a survey more favourable to claims for very early hominids in Europe.

Clark (1985) is a useful introduction to the search for eoliths in East Anglia (the John Evans quotation in Chapter 30 is from Evans [1859], listed in 'Discovering the Antiquity of Human Ancestry'). The West Runton elephant (Chapter 30) is well described in a poster published by Norfolk Museums Service, and his bones can be seen in Norwich City Museum. Palaeolithic wooden spears (Chapter 49) are described in Movius (1950) and Oakley et al (1977). The English Rivers Project (Chapter 37) is described in Wymer (1996). See also references in 'Discovering the Ice Ages', (including Bridgland [1994] for the Swanscombe quarries).

Ashton, N M, Cook, J, Lewis, S G & Rose, J 1992. *High Lodge: Excavations by G de G Sieveking, 1962–8, and J Cook, 1988.* London: British Museum Press.

Bishop, M J 1975. Earliest record of man's presence in Britain. *Nature* 253, 95–97.

Bonifay, E & Vandermeersch, B (eds) 1991. *Les Premiers Européens.* Paris: Éditions C T H S.

Bridgland, D R 1994. Dating of the lower palaeolithic industries within the framework of the lower Thames terrace sequence. In Ashton, N & David, A (eds) *Stories in Stone* (London: Lithic Studies Society), 28–40.

Clark, J G D 1985. The Prehistoric Society: from East Anglia to the world. *Proceedings of the Prehistoric Society* 51, 1–13.

Conway, B, McNabb, J & Ashton, N 1996. *Excavations at Barnfield Pit, Swanscombe, 1968–72* (London: British Museum Occasional Paper 94).

Dennell, R 1983. *European Economic Prehistory. A New Approach.* London: Academic Press.

Dennell, R & Roebroeks, W 1996. The earliest colonization of Europe: the short chronology revisited. *Antiquity* 70, 535–42.

Hublin, J-J 1996. The first Europeans. *Archaeology* 49, 36–44.

Mellars, P A 1992. Archaeology and the population-dispersal hypothesis of modern human origins in Europe. *Philosophical Transactions of the Royal Society of London B* 337, 225–34.

Mellars, P A & Stringer, C B (eds) 1989. *The Human Revolution.* Edinburgh: Edinburgh University Press.

Movius, H L 1950. A wooden spear of third interglacial age from Lower Saxony. *South Western Journal of Anthropology* 6, 139–42.

Oakley, K P, Andrews, P, Keeley, L H & Clark, J D 1977. A reappraisal of the Clacton spearpoint. *Proceedings of the Prehistoric Society* 43, 13–30.

Roberts, M B, Gamble, C S & Bridgland, D R 1995. The earliest occupation of Europe: the British Isles. In Roebroeks & Kolfschoten (eds), 165–91.

Roe, D A 1981. *The Lower and Middle Palaeolithic Periods in Britain.* London: Routledge & Kegan Paul.

Roe, D A 1996. Artefact distributions and the British palaeolithic. In Gamble, C & Lawson, A (eds) *The English Palaeolithic Reviewed* (Salisbury: Trust for Wessex Archaeology), 1–6.

Roebroeks, W 1988. *From Find Scatters to Early Hominid Behaviour: a Study of Middle Palaeolithic Riverside Settlements at Maastricht-*

Belvédère (The Netherlands). Leiden: Analecta Praehistorica Leidensia 21.

Roebroeks, W 1996. The English palaeolithic record: absence of evidence, evidence of absence and the first occupation of Europe. In Gamble, C & Lawson, A (eds) *The English Palaeolithic Reviewed* (Salisbury: Trust for Wessex Archaeology), 57–62.

Roebroeks, W, Conard, N J & van Kolfschoten, T 1992. Dense forests, cold steppes and the palaeolithic settlement of northern Europe. *Current Anthropology* 33, 551–86.

Roebroeks, W & van Kolfschoten, T 1994. The earliest occupation of Europe: a short chronology. *Antiquity* 68, 489–503.

Singer, R, Gladfelter, B G, & Wymer, J J 1993. *The Lower Paleolithic Site at Hoxne, England*. Chicago: University of Chicago Press.

Smith, W G 1894. *Man the Primeval Savage: his Haunts and Relics from the Hill-tops of Bedfordshire to Blackwall*. London: Edward Stanford.

Stringer, C B & Gamble, C 1993. *In Search of the Neanderthals: Solving the Puzzle of Human Origins*. London: Thames & Hudson. (see also review feature in *Cambridge Archaeological Journal* 4 [1994], 95–119)

Trinkaus, E & Shipman, P 1993. *The Neandertals: Changing the Image of Mankind*. London: Pimlico.

Turner, A 1992. Large carnivores and earliest European hominids: changing determinants of resource availability during the lower and middle pleistocene. *Journal of Human Evolution* 22, 109–26.

Turner, A 1995. Evidence for pleistocene contact between the British isles and the European continent based on distributions of larger carnivores. In Preece, R C (ed) *Island Britain: a Quaternary Perspective* (London: Geological Society Special Publication 96), 141–9.

Wymer, J J 1996. The English Rivers Palaeolithic Survey. In Gamble, C & Lawson, A (eds) *The English Palaeolithic Reviewed* (Salisbury: Trust for Wessex Archaeology), 7–22.

Making and Thinking About Stone Tools (Chs 32, 36, 41, 53, 54)
The key text for stone tool microwear studies remains Keeley (1980). The late Irene Sala's study (1996) is an eloquent and useful critical review: there are still many unresolved questions in this field, and she well reflects the doubts felt amongst many students at the London Institute of Archaeology in the 1980s. The growing interest in Britain in early stone working technology can be followed in *Lithics*, the

newsletter of the Lithic Studies Society (ISSN 0262–7817). Lord (1993) is an excellent little introduction to the art of flint knapping (ISBN 0–9521356–0–4). See also references in 'The Boxgrove Excavation'.

Ashton, N & McNabb, J 1994. Bifaces in perspective. In Ashton, N & David, A (eds), *Stories in Stone* (London: Lithic Studies Society), 182–91.

Binneman, J & Beaumont, P 1992. Use-wear analysis of two acheulean handaxes from Wonderwerk Cave, Northern Cape. *Southern African Field Archaeology* 1, 92–7.

Brown, K R 1993. An alternative approach to cognition in the lower palaeolithic: the modular view. *Cambridge Archaeological Journal* 3, 231–45.

Calvin, W H 1994. The emergence of intelligence. *Scientific American* 271, 101–113.

Davidson, I & Noble, W 1993. Tools and language in human evolution. In Gibson, K R & Ingold, T (eds), 363–88.

Gibson, K R & Ingold, T (eds) 1993. *Tools, Language & Cognition in Human Evolution*. Cambridge: Cambridge University Press.

Gowlett, J A J 1986. Culture and conceptualisation: the Oldowan-Acheulean gradient. In Bailey, G N & Callow, P (eds) *Stone Age Prehistory* (Cambridge: Cambridge University Press), 243–60.

Jones, P 1980. Experimental butchery with modern stone tools and its relevance for palaeolithic archaeology. *World Archaeology* 12, 153–65.

Keeley, L H 1980. *Experimental Determination of Stone Tool Uses*. Chicago: University of Chicago Press.

Lord, J W 1993. *The Nature and Subsequent Uses of Flint 1: The Basics of Lithic Technology*. Brandon: John Lord.

McNabb, J & Ashton, N 1994. Thoughtful flakers. *Cambridge Archaeological Journal* 4, 289–98.

Mithen, S 1994. Technology and society during the middle pleistocene: hominid group size, social learning and industrial variability. *Cambridge Archaeological Journal* 4, 3–32.

Newcomer, M H & Sieveking, G de G 1980. Experimental flake scatter-patterns: a new interpretative technique. *Journal of Field Archaeology* 7, 346–52.

Pelegrin, J 1993. A framework for analysing prehistoric stone tool manufacture and a tentative application to some early stone industries.

In Berthelet, A & Chavaillon, J (eds) *The Use of Tools by Human and Non-human Primates* (Oxford: Clarendon Press), 302–17.

Robson Brown, K 1993. An alternative approach to cognition in the lower palaeolithic: the modular view. *Cambridge Archaeological Journal* 3, 231–45.

Sala, I L 1996. *A Study of Microscopic Polish on Flint Implements.* (British Archaeological Reports International Series 629, Oxford).

Steele, J, Quinlan, A & Wenban-Smith, F 1995. Stone tools and the linguistic capabilities of earlier hominids. *Cambridge Archaeological Journal* 5, 245–56.

Toth, N 1985. Archaeological evidence for preferential right-handedness in the lower and middle pleistocene, and its possible implications. *Journal of Human Evolution* 14, 607–14.

Toth, N, Schick, K D, Savage-Rumbaugh, E S, Sevcik, R A & Rumbaugh, D M 1993. Pan the tool-maker: investigations into the stone tool-making and tool-using capabilities of bonobos *(Pan paniscus)*. *Journal of Archaeological Science* 20, 81–91.

Wenban-Smith, F 1996. *The Palaeolithic Archaeology of Baker's Hole: a Case Study for Focus in Lithic Analysis.* Unpublished PhD thesis, University of Southampton.

White, M J 1995. Raw materials and biface variability in southern Britain: a preliminary examination. *Lithics* 15, 1–20.

Wright, R V S 1972. Imitative learning of a flaked stone technology – the case of an orangutan. *Mankind* 8, 296–306.

Wynn, T 1979. The intelligence of later acheulean hominids. *Man* 14, 371–91.

Wynn, T 1985. Stone tools and the evolution of human intelligence. *World Archaeology* 17, 32–43.

Wynn, T 1995. Handaxe enigmas. *World Archaeology* 27, 10–24.

Modern Hunters and Gatherers (Ch 31)

The Métis quotation is from York (1990), and the two Presidential remarks are taken from Diamond (1991: reference in 'Hominid Fossils ...'). The Duke of Argyll is cited by Lubbock (1882). The sexual antics of anthropologists are described in Dean Falk's eccentric book (Falk 1992). The closing comment by Foley is taken from his useful paper in Ingold et al (1988), 'Hominids, humans and hunter-gatherers: an evolutionary perspective'. See also Bender & Morris, 'Twenty years of history, evolution and social change in gatherer-hunter studies' in the same volume.

Dahlberg, F (ed) 1981. *Woman the Gatherer*. New Haven: Yale University Press.

Dawson, J W 1888. *Fossil Men and their Modern Representatives* (3rd ed). London: Hodder & Stoughton.

Falk, D 1992. *Braindance*. New York: Henry Holt.

Ingold, T, Riches, D & Woodburn J (eds) 1988. *Hunters and Gatherers*. New York: Berg.

Lee, R B & De Vore, I (eds) 1968. *Man the Hunter*. New York: Aldine Publishing.

Lubbock J 1882. *On the Origin of Civilisation and Primitive Condition of Man* (4th ed). London: Longmans.

Sollas, W J 1911. *Ancient Hunters and their Modern Representatives*. London: Macmillan.

York, G 1990. *The Dispossessed*. London: Vintage.

Chimpanzee Behaviour (Ch 33)

National Geographic has published well illustrated articles covering Jane Goodall's work with chimpanzees at Gombe (Aug. 1963, Dec. 1965 and Dec. 1995), the Boeschs' work in Côte d'Ivoire and the relationship between apes and humans (Mar. 1992), and Takayoshi Kano's study of bonobos (Mar. 1992). For experiments teaching animals to make stone tools, see Toth et al (1993) and Wright (1972) in the section 'Making and Thinking About Stone Tools'.

Boesch, C 1993. Aspects of transmission of tool-use in wild chimpanzees. In Gibson, K R & Ingold, T (eds) *Tools, Language & Cognition in Human Evolution* (Cambridge: Cambridge University Press), 171–83.

Boesch, C & Boesch, H 1993. Diversity of tool use and tool-making in wild chimpanzees. In Berthelet, A & Chavaillon, J (eds) *The Use of Tools by Human and Non-human Primates* (Oxford: Clarendon Press), 158–74.

Boesch, C, Marchesi, P, Marchesi, N, Fruth, B & Joulian, F 1994. Is nut cracking in wild chimpanzees a cultural behaviour? *Journal of Human Evolution* 26, 325–338.

Goodall, J 1986. *The Chimpanzees of Gombe: Patterns of Behaviour*. Cambridge, Mass: Belknap Press, Harvard University.

Goodall, J 1990. *Through a Window: My Thirty Years with the Chimpanzees of Gombre*. London: Weidenfeld & Nicolson. Chapters on chimpanzee and human minds should be required reading for archaeologists concerned with early hominids.

Kano, T 1991. *The Last Ape: Pygmy Chimpanzee Behaviour & Ecology.* Stanford: Stanford University Press.

McGrew, W C 1992. *Chimpanzee Material Culture: Implications for Human Evolution.* Cambridge: Cambridge University Press.

McGrew, W C, Tutin, C E G & Baldwin, P J 1979. Chimpanzees, tools, and termites: cross-cultural comparisons of Senegal, Tanzania, and Rio Muni. *Man* 14, 185–214.

Stanford, C B 1996. The hunting ecology of wild chimpanzees: implications for the evolutionary ecology of pliocene hominids. *American Anthropologist* 98, 96–113.

Sugiyama, J 1993. Local variation of tools and tool use among wild chimpanzees. In Berthelet, A & Chavaillon, J (eds) *The Use of Tools by Human and Non-human Primates* (Oxford: Clarendon Press), 175–90.

The Boxgrove Excavation

The names used in this book to describe the excavations are not always those used on the dig or in the technical publications. A concordance follows. 'Project A', which does not appear in this list, was the name given retrospectively to everything that occurred before Project B.

The feature described here as . . .	*Appears elsewhwere as . . .*
The West Quarry	Quarry 1
The East Quarry	Quarry 2
The Sand Project	Project B
Greg's Project	Project C *or* the Eartham Quarry Project (EQP)
The Hominid Project	Project D *or* the Hominid Project
The First (Handaxe) Trench	Q2A (Quarry 2, Area A)
Louise's Trench	Q1A (Quarry 1, Area A)
The L-Shape	Q1B
Sharon and Simon's Trench	GTP3 (Geological Test Pit 3)
Simon Colcutt's Trench	GTP13
Indira's Trench *or* the Horse Butchery Site	GTP17
The Beach Section	GTP25
Roger's Trenches	Q1B Trenches 1 to 5

Annual reports in *The Archaeology of Chichester & District* (1985–92) are useful for anyone interested in the history of the dig. Much work is currently in the publication pipeline. The Prehistoric Society report referred to in Chapter 18 appears in the *Proceedings* of that body for 1984 (volume 50). The Boxgrove web site is at http://www.ucl.ac.uk/boxgrove.

Austin, L 1994. The life and death of a Boxgrove biface. In Ashton, N & David, A (eds), *Stories in Stone* (London: Lithic Studies Society), 119–26.

Bergman, C A & Roberts, M B 1988. Flaking technology at the Acheulean site of Boxgrove, West Sussex (England). *Revue Archéologique de Picardie* 1–2, 105–13.

Bergman, C A, Roberts, M B, Collcutt, S N & Barlow, P 1990. Refitting and spatial analysis of artefacts from Quarry 2 at the middle pleistocene acheulean site of Boxgrove, West Sussex, England. In Cziesla, E, Eickhoff, S, Arts, N & Winter, D (eds.) *The Big Puzzle* (Bonn: Holos), 265–82.

Bowen, D Q & Sykes, G A 1994. How old is 'Boxgrove man'? *Nature* 371, 751.

Gamble, C S 1994. Time for Boxgrove man. *Nature* 369, 275–76.

Goldberg, P & Macphail, R 1990. Micromorphological evidence of middle pleistocene landscape changes from southern England, Westbury-sub-Mendip, Somerset and Boxgrove. In Douglas, L A (ed) *Soil Micromorphology*, 441–7.

Macphail, R I 1996. The soil micromorphological reconstruction of the 500,000-year-old hominid environment at Boxgrove, West Sussex, UK. In Castelletti, L & Cremaschi (eds) *Micromorphology of Deposits of Anthropogenic Origin*, 133–42.

Mitchell, J C 1995. Studying biface utilisation at Boxgrove: roe deer butchery with replica handaxes. *Lithics* 16, 64–9.

Roberts, M B 1986. Excavation of the lower palaeolithic site at Amey's Eartham Pit, Boxgrove, West Sussex: a preliminary report. *Proceedings of the Prehistoric Society* 52, 215–45.

Roberts, M B 1994. How old is 'Boxgrove Man'? Reply to Bowen and Sykes. *Nature* 371, 751.

Roberts, M B 1996. The age and significance of the Middle Pleistocene sediments at Boxgrove, West Sussex, UK and their associated archaeology. In Beinhauer, K W, Kraatz, R & Wagner, G A (eds) *Neuerfunde und forschungen zur Frühen Menscheitsgeschichte*

Eurasiens mit einem Ausblick alf Afrika (Sigmaringen: Thorbecke Verlag).

Roberts, M B & Parfitt, S 1997. *The Middle Pleistocene Hominid Site at ARC Eartham Quarry, Boxgrove, West Sussex, UK.* London: English Heritage.

Roberts, M B, Stringer, C B & Parfitt, S A 1994. A hominid tibia from middle Pleistocene sediments at Boxgrove, UK. *Nature* 369, 311–13.

Stringer, C B 1996. The Boxgrove tibia: Britain's oldest hominid and its place in the Middle Pleistocene record. In Gamble, C S & Lawson, A J (eds) *The English Palaeolithic Reviewed* (Salisbury: Trust for Wessex Archaeology), 52–56.

Stringer, C B, Trinkaus, E, Roberts, M B, Parfitt, S A & Macphail, R I 1997. The Middle Pleistocene human tibia from Boxgrove. *Journal of Human Evolution* 32.

Wenban-Smith, F 1989. The use of canonical variates for determination of biface manufacturing technology at Boxgrove lower palaeolithic site and the behavioural implications of this technology. *Journal of Archaeological Science* 16, 17–26.

Woodcock, A 1981. *The Lower and Middle Palaeolithic Periods in Sussex.* Oxford: British Archaeological Reports British Series 94.

Acknowledgements

The following have all helped with piecing together the story of the Boxgrove dig and/or the archaeological background for the book, for which many thanks: Con Ainsworth, Nick Ashton, Louise Austin, Laura Basel, Martin Bates, Greg Bell, Mike Bishop, Don Brothwell, Amanda Chadburn (English Heritage), Richard Champion, Chris Chippindale, John Cooper, Lorraine Cornish, Tim Cromack (English Heritage), Andy Currant, Andrew David (English Heritage), Robin Dennel, Simon Denison, Peter Drewett, Frank Fagan (ARC), Rob Foley, Henry Gee, Sharon Gerber, Lucy Gibbons, Stephen Aldhouse Green, Chris Hale, Norman Hammond, Phil Harding, John Humble (English Heritage), Mike Jones, Geoff Kellaway, David Keys, Sir Bernard Knight, Thys van Kolfschoten, Andrew Lawson, Duncan Lees, Jamie Mackenzie, Richard Macphail, Indira Mann, John McNabb, Paul Mellars, John Mitchell, Roger Pedersen, Christopher Pitts, Derek Roe, Wil Roebroeks, Antonio Rosas, Clare de Rouffignac (English Heritage), Nick Shackleton, Joan Sheldon, Roy Shephard-Thorn, Bob Smith (ARC), John Stewart, Erik Trinkaus, Tony Tynan, Geoff Wainwright (English Heritage), Francis Wenban-Smith, John Whittaker, Andrew Woodcock, John Wymer.

The excavations, funded since 1984 by English Heritage, would not have been possible without the cooperation of ARC. Mark Roberts would like to thank them for going out of their way to faciliate fieldwork, and for the use of facilities.

Mark would also like to thank all his colleagues, friends, family, and especially Julie, Harriet and Sidney for putting up with Boxgrove for the past fourteen years. Particular thanks are due to Simon Parfitt, my Assistant Director, for many years of enjoyable and profitable help and stimulation. Jules Tipper and Tony Tynan, the Boxgrove site managers, showed dedication beyond the call of duty in their long stewardship at the site, which included some particularly foul winters in the barns. They and all my staff epitomized for me, what made Boxgrove special.

Mike Pitts would particularly like to thank Clive Gamble, for inviting him into the world of Boxgrove and for his constant support, Chris Stringer for repeated help with bones, and above all Simon Parfitt, without whom the book would never have been finished. Much welcome editorial help was received from Mark Booth and Roderick Brown. Credit is due to Elaine Morris, who first reported the story of the key ring at the 1993 Christmas party for *Past* magazine, and who lent me her taped interviews. Barbara West showed her usual dedication to the Boxgrove Project by preparing many of the illustrations. The drawings of artefacts from Boxgrove are by Julian Cross, the butchered bones by Phil Rye and the animals by Ray Burrows. I am truly grateful to the diggers at Boxgrove in 1995 and 1996 who always made me feel welcome, although they clearly sometimes wondered what I was doing there; and my friends at Stones Restaurant in Avebury who must also have wondered what I wasn't doing *there* – in particular Debbie Iles, Lynda Murray, Gavin Topham and Andrew Webb. My work in London would have been impossible without the generous forebearance of my old friends Tom Blagg and Judy Medrington. Finally, thank you Hilary, for support and encouragement throughout everything.

Index